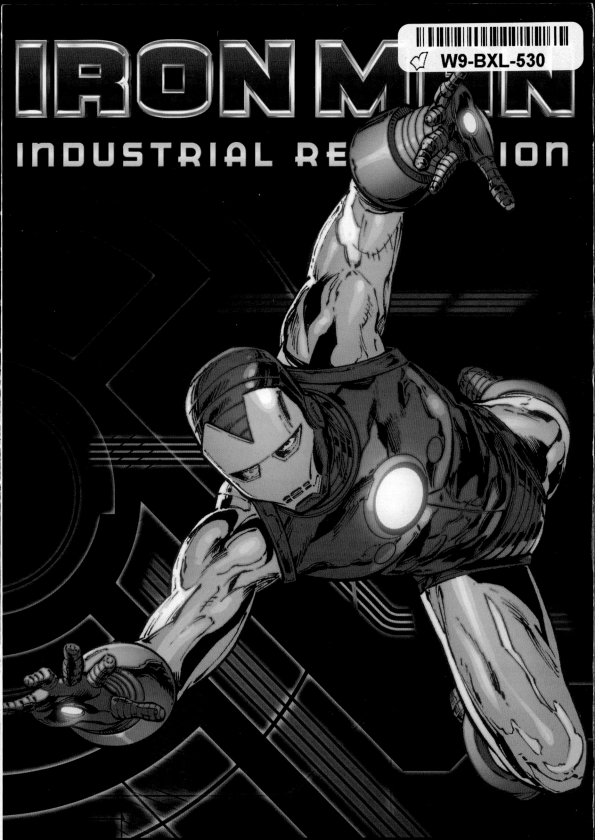

IRON MAN
INDUSTRIAL REVOLUTION

W9-BXL-530

IRON MAN: INDUSTRIAL REVOLUTION. Contains material originally published in magazine form as IRON MAN LEGACY #6-11. First printing 2011. Hardcover ISBN# 978-0-7851-4731-2. Softcover ISBN# 978-0-7851-4732-9. Published by MARVEL WORLDWIDE, INC., a subsidiary of MARVEL ENTERTAINMENT, LLC. OFFICE OF PUBLICATION: 135 West 50th Street, New York, NY 10020. Copyright © 2010 and 2011 Marvel Characters, Inc. All rights reserved. Hardcover: $19.99 per copy in the U.S. and $21.99 in Canada (GST #R127032852). Softcover: $16.99 per copy in the U.S. and $18.50 in Canada (GST #R127032852). Canadian Agreement #40668537. All characters featured in this issue and the distinctive names and likenesses thereof, and all related indicia are trademarks of Marvel Characters, Inc. No similarity between any of the names, characters, persons, and/or institutions in this magazine with those of any living or dead person or institution is intended, and any such similarity which may exist is purely coincidental. **Printed in the U.S.A.** ALAN FINE, EVP - Office of the President, Marvel Worldwide, Inc. and EVP & CMO Marvel Characters B.V.; DAN BUCKLEY, Publisher & President - Print, Animation & Digital Divisions; JOE QUESADA, Chief Creative Officer; JIM SOKOLOWSKI, Chief Operating Officer; DAVID BOGART, SVP of Business Affairs & Talent Management; TOM BREVOORT, SVP of Publishing; C.B. CEBULSKI, SVP of Creator & Content Development; DAVID GABRIEL, SVP of Publishing Sales & Circulation; MICHAEL PASCIULLO, SVP of Brand Planning & Communications; JIM O'KEEFE, VP of Operations & Logistics; DAN CARR, Executive Director of Publishing Technology; JUSTIN F. GABRIE, Director of Publishing & Editorial Operations; SUSAN CRESPI, Editorial Operations Manager; ALEX MORALES, Publishing Operations Manager; STAN LEE, Chairman Emeritus. For information regarding advertising in Marvel Comics or on Marvel.com, please contact Ron Stern, VP of Business Development, at rstern@marvel.com. For Marvel subscription inquiries, please call 800-217-9158. Manufactured between 2/21/2011 and 3/21/2011 (hardcover), and 2/21/2011 and 9/19/2011 (softcover), by R.R. DONNELLEY, INC., SALEM, VA, USA.

10 9 8 7 6 5 4 3 2 1

IRON MAN
INDUSTRIAL REVOLUTION

WRITER: **FRED VAN LENTE**
PENCILERS: **STEVE KURTH** (ISSUES #6-9)
& PHILIPPE BRIONES (ISSUES #10-11)
INKERS: **ALLEN MARTINEZ** (ISSUES #6-9) **& JEFF HUET** (ISSUES #10-11)
COLORIST: **JOHN RAUCH**
LETTERER: **DAVE SHARPE**
COVER ARTIST: **JUAN DOE**
ASSISTANT EDITOR: **CHARLIE BECKERMAN**
EDITOR: **RALPH MACCHIO**

COLLECTION EDITOR: **CORY LEVINE**
EDITORIAL ASSISTANTS: **JAMES EMMETT & JOE HOCHSTEIN**
ASSISTANT EDITORS: **MATT MASDEU, ALEX STARBUCK & NELSON RIBEIRO**
EDITORS, SPECIAL PROJECTS: **JENNIFER GRÜNWALD & MARK D. BEAZLEY**
SENIOR EDITOR, SPECIAL PROJECTS: **JEFF YOUNGQUIST**
SENIOR VICE PRESIDENT OF SALES: **DAVID GABRIEL**
BOOK DESIGNER: **RODOLFO MURAGUCHI**

EDITOR IN CHIEF: **AXEL ALONSO**
CHIEF CREATIVE OFFICER: **JOE QUESADA**
PUBLISHER: **DAN BUCKLEY**
EXECUTIVE PRODUCER: **ALAN FINE**

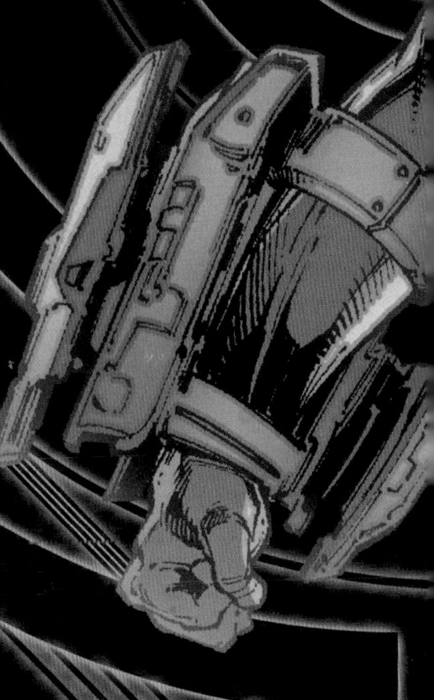

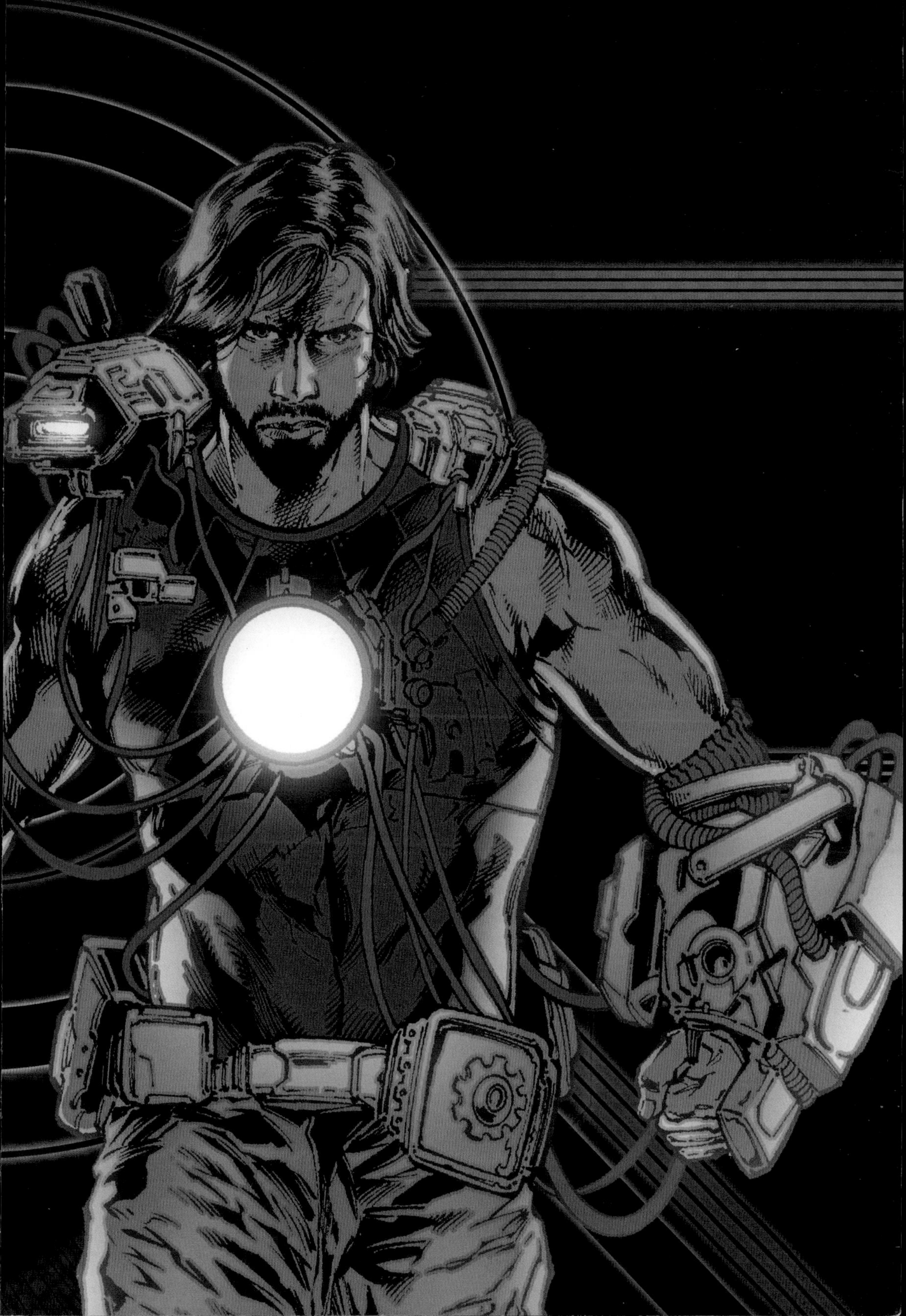

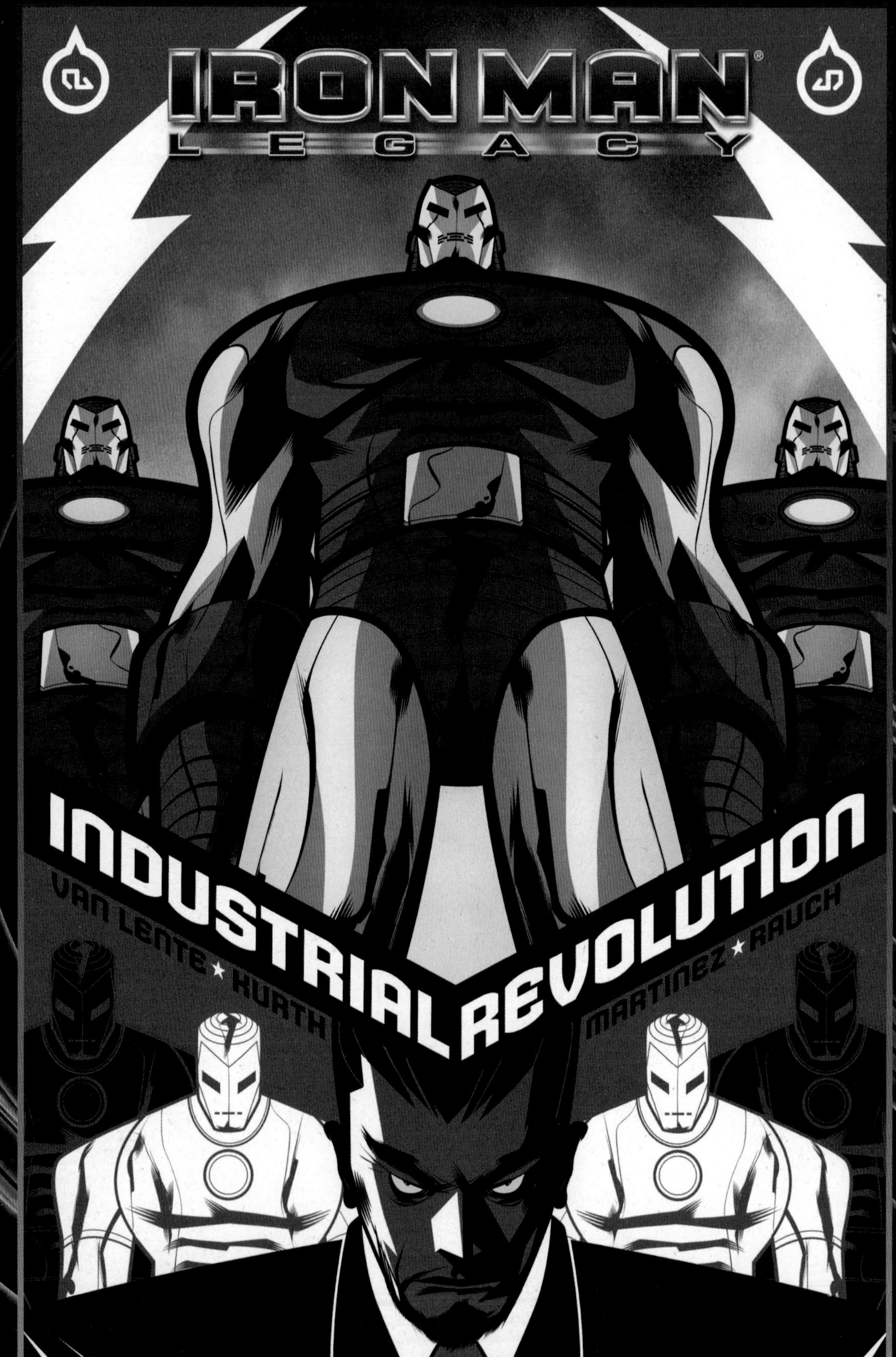
IRON MAN
LEGACY
INDUSTRIAL REVOLUTION
VAN LENTE ★ KURTH
MARTINEZ ★ RAUCH

IRON MAN LEGACY 6

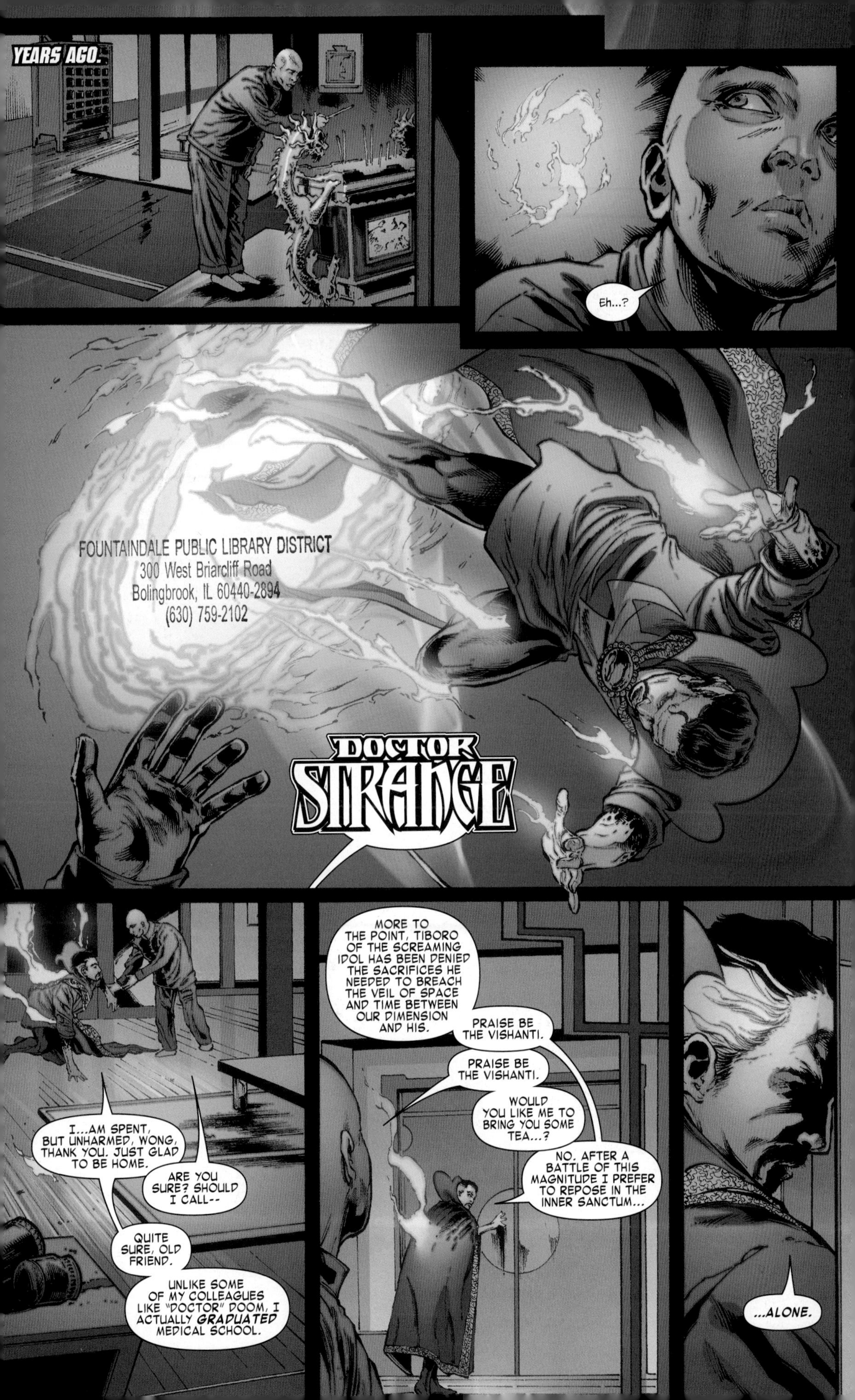

YEARS AGO.
Eh...?
DOCTOR STRANGE
I...AM SPENT, BUT UNHARMED, WONG, THANK YOU. JUST GLAD TO BE HOME.
ARE YOU SURE? SHOULD I CALL--
QUITE SURE, OLD FRIEND.
UNLIKE SOME OF MY COLLEAGUES LIKE "DOCTOR" DOOM, I ACTUALLY GRADUATED MEDICAL SCHOOL.
MORE TO THE POINT, TIBORO OF THE SCREAMING IDOL HAS BEEN DENIED THE SACRIFICES HE NEEDED TO BREACH THE VEIL OF SPACE AND TIME BETWEEN OUR DIMENSION AND HIS.
PRAISE BE THE VISHANTI.
PRAISE BE THE VISHANTI.
WOULD YOU LIKE ME TO BRING YOU SOME TEA...?
NO. AFTER A BATTLE OF THIS MAGNITUDE I PREFER TO REPOSE IN THE INNER SANCTUM...
...ALONE.

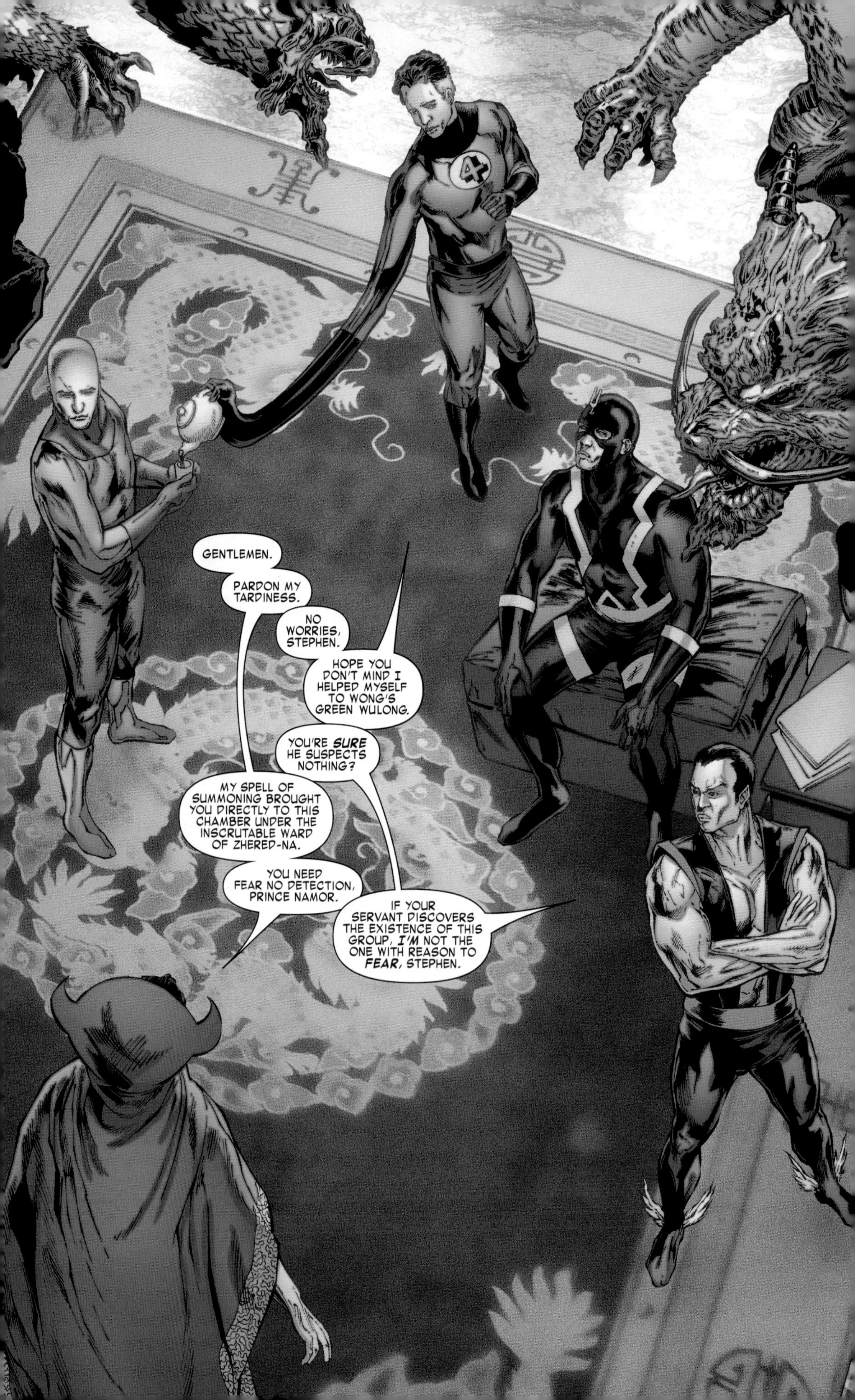
GENTLEMEN.
PARDON MY TARDINESS.
NO WORRIES, STEPHEN.
HOPE YOU DON'T MIND I HELPED MYSELF TO WONG'S GREEN WULONG.
YOU'RE SURE HE SUSPECTS NOTHING?
MY SPELL OF SUMMONING BROUGHT YOU DIRECTLY TO THIS CHAMBER UNDER THE INSCRUTABLE WARD OF ZHERED-NA.
YOU NEED FEAR NO DETECTION, PRINCE NAMOR.
IF YOUR SERVANT DISCOVERS THE EXISTENCE OF THIS GROUP, I'M NOT THE ONE WITH REASON TO FEAR, STEPHEN.

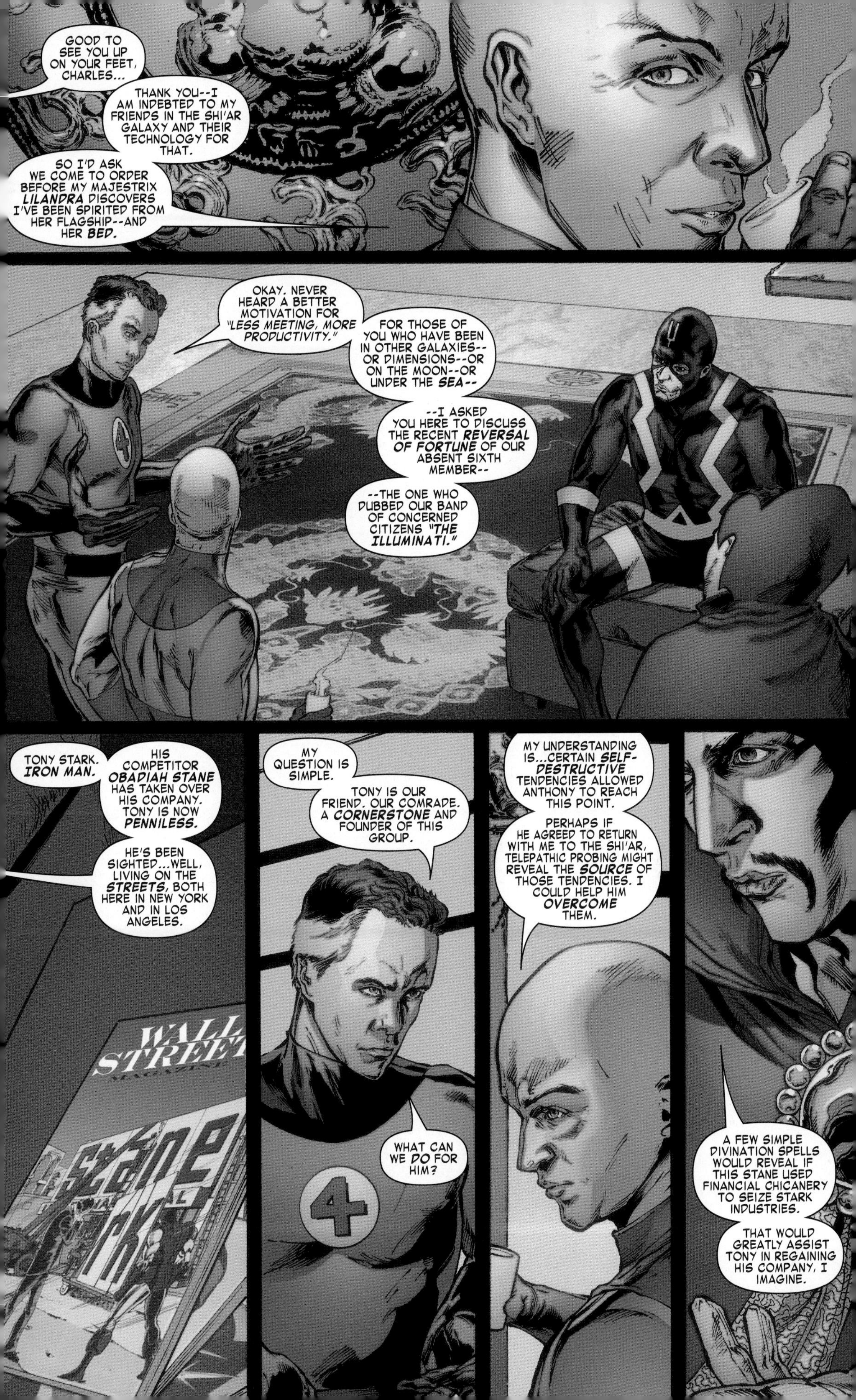
GOOD TO SEE YOU UP ON YOUR FEET, CHARLES...
THANK YOU--I AM INDEBTED TO MY FRIENDS IN THE SHI'AR GALAXY AND THEIR TECHNOLOGY FOR THAT.
SO I'D ASK WE COME TO ORDER BEFORE MY MAJESTRIX LILANDRA DISCOVERS I'VE BEEN SPIRITED FROM HER FLAGSHIP--AND HER BED.
OKAY. NEVER HEARD A BETTER MOTIVATION FOR "LESS MEETING, MORE PRODUCTIVITY."
FOR THOSE OF YOU WHO HAVE BEEN IN OTHER GALAXIES--OR DIMENSIONS--OR ON THE MOON--OR UNDER THE SEA--
--I ASKED YOU HERE TO DISCUSS THE RECENT REVERSAL OF FORTUNE OF OUR ABSENT SIXTH MEMBER--
--THE ONE WHO DUBBED OUR BAND OF CONCERNED CITIZENS "THE ILLUMINATI."
TONY STARK. IRON MAN.
HIS COMPETITOR OBADIAH STANE HAS TAKEN OVER HIS COMPANY. TONY IS NOW PENNILESS.
HE'S BEEN SIGHTED...WELL, LIVING ON THE STREETS, BOTH HERE IN NEW YORK AND IN LOS ANGELES.
MY QUESTION IS SIMPLE.
TONY IS OUR FRIEND. OUR COMRADE. A CORNERSTONE AND FOUNDER OF THIS GROUP.
WHAT CAN WE DO FOR HIM?
MY UNDERSTANDING IS...CERTAIN SELF-DESTRUCTIVE TENDENCIES ALLOWED ANTHONY TO REACH THIS POINT.
PERHAPS IF HE AGREED TO RETURN WITH ME TO THE SHI'AR, TELEPATHIC PROBING MIGHT REVEAL THE SOURCE OF THOSE TENDENCIES. I COULD HELP HIM OVERCOME THEM.
A FEW SIMPLE DIVINATION SPELLS WOULD REVEAL IF THIS STANE USED FINANCIAL CHICANERY TO SEIZE STARK INDUSTRIES.
THAT WOULD GREATLY ASSIST TONY IN REGAINING HIS COMPANY, I IMAGINE.

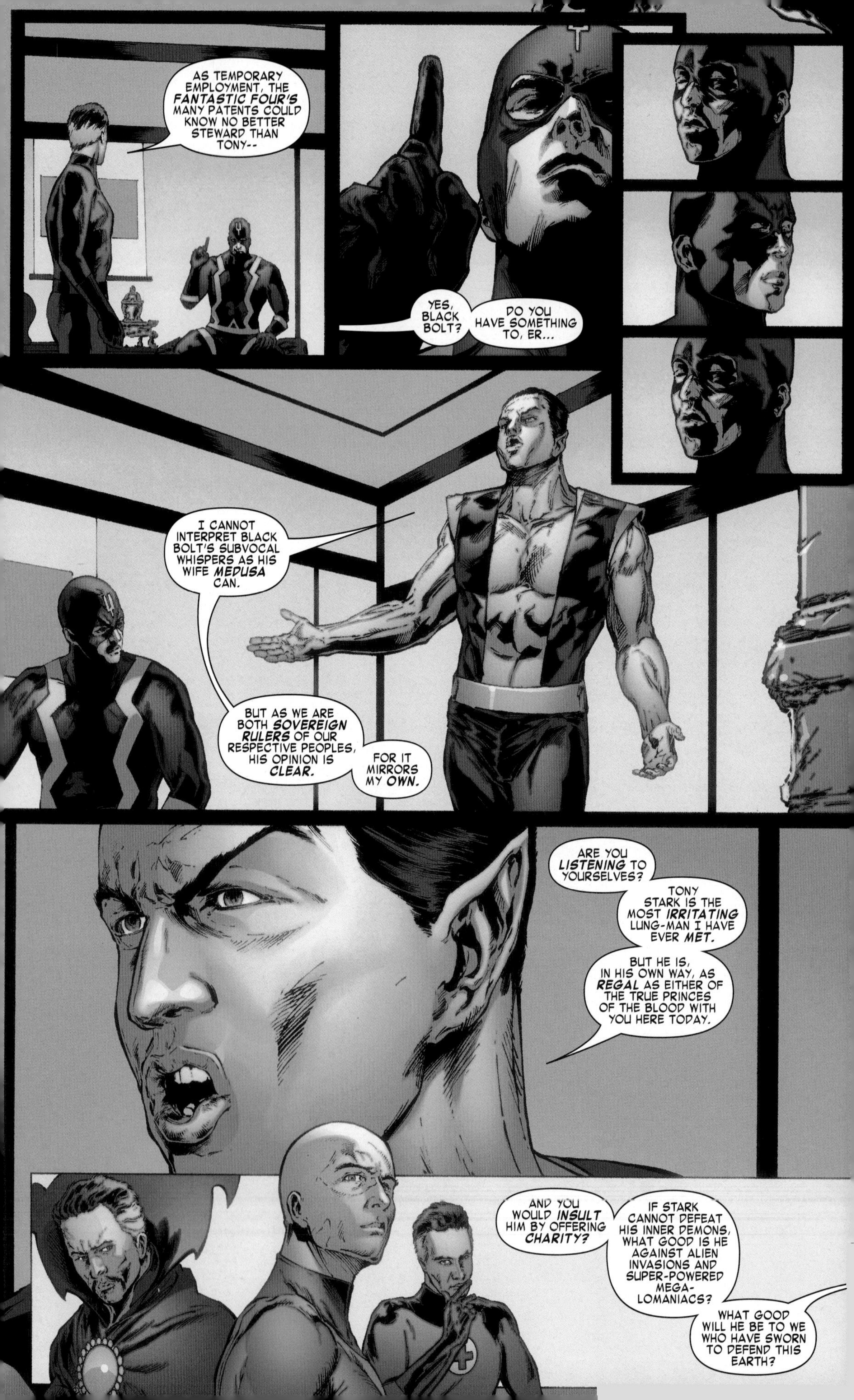
AS TEMPORARY EMPLOYMENT, THE FANTASTIC FOUR'S MANY PATENTS COULD KNOW NO BETTER STEWARD THAN TONY--
YES, BLACK BOLT?
DO YOU HAVE SOMETHING TO, ER...
I CANNOT INTERPRET BLACK BOLT'S SUBVOCAL WHISPERS AS HIS WIFE MEDUSA CAN.
BUT AS WE ARE BOTH SOVEREIGN RULERS OF OUR RESPECTIVE PEOPLES, HIS OPINION IS CLEAR.
FOR IT MIRRORS MY OWN.
ARE YOU LISTENING TO YOURSELVES?
TONY STARK IS THE MOST IRRITATING LUNG-MAN I HAVE EVER MET.
BUT HE IS, IN HIS OWN WAY, AS REGAL AS EITHER OF THE TRUE PRINCES OF THE BLOOD WITH YOU HERE TODAY.
AND YOU WOULD INSULT HIM BY OFFERING CHARITY?
IF STARK CANNOT DEFEAT HIS INNER DEMONS, WHAT GOOD IS HE AGAINST ALIEN INVASIONS AND SUPER-POWERED MEGA-LOMANIACS?
WHAT GOOD WILL HE BE TO WE WHO HAVE SWORN TO DEFEND THIS EARTH?

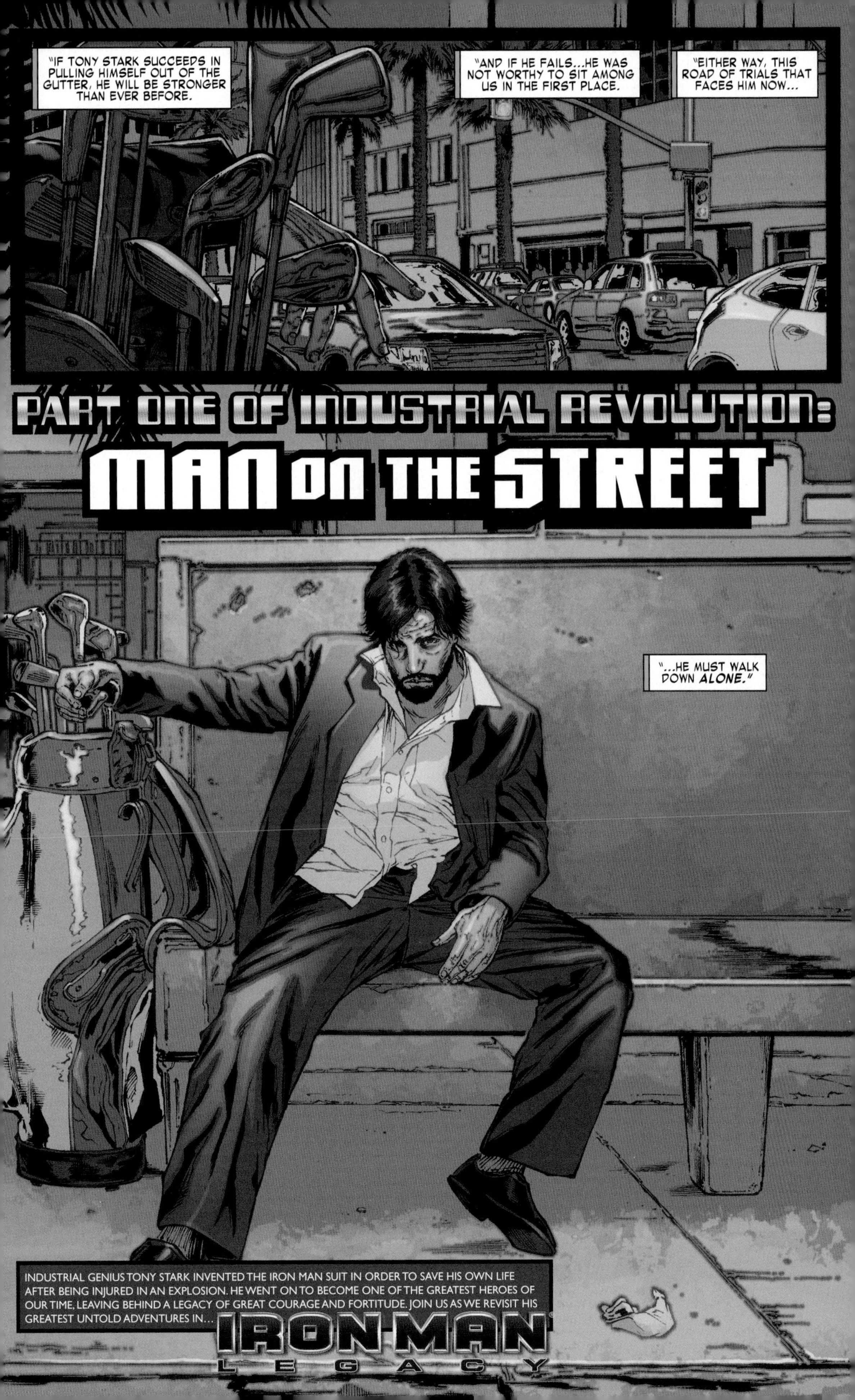
"IF TONY STARK SUCCEEDS IN PULLING HIMSELF OUT OF THE GUTTER, HE WILL BE STRONGER THAN EVER BEFORE.
"AND IF HE FAILS...HE WAS NOT WORTHY TO SIT AMONG US IN THE FIRST PLACE.
"EITHER WAY, THIS ROAD OF TRIALS THAT FACES HIM NOW...
PART ONE OF INDUSTRIAL REVOLUTION:
MAN ON THE STREET
"...HE MUST WALK DOWN ALONE."
INDUSTRIAL GENIUS TONY STARK INVENTED THE IRON MAN SUIT IN ORDER TO SAVE HIS OWN LIFE AFTER BEING INJURED IN AN EXPLOSION. HE WENT ON TO BECOME ONE OF THE GREATEST HEROES OF OUR TIME, LEAVING BEHIND A LEGACY OF GREAT COURAGE AND FORTITUDE. JOIN US AS WE REVISIT HIS GREATEST UNTOLD ADVENTURES IN...
IRON MAN
LEGACY

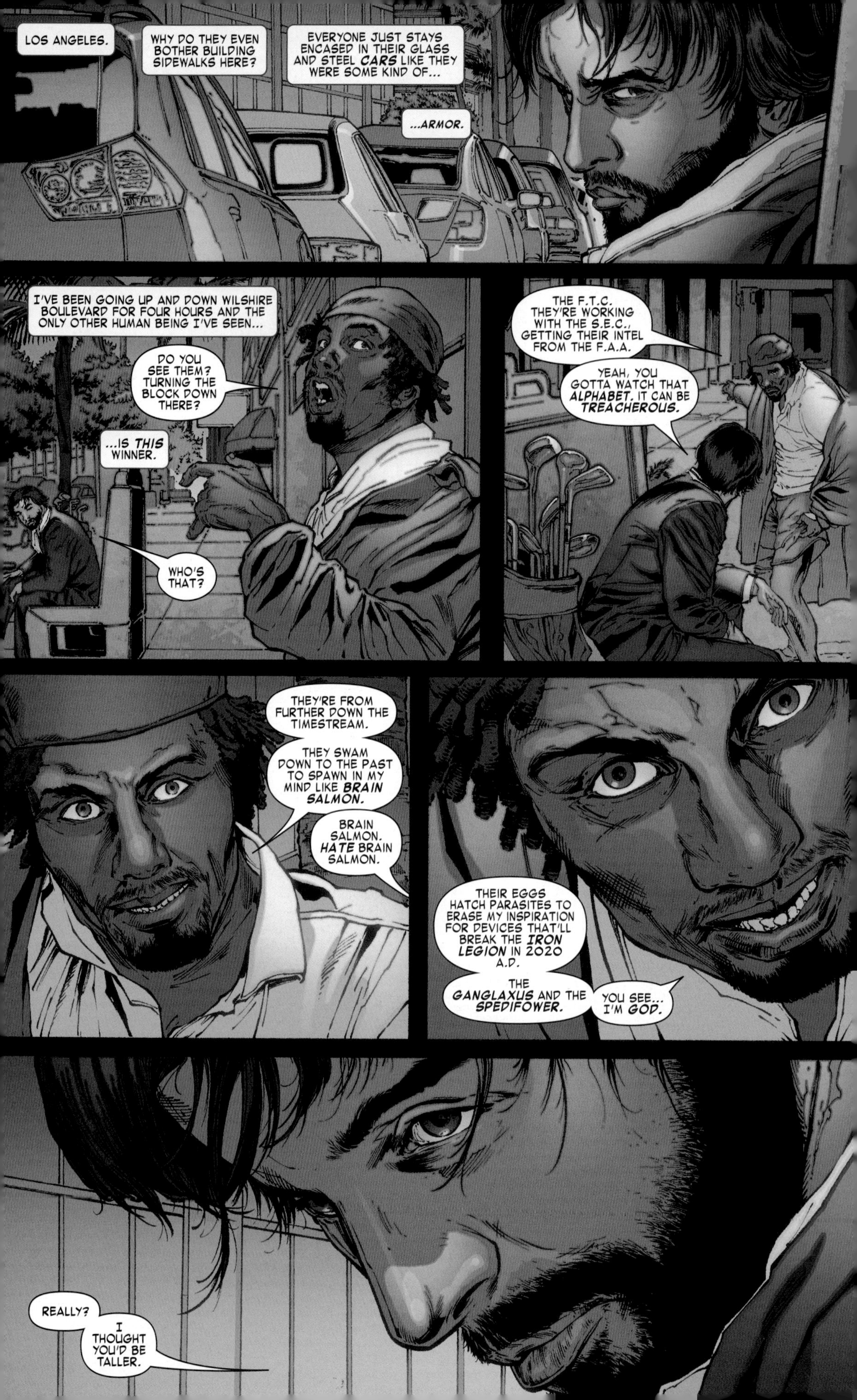
LOS ANGELES.
WHY DO THEY EVEN BOTHER BUILDING SIDEWALKS HERE?
EVERYONE JUST STAYS ENCASED IN THEIR GLASS AND STEEL CARS LIKE THEY WERE SOME KIND OF...
...ARMOR.
I'VE BEEN GOING UP AND DOWN WILSHIRE BOULEVARD FOR FOUR HOURS AND THE ONLY OTHER HUMAN BEING I'VE SEEN...
DO YOU SEE THEM? TURNING THE BLOCK DOWN THERE?
...IS THIS WINNER.
WHO'S THAT?
THE F.T.C. THEY'RE WORKING WITH THE S.E.C., GETTING THEIR INTEL FROM THE F.A.A.
YEAH, YOU GOTTA WATCH THAT ALPHABET. IT CAN BE TREACHEROUS.
THEY'RE FROM FURTHER DOWN THE TIMESTREAM.
THEY SWAM DOWN TO THE PAST TO SPAWN IN MY MIND LIKE BRAIN SALMON.
BRAIN SALMON. HATE BRAIN SALMON.
THEIR EGGS HATCH PARASITES TO ERASE MY INSPIRATION FOR DEVICES THAT'LL BREAK THE IRON LEGION IN 2020 A.D.
THE GANGLAXUS AND THE SPEDIFOWER.
YOU SEE... I'M GOD.
REALLY?
I THOUGHT YOU'D BE TALLER.

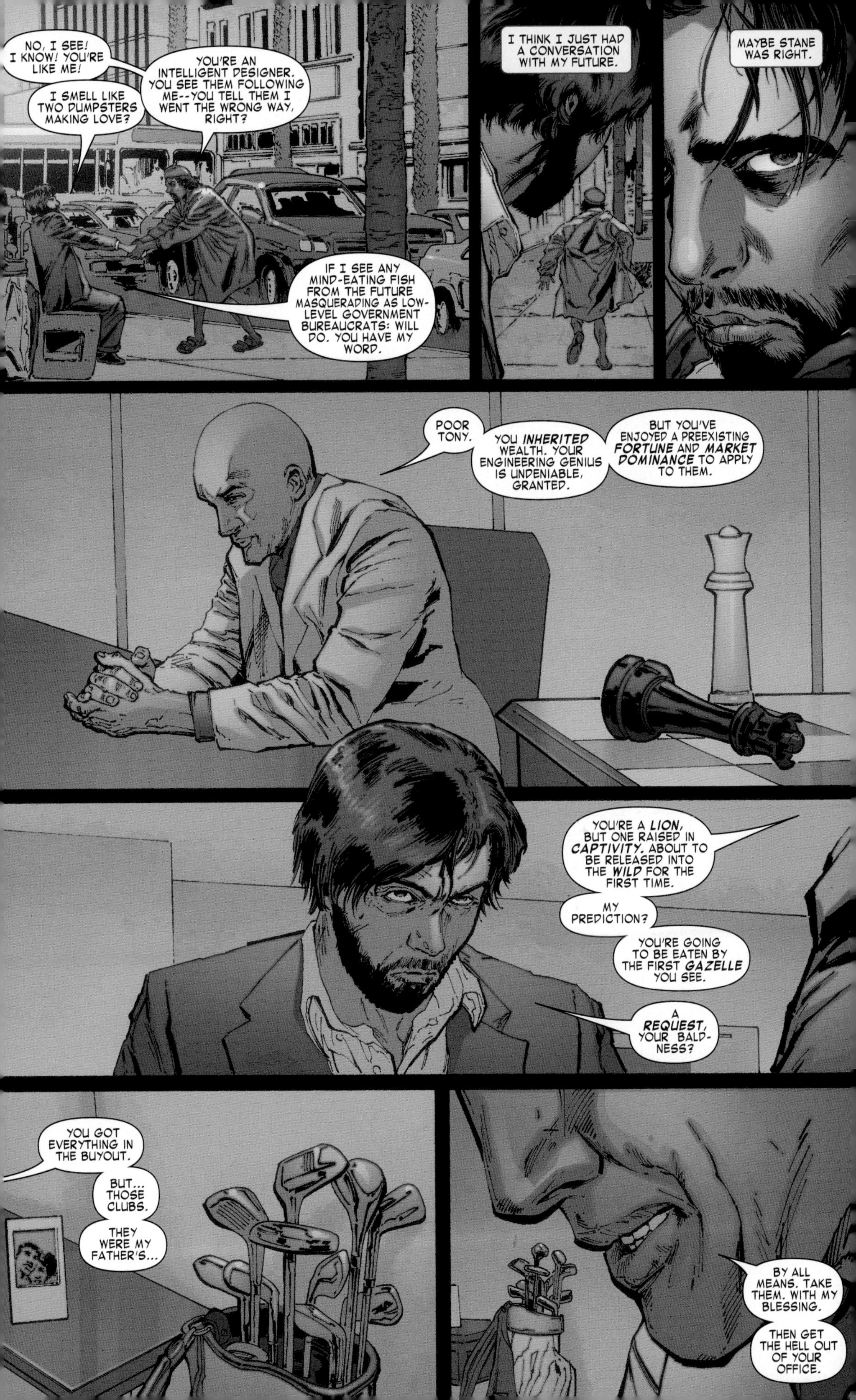
NO, I SEE! I KNOW! YOU'RE LIKE ME!
YOU'RE AN INTELLIGENT DESIGNER. YOU SEE THEM FOLLOWING ME--YOU TELL THEM I WENT THE WRONG WAY, RIGHT?
I SMELL LIKE TWO DUMPSTERS MAKING LOVE?
IF I SEE ANY MIND-EATING FISH FROM THE FUTURE MASQUERADING AS LOW-LEVEL GOVERNMENT BUREAUCRATS: WILL DO. YOU HAVE MY WORD.
I THINK I JUST HAD A CONVERSATION WITH MY FUTURE.
MAYBE STANE WAS RIGHT.
POOR TONY.
YOU *INHERITED* WEALTH. YOUR ENGINEERING GENIUS IS UNDENIABLE, GRANTED.
BUT YOU'VE ENJOYED A PREEXISTING ***FORTUNE*** AND ***MARKET DOMINANCE*** TO APPLY TO THEM.
YOU'RE A ***LION,*** BUT ONE RAISED IN ***CAPTIVITY.*** ABOUT TO BE RELEASED INTO THE ***WILD*** FOR THE FIRST TIME.
MY PREDICTION?
YOU'RE GOING TO BE EATEN BY THE FIRST ***GAZELLE*** YOU SEE.
A ***REQUEST,*** YOUR BALD-NESS?
YOU GOT EVERYTHING IN THE BUYOUT.
BUT... THOSE CLUBS.
THEY WERE MY FATHER'S...
BY ALL MEANS. TAKE THEM. WITH MY BLESSING.
THEN GET THE HELL OUT OF YOUR OFFICE.

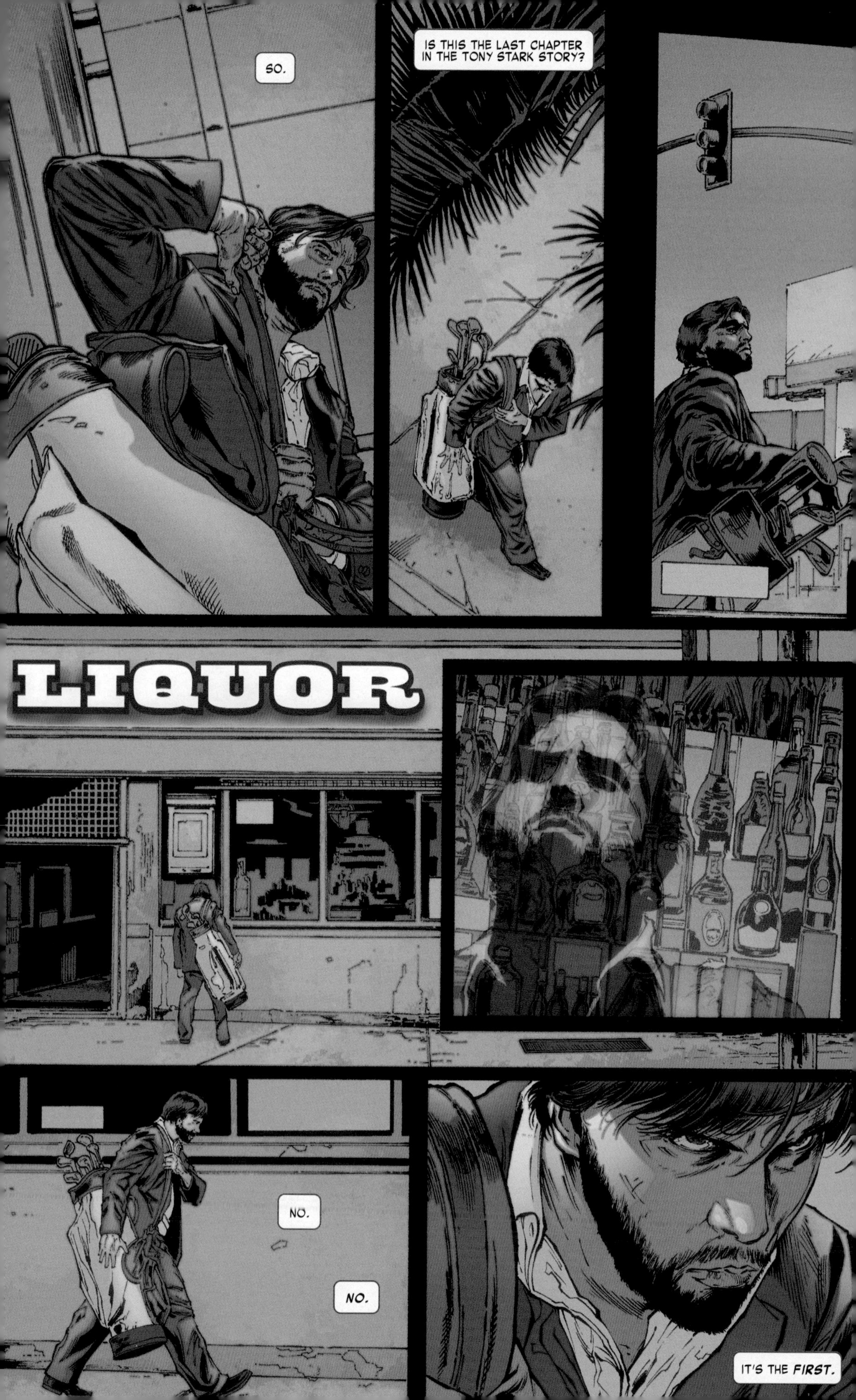
SO.
IS THIS THE LAST CHAPTER IN THE TONY STARK STORY?
LIQUOR
NO.
NO.
IT'S THE FIRST.

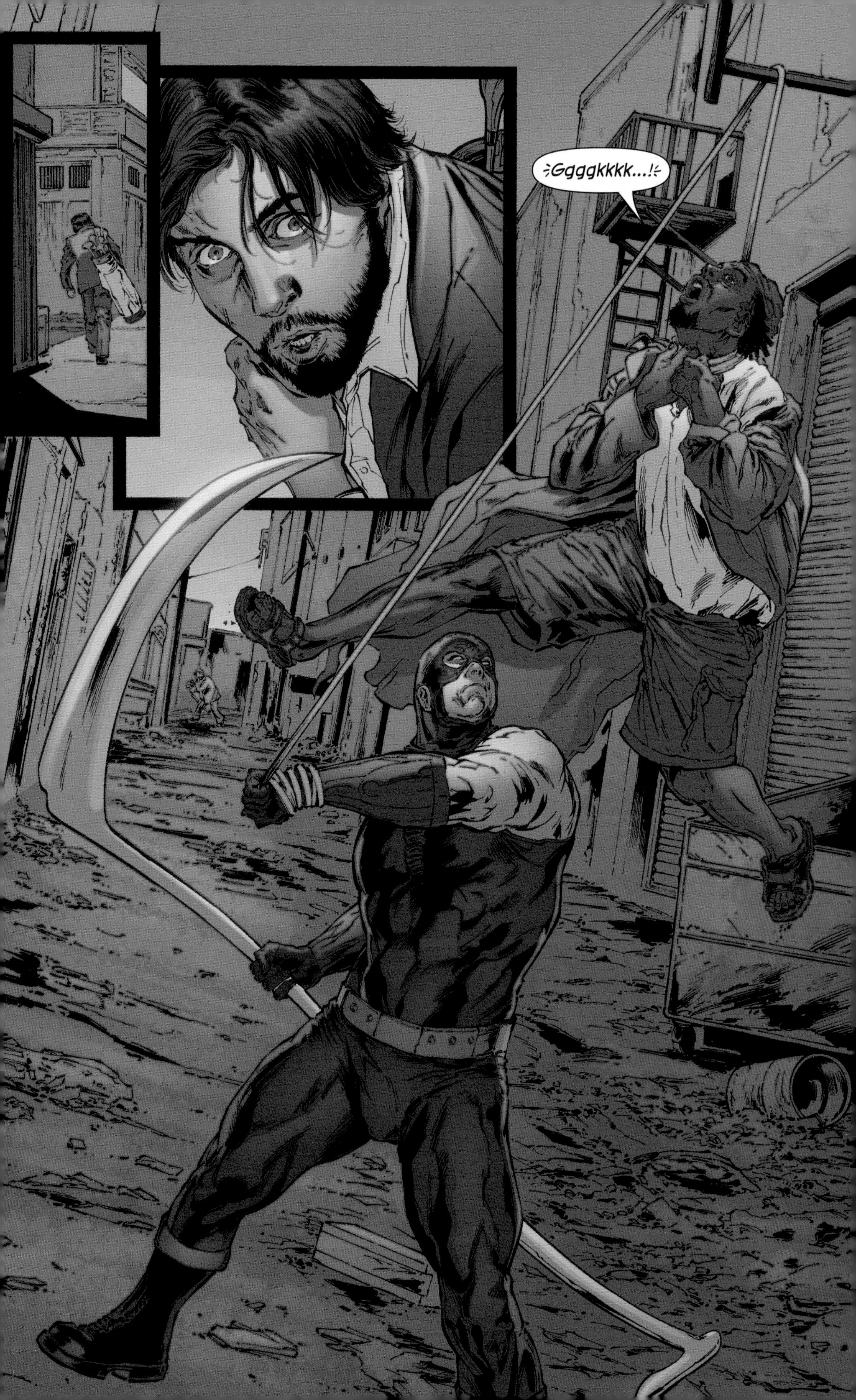
Ggggkkkk...!

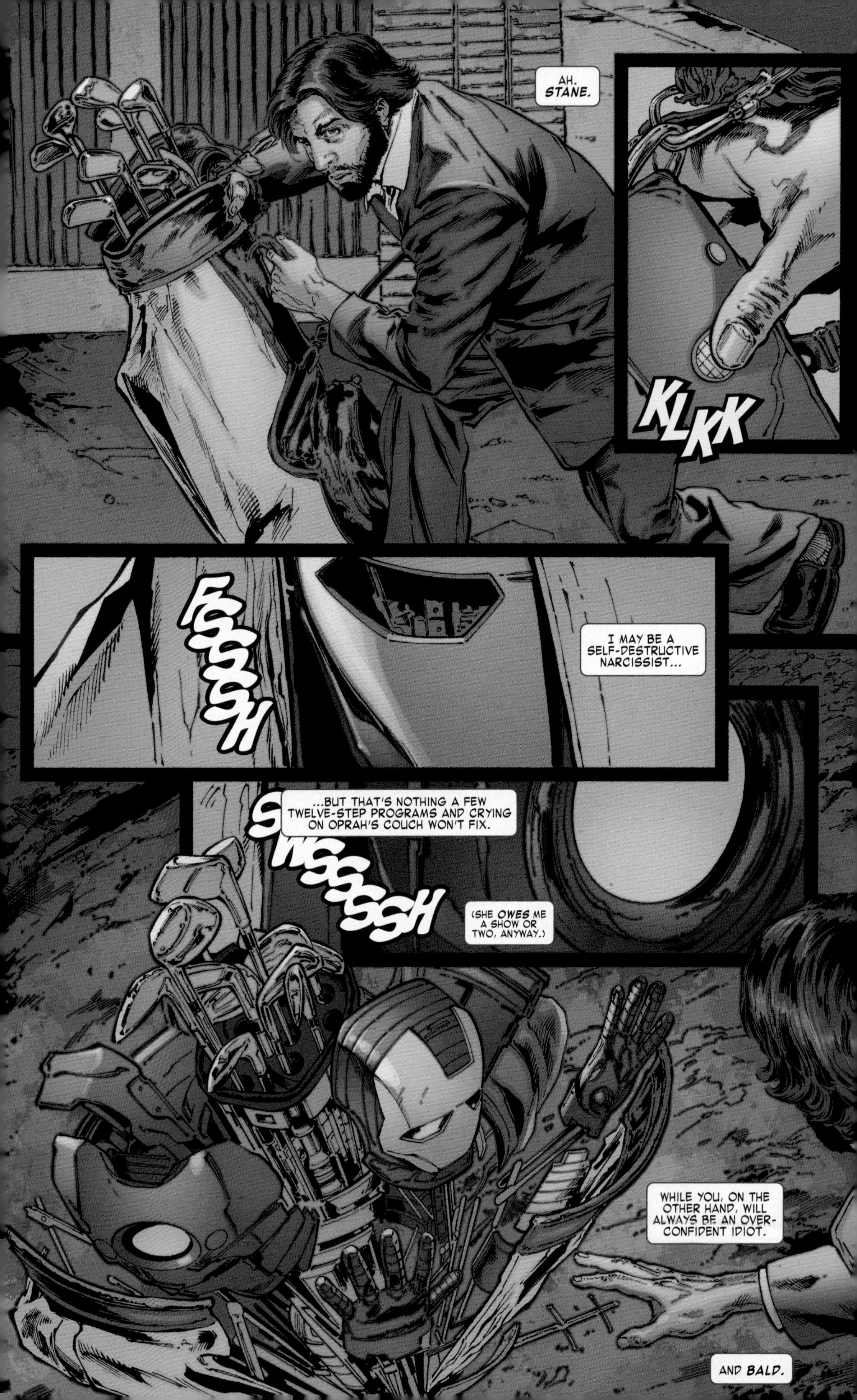
AH. STANE.
KLKK
FSSSSH
I MAY BE A SELF-DESTRUCTIVE NARCISSIST...
...BUT THAT'S NOTHING A FEW TWELVE-STEP PROGRAMS AND CRYING ON OPRAH'S COUCH WON'T FIX.
SWSSSSH
(SHE OWES ME A SHOW OR TWO, ANYWAY.)
WHILE YOU, ON THE OTHER HAND, WILL ALWAYS BE AN OVER-CONFIDENT IDIOT.
AND BALD.

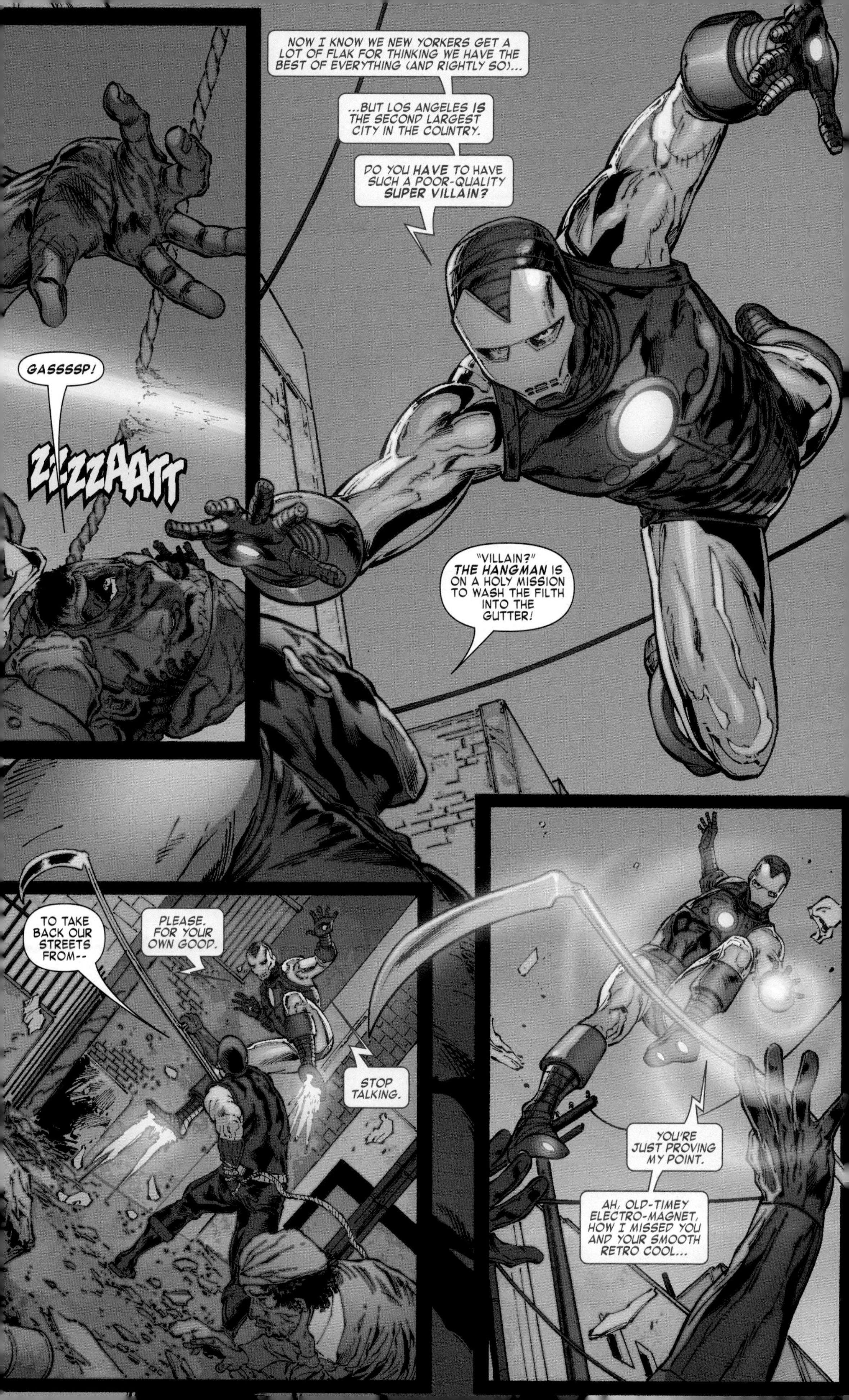
NOW I KNOW WE NEW YORKERS GET A LOT OF FLAK FOR THINKING WE HAVE THE BEST OF EVERYTHING (AND RIGHTLY SO)...
...BUT LOS ANGELES IS THE SECOND LARGEST CITY IN THE COUNTRY.
DO YOU HAVE TO HAVE SUCH A POOR-QUALITY SUPER VILLAIN?
GASSSSP!
ZZZZAATT
"VILLAIN?" THE HANGMAN IS ON A HOLY MISSION TO WASH THE FILTH INTO THE GUTTER!
TO TAKE BACK OUR STREETS FROM--
PLEASE. FOR YOUR OWN GOOD.
STOP TALKING.
YOU'RE JUST PROVING MY POINT.
AH, OLD-TIMEY ELECTRO-MAGNET, HOW I MISSED YOU AND YOUR SMOOTH RETRO COOL...

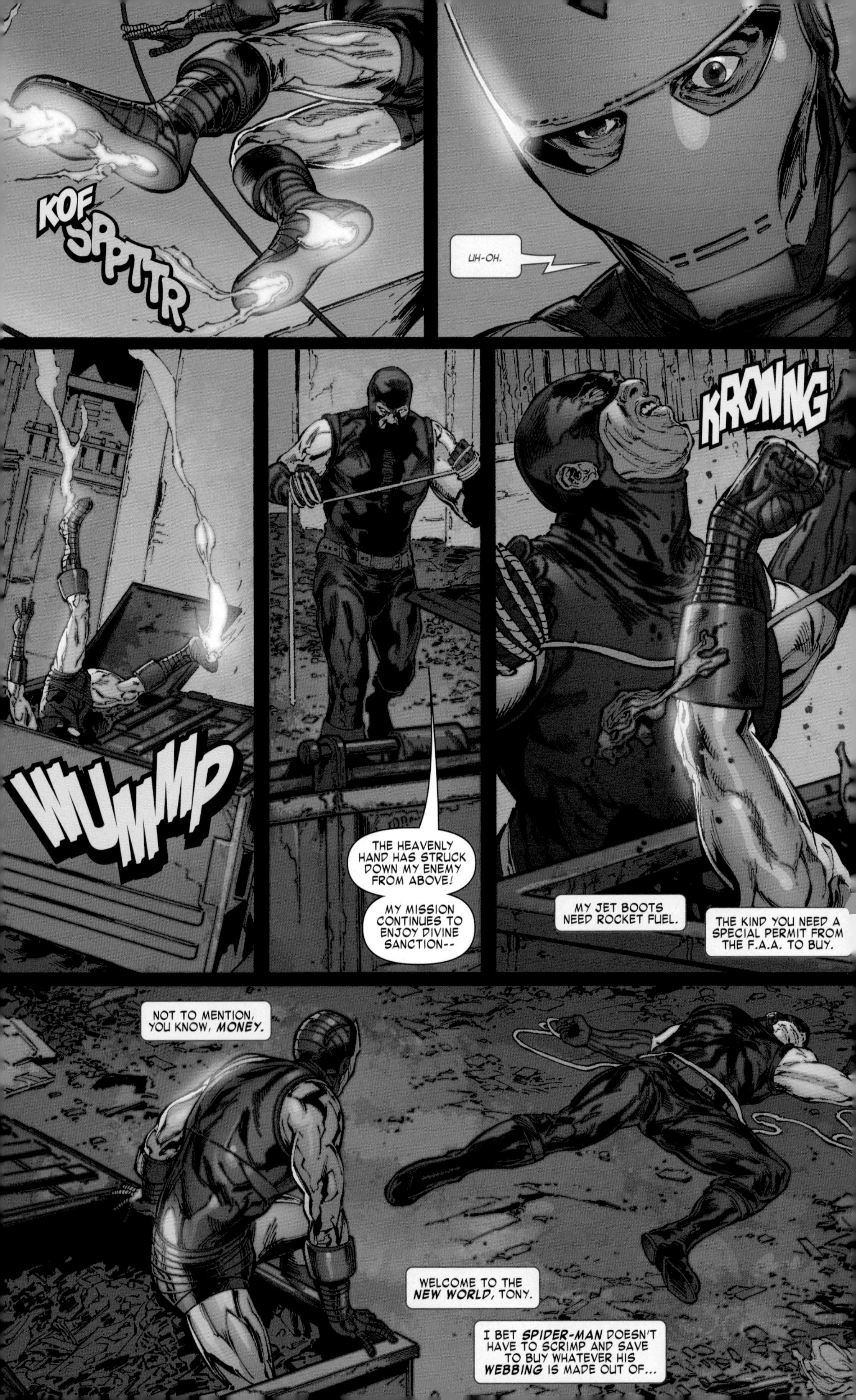
KOF
SPPTTTR
UH-OH.
WUMMP
THE HEAVENLY HAND HAS STRUCK DOWN MY ENEMY FROM ABOVE!
MY MISSION CONTINUES TO ENJOY DIVINE SANCTION--
KRONNG
MY JET BOOTS NEED ROCKET FUEL.
THE KIND YOU NEED A SPECIAL PERMIT FROM THE F.A.A. TO BUY.
NOT TO MENTION, YOU KNOW, MONEY.
WELCOME TO THE NEW WORLD, TONY.
I BET SPIDER-MAN DOESN'T HAVE TO SCRIMP AND SAVE TO BUY WHATEVER HIS WEBBING IS MADE OUT OF...

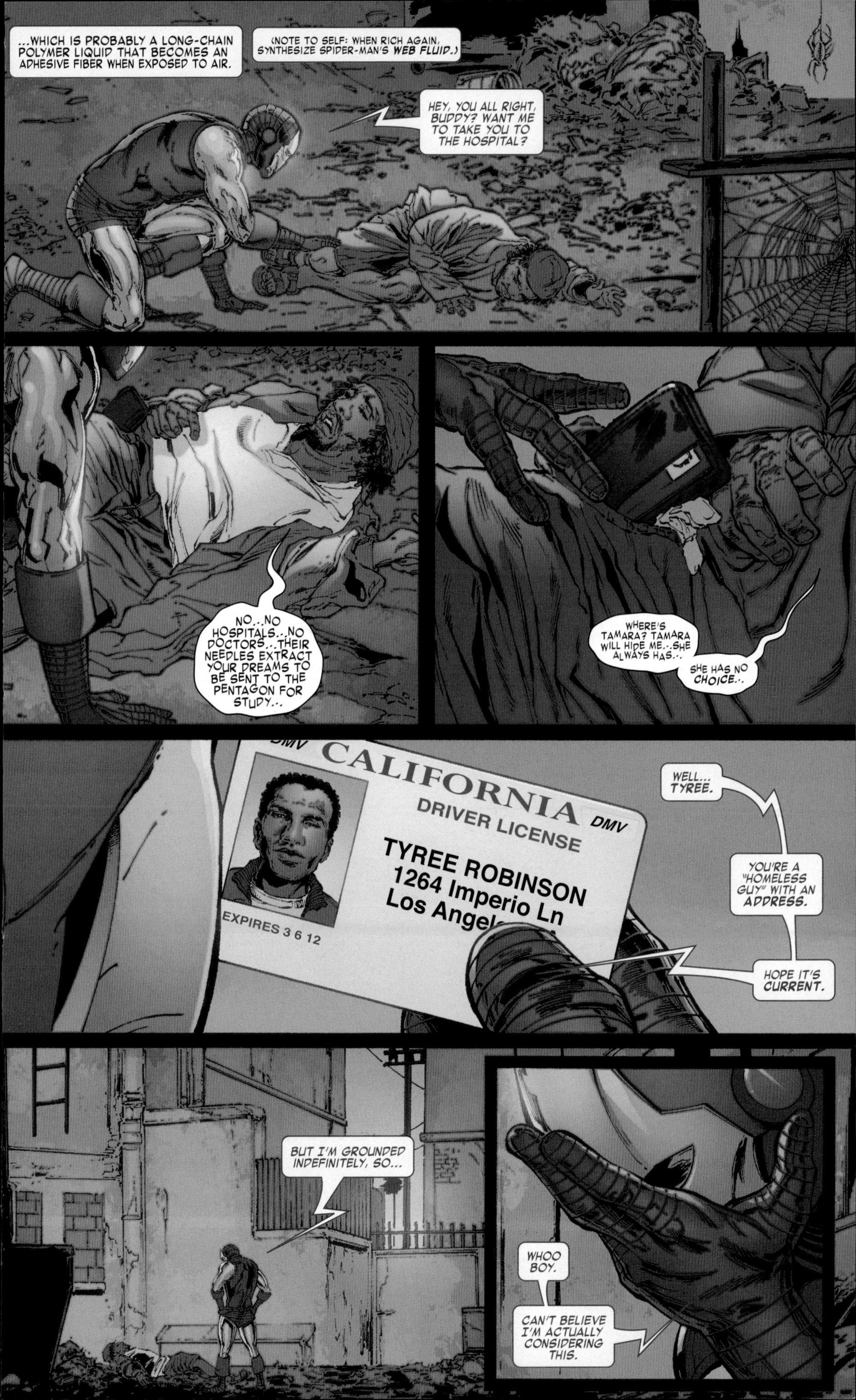
...WHICH IS PROBABLY A LONG-CHAIN POLYMER LIQUID THAT BECOMES AN ADHESIVE FIBER WHEN EXPOSED TO AIR.
(NOTE TO SELF: WHEN RICH AGAIN, SYNTHESIZE SPIDER-MAN'S WEB FLUID.)
HEY, YOU ALL RIGHT, BUDDY? WANT ME TO TAKE YOU TO THE HOSPITAL?
NO...NO HOSPITALS...NO DOCTORS...THEIR NEEDLES EXTRACT YOUR DREAMS TO BE SENT TO THE PENTAGON FOR STUDY...
WHERE'S TAMARA? TAMARA WILL HIDE ME...SHE ALWAYS HAS...
SHE HAS NO CHOICE...
DMV CALIFORNIA DMV
DRIVER LICENSE
TYREE ROBINSON
1264 Imperio Ln
Los Angel
EXPIRES 3 6 12
WELL... TYREE.
YOU'RE A "HOMELESS GUY" WITH AN ADDRESS.
HOPE IT'S CURRENT.
BUT I'M GROUNDED INDEFINITELY, SO...
WHOO BOY.
CAN'T BELIEVE I'M ACTUALLY CONSIDERING THIS.

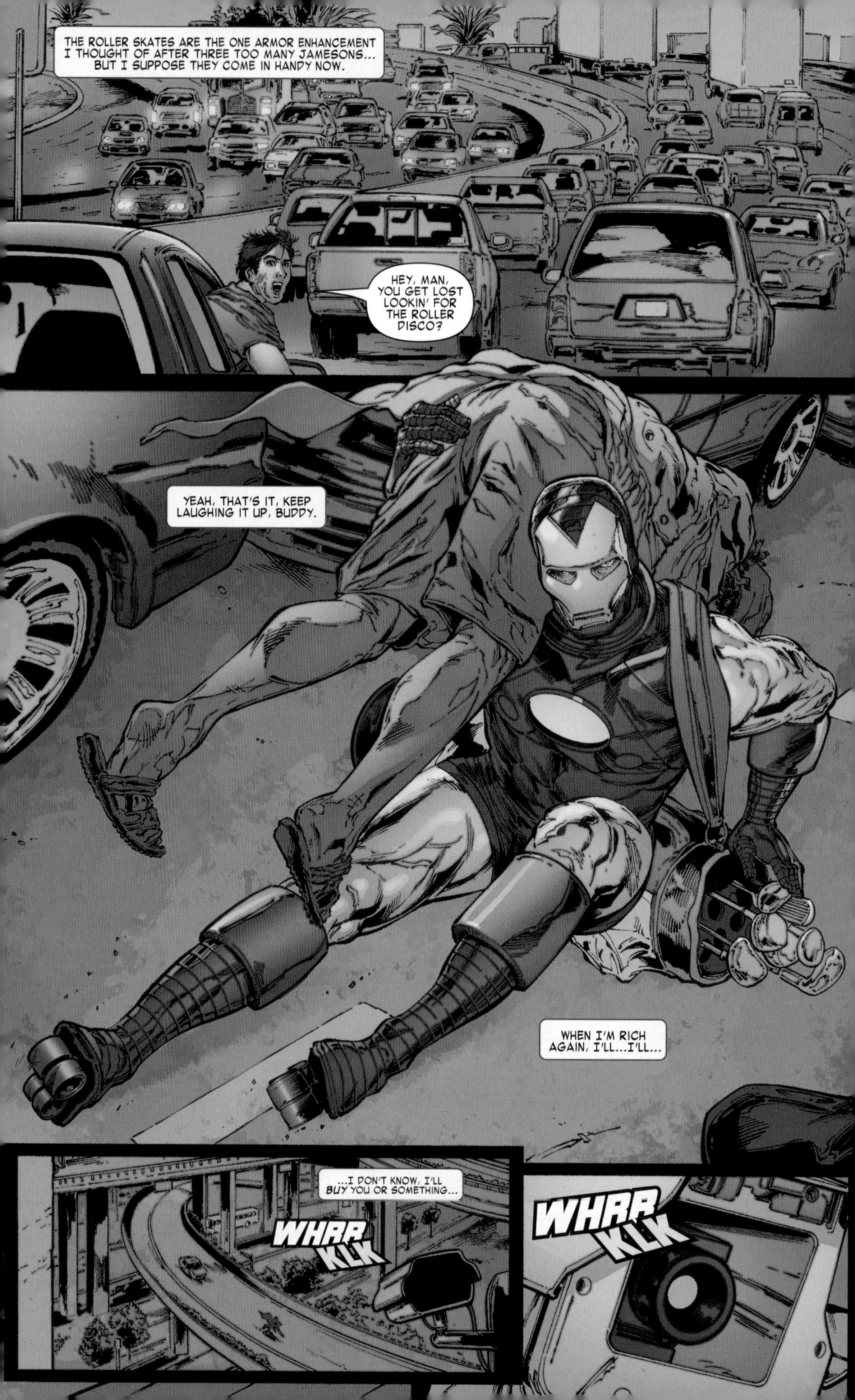
THE ROLLER SKATES ARE THE ONE ARMOR ENHANCEMENT I THOUGHT OF AFTER THREE TOO MANY JAMESONS... BUT I SUPPOSE THEY COME IN HANDY NOW.
HEY, MAN, YOU GET LOST LOOKIN' FOR THE ROLLER DISCO?
YEAH, THAT'S IT, KEEP LAUGHING IT UP, BUDDY.
WHEN I'M RICH AGAIN, I'LL...I'LL...
...I DON'T KNOW, I'LL BUY YOU OR SOMETHING...
WHRR KLK
WHRR KLK

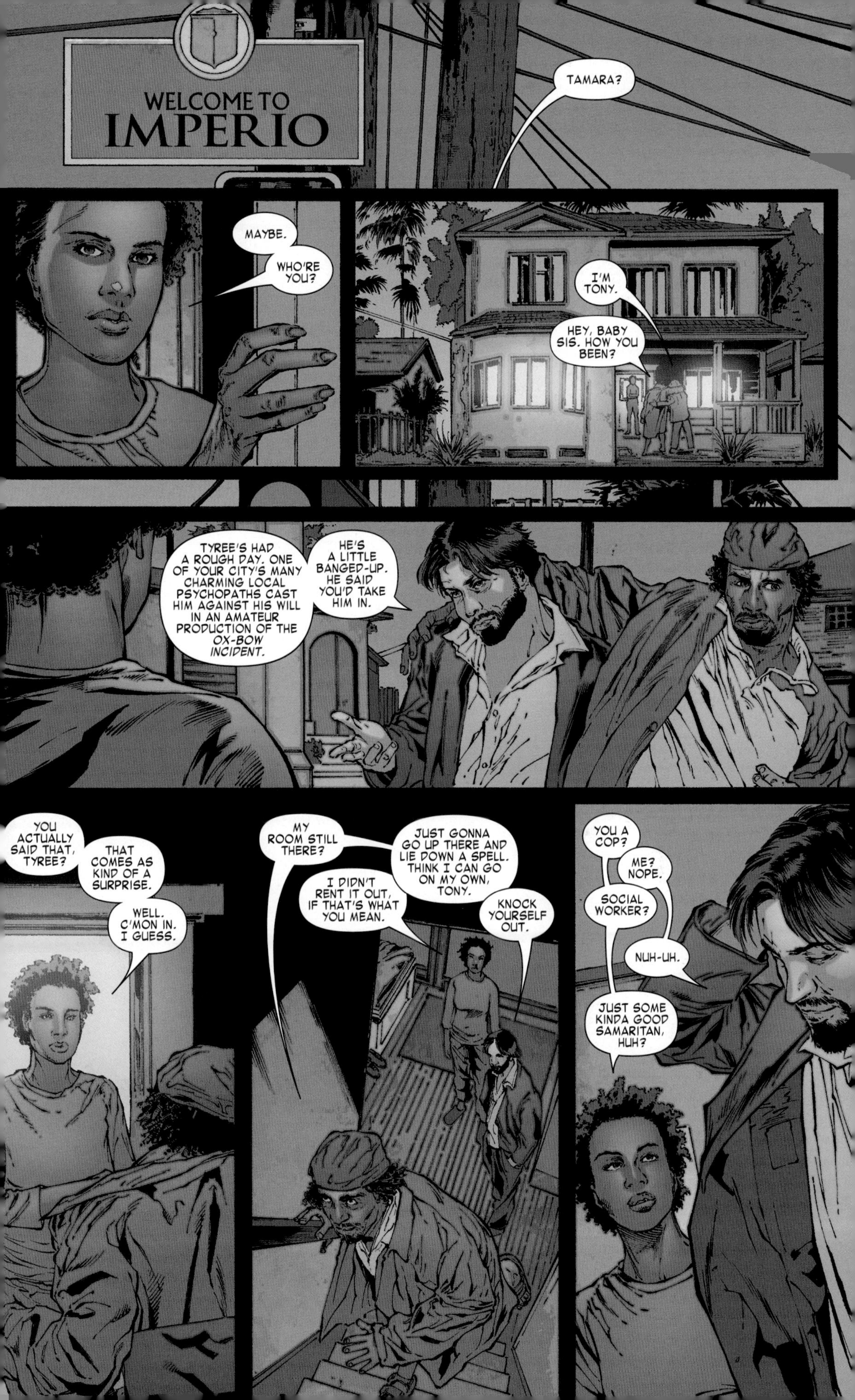
WELCOME TO
IMPERIO
TAMARA?
MAYBE.
WHO'RE YOU?
I'M TONY.
HEY, BABY SIS. HOW YOU BEEN?
TYREE'S HAD A ROUGH DAY. ONE OF YOUR CITY'S MANY CHARMING LOCAL PSYCHOPATHS CAST HIM AGAINST HIS WILL IN AN AMATEUR PRODUCTION OF THE *OX-BOW INCIDENT.*
HE'S A LITTLE BANGED-UP. HE SAID YOU'D TAKE HIM IN.
YOU ACTUALLY SAID THAT, TYREE?
THAT COMES AS KIND OF A SURPRISE.
WELL. C'MON IN. I GUESS.
MY ROOM STILL THERE?
I DIDN'T RENT IT OUT, IF THAT'S WHAT YOU MEAN.
JUST GONNA GO UP THERE AND LIE DOWN A SPELL. THINK I CAN GO ON MY OWN, TONY.
KNOCK YOURSELF OUT.
YOU A COP?
ME? NOPE.
SOCIAL WORKER?
NUH-UH.
JUST SOME KINDA GOOD SAMARITAN, HUH?

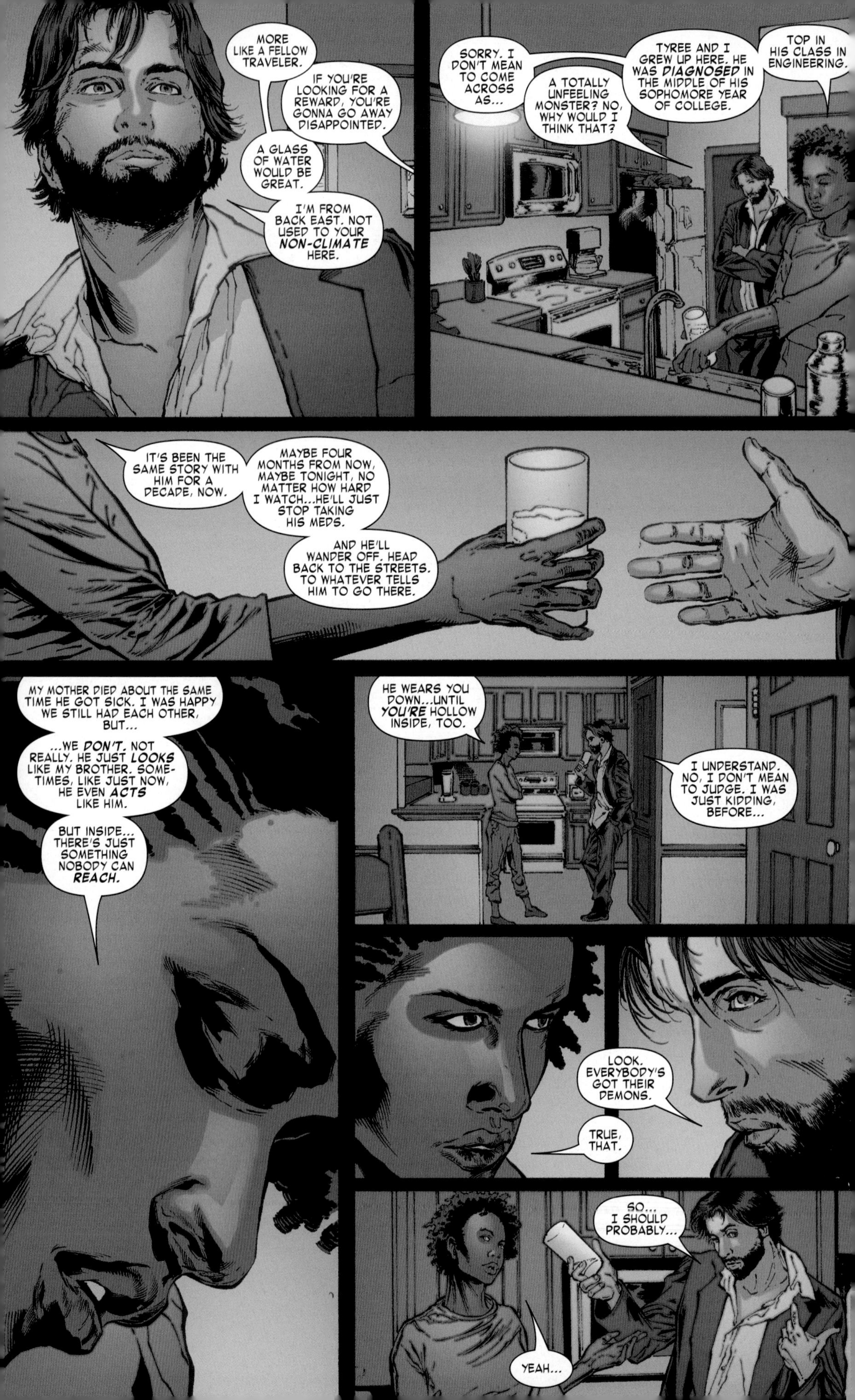
MORE LIKE A FELLOW TRAVELER.
IF YOU'RE LOOKING FOR A REWARD, YOU'RE GONNA GO AWAY DISAPPOINTED.
A GLASS OF WATER WOULD BE GREAT.
I'M FROM BACK EAST. NOT USED TO YOUR NON-CLIMATE HERE.
SORRY. I DON'T MEAN TO COME ACROSS AS...
A TOTALLY UNFEELING MONSTER? NO, WHY WOULD I THINK THAT?
TYREE AND I GREW UP HERE. HE WAS DIAGNOSED IN THE MIDDLE OF HIS SOPHOMORE YEAR OF COLLEGE.
TOP IN HIS CLASS IN ENGINEERING.
IT'S BEEN THE SAME STORY WITH HIM FOR A DECADE, NOW.
MAYBE FOUR MONTHS FROM NOW, MAYBE TONIGHT, NO MATTER HOW HARD I WATCH...HE'LL JUST STOP TAKING HIS MEDS.
AND HE'LL WANDER OFF. HEAD BACK TO THE STREETS. TO WHATEVER TELLS HIM TO GO THERE.
MY MOTHER DIED ABOUT THE SAME TIME HE GOT SICK. I WAS HAPPY WE STILL HAD EACH OTHER, BUT...
...WE DON'T. NOT REALLY. HE JUST LOOKS LIKE MY BROTHER. SOME-TIMES, LIKE JUST NOW, HE EVEN ACTS LIKE HIM.
BUT INSIDE... THERE'S JUST SOMETHING NOBODY CAN REACH.
HE WEARS YOU DOWN...UNTIL YOU'RE HOLLOW INSIDE, TOO.
I UNDERSTAND. NO, I DON'T MEAN TO JUDGE. I WAS JUST KIDDING, BEFORE...
LOOK. EVERYBODY'S GOT THEIR DEMONS.
TRUE, THAT.
SO... I SHOULD PROBABLY...
YEAH...

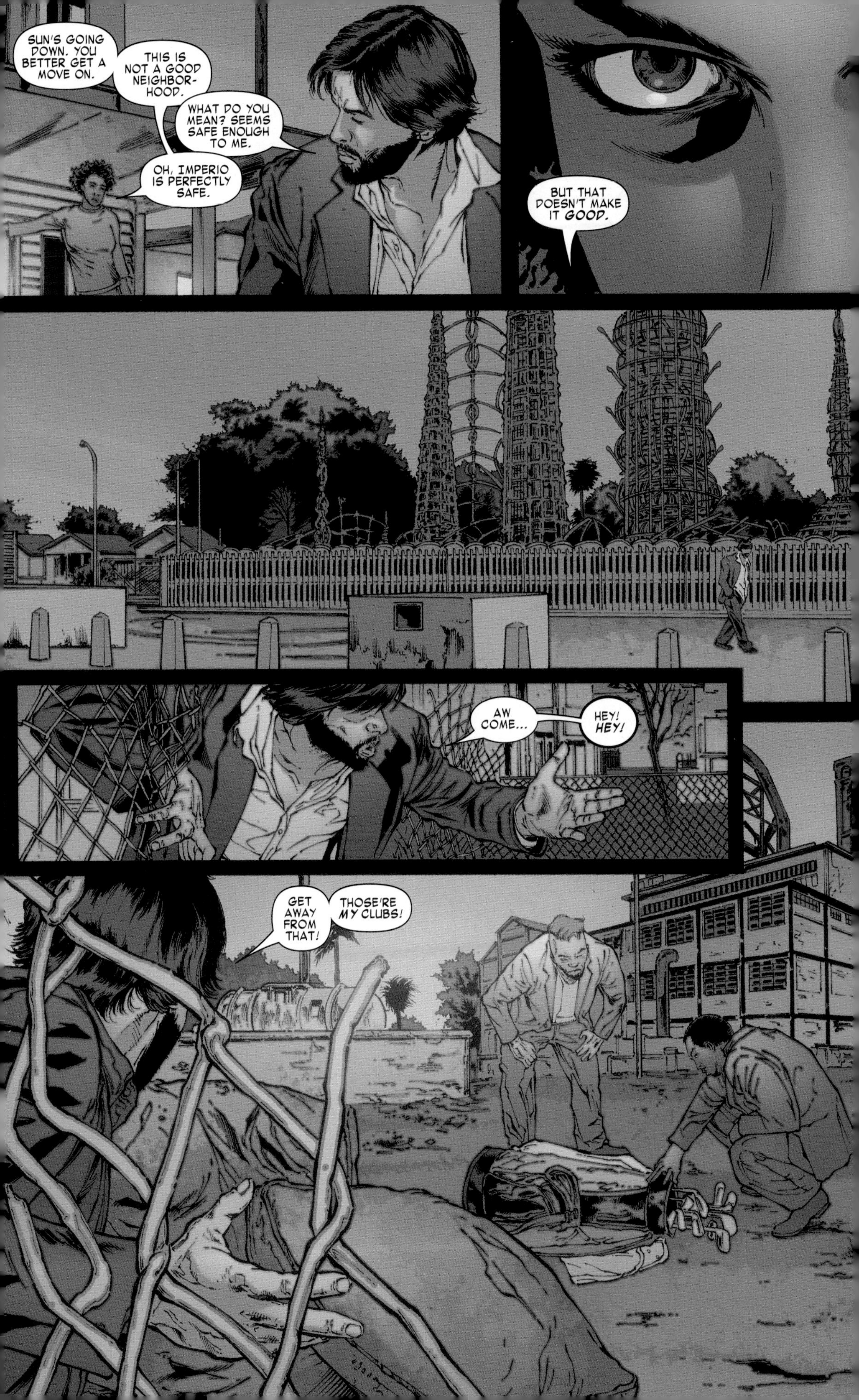
SUN'S GOING DOWN. YOU BETTER GET A MOVE ON.
THIS IS NOT A GOOD NEIGHBOR-HOOD.
WHAT DO YOU MEAN? SEEMS SAFE ENOUGH TO ME.
OH, IMPERIO IS PERFECTLY SAFE.
BUT THAT DOESN'T MAKE IT GOOD.
AW COME...
HEY! HEY!
GET AWAY FROM THAT!
THOSE'RE MY CLUBS!

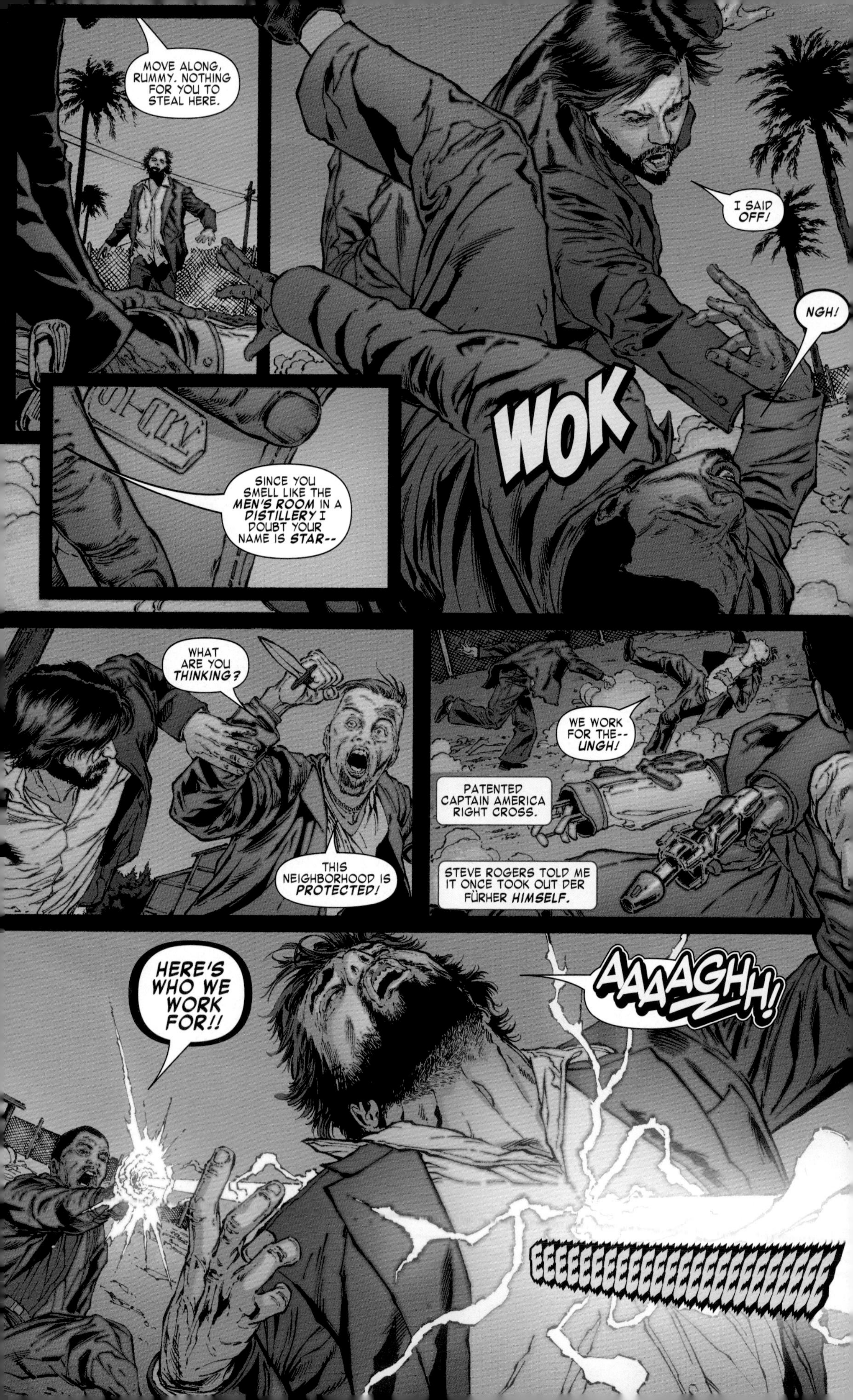
MOVE ALONG, RUMMY. NOTHING FOR YOU TO STEAL HERE.
SINCE YOU SMELL LIKE THE MEN'S ROOM IN A DISTILLERY I DOUBT YOUR NAME IS STAR--
I SAID OFF!
NGH!
WOK
WHAT ARE YOU THINKING?
THIS NEIGHBORHOOD IS PROTECTED!
WE WORK FOR THE-- UNGH!
PATENTED CAPTAIN AMERICA RIGHT CROSS.
STEVE ROGERS TOLD ME IT ONCE TOOK OUT DER FÜRHER HIMSELF.
HERE'S WHO WE WORK FOR!!
AAAAGHH!
EEEEEEEEEEEEEEEEEEEEEE

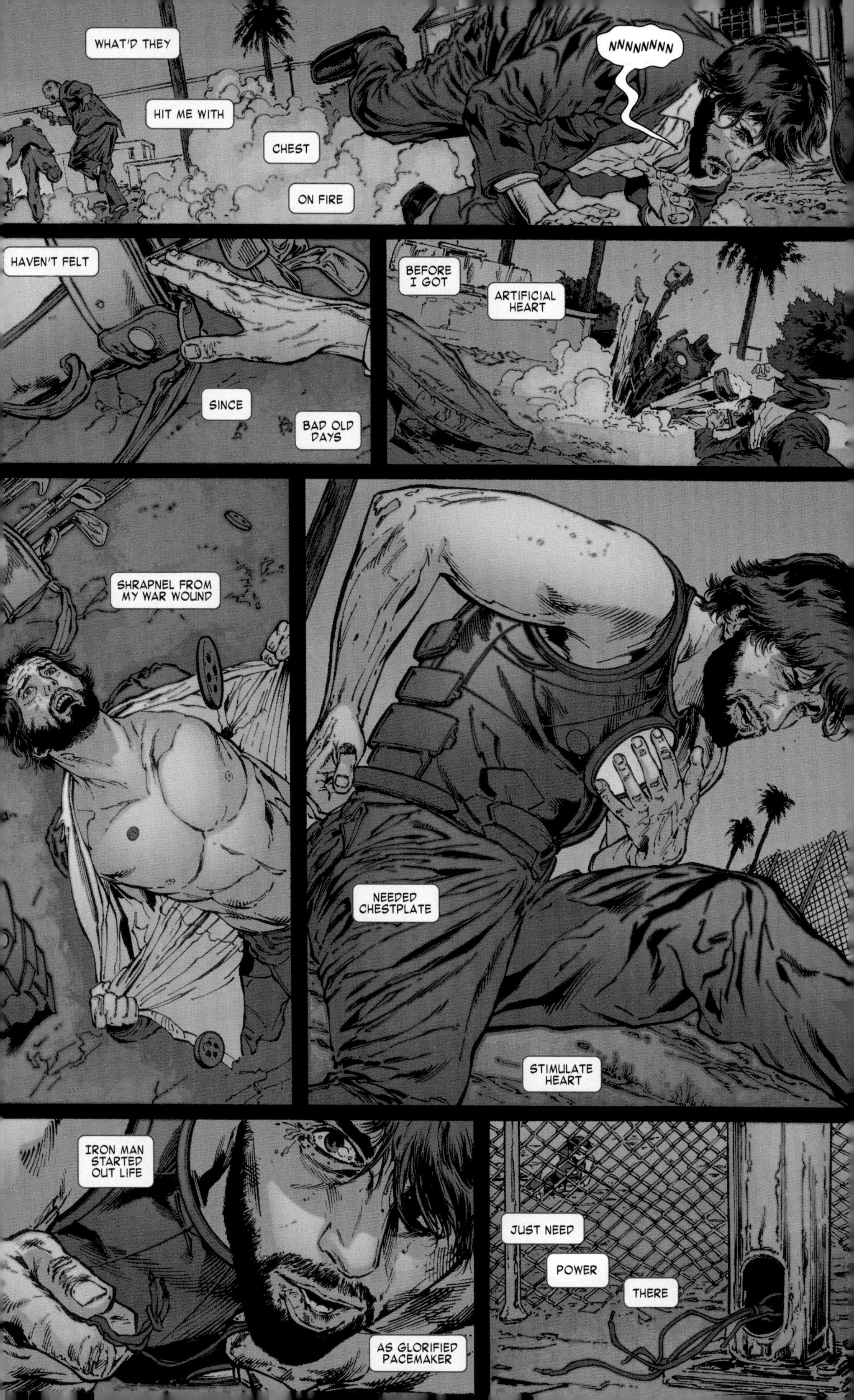
WHAT'D THEY
HIT ME WITH
CHEST
ON FIRE
NNNNNNNN
HAVEN'T FELT
SINCE
BAD OLD DAYS
BEFORE I GOT
ARTIFICIAL HEART
SHRAPNEL FROM MY WAR WOUND
NEEDED CHESTPLATE
STIMULATE HEART
IRON MAN STARTED OUT LIFE
AS GLORIFIED PACEMAKER
JUST NEED
POWER
THERE

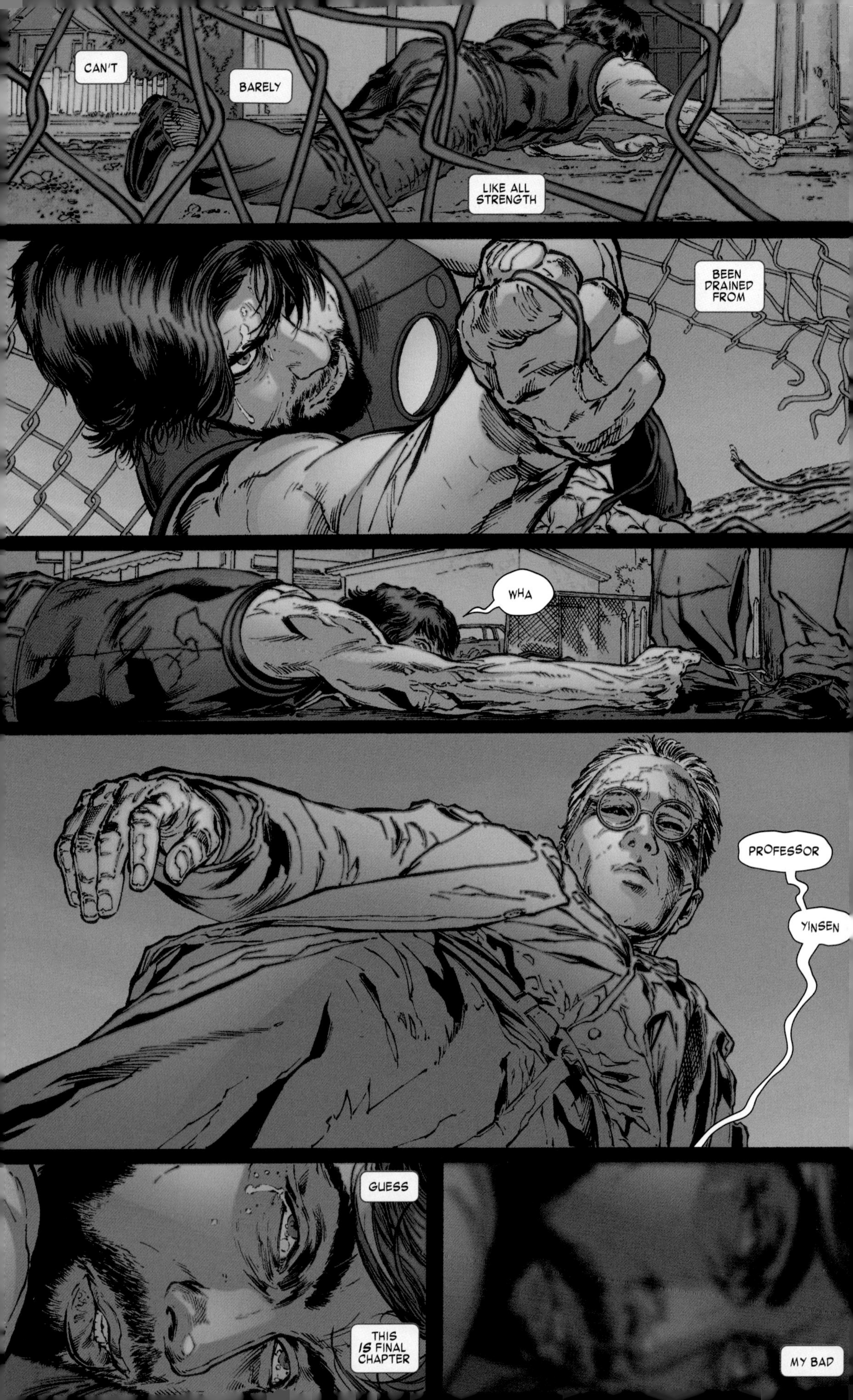
CAN'T
BARELY
LIKE ALL STRENGTH
BEEN DRAINED FROM
WHA
PROFESSOR
YINSEN
GUESS
THIS IS FINAL CHAPTER
MY BAD

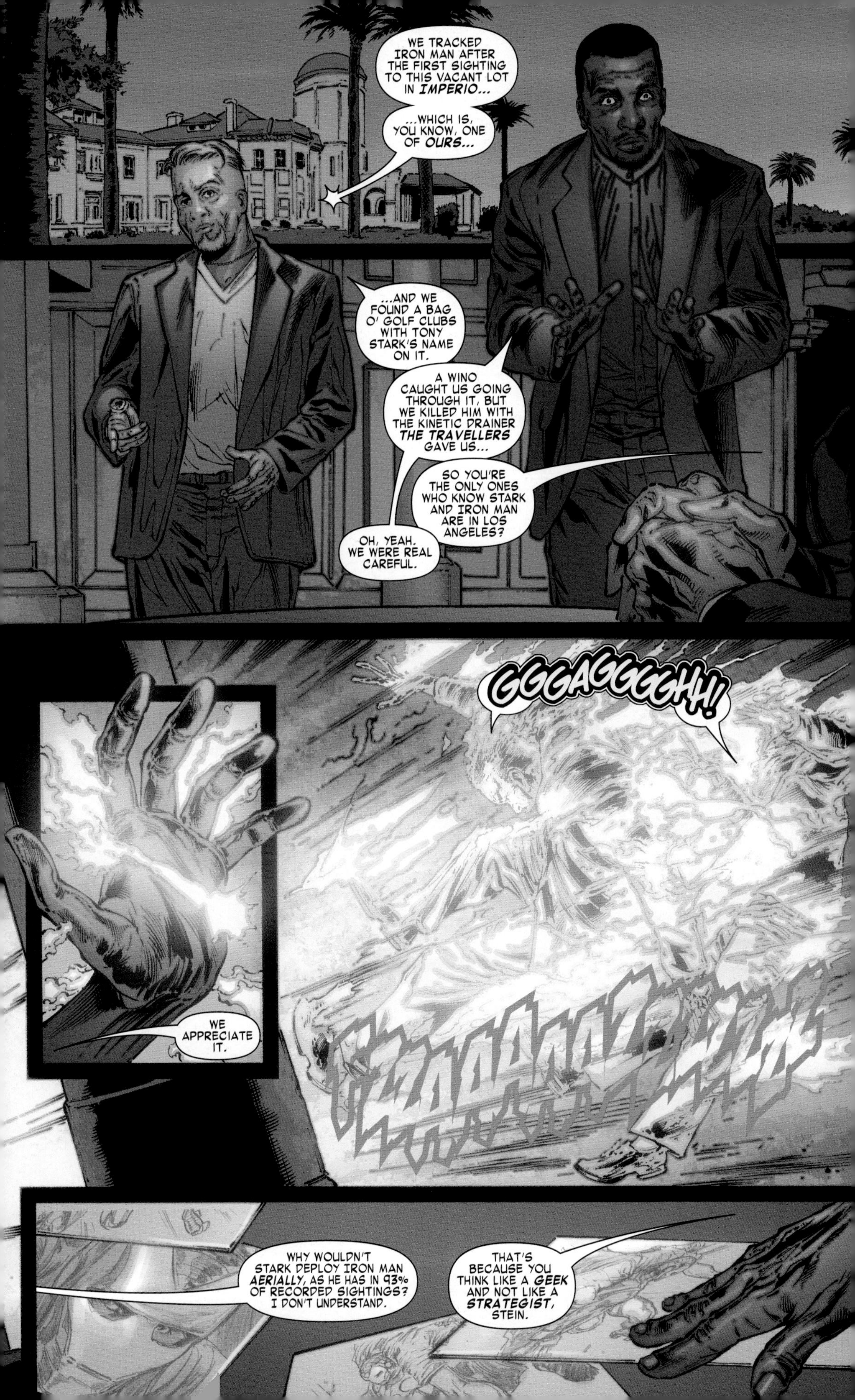
WE TRACKED IRON MAN AFTER THE FIRST SIGHTING TO THIS VACANT LOT IN IMPERIO...
...WHICH IS, YOU KNOW, ONE OF OURS...
...AND WE FOUND A BAG O' GOLF CLUBS WITH TONY STARK'S NAME ON IT.
A WINO CAUGHT US GOING THROUGH IT, BUT WE KILLED HIM WITH THE KINETIC DRAINER THE TRAVELLERS GAVE US...
SO YOU'RE THE ONLY ONES WHO KNOW STARK AND IRON MAN ARE IN LOS ANGELES?
OH, YEAH. WE WERE REAL CAREFUL.
WE APPRECIATE IT.
GGGAGGGGHH!
WHY WOULDN'T STARK DEPLOY IRON MAN AERIALLY, AS HE HAS IN 93% OF RECORDED SIGHTINGS? I DON'T UNDERSTAND.
THAT'S BECAUSE YOU THINK LIKE A GEEK AND NOT LIKE A STRATEGIST, STEIN.

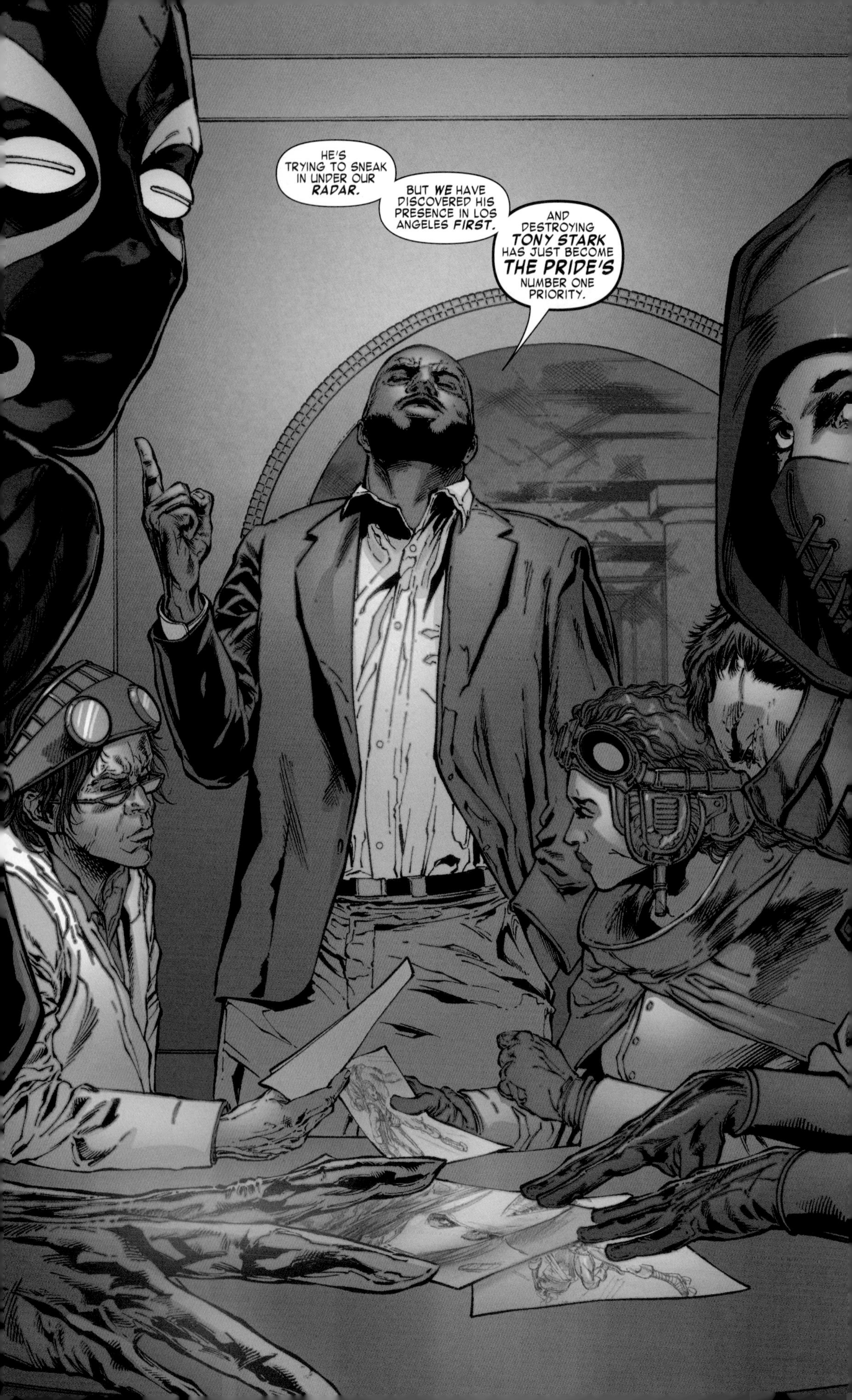
HE'S TRYING TO SNEAK IN UNDER OUR RADAR.
BUT WE HAVE DISCOVERED HIS PRESENCE IN LOS ANGELES FIRST.
AND DESTROYING TONY STARK HAS JUST BECOME THE PRIDE'S NUMBER ONE PRIORITY.

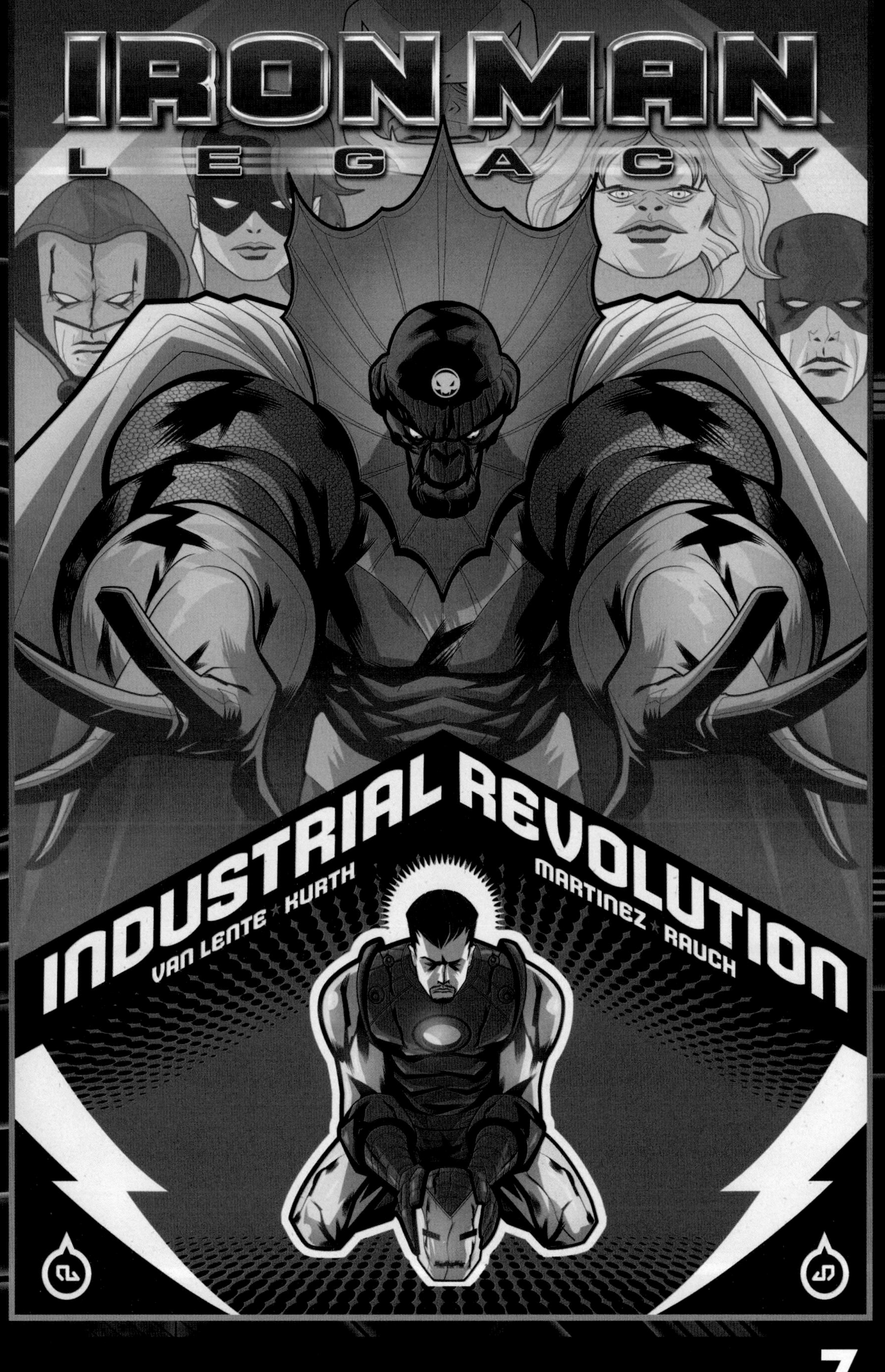
IRON MAN
LEGACY
INDUSTRIAL REVOLUTION
VAN LENTE KURTH
MARTINEZ RAUCH

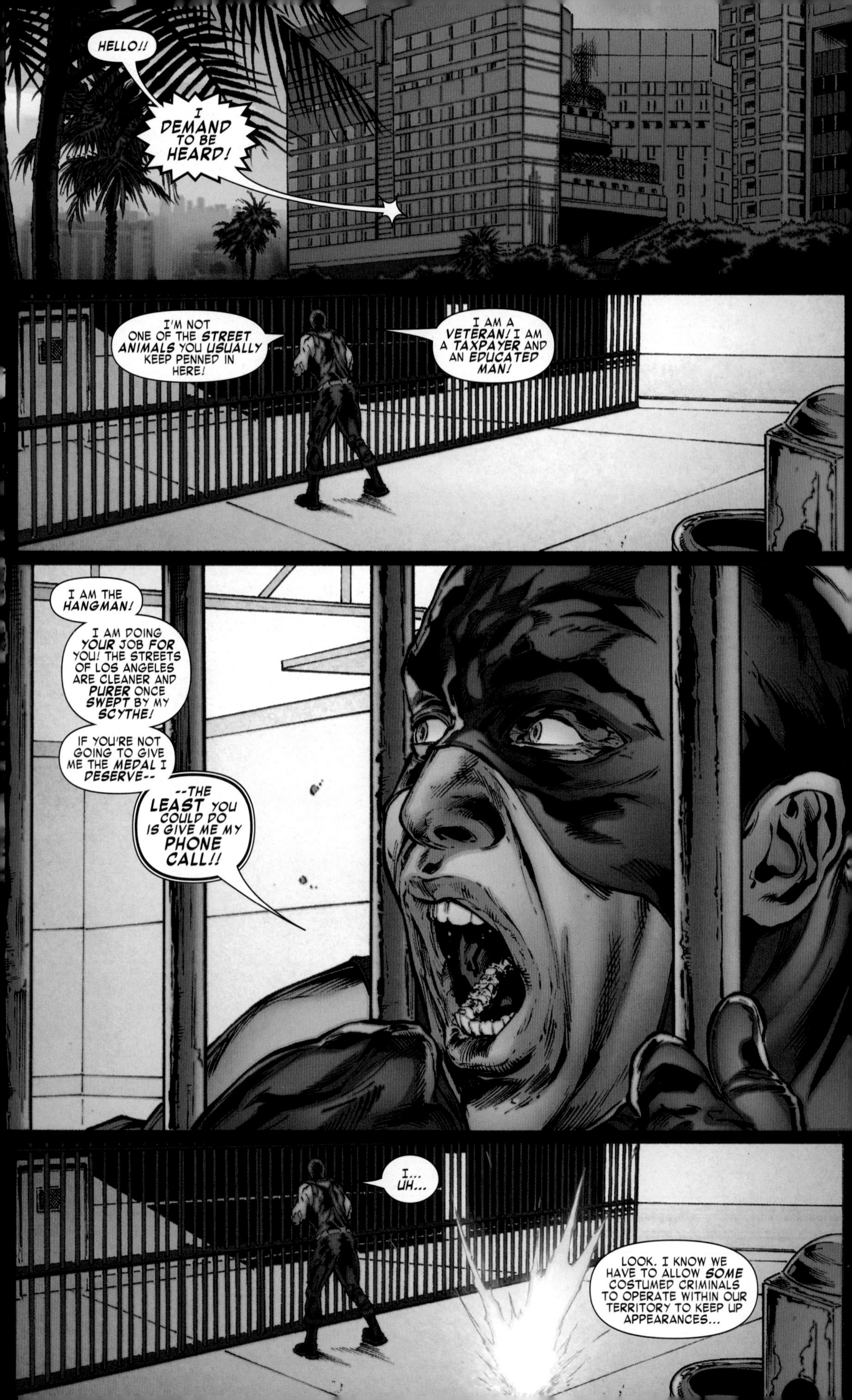
HELLO!!
I DEMAND TO BE HEARD!
I'M NOT ONE OF THE STREET ANIMALS YOU USUALLY KEEP PENNED IN HERE!
I AM A VETERAN! I AM A TAXPAYER AND AN EDUCATED MAN!
I AM THE HANGMAN!
I AM DOING YOUR JOB FOR YOU! THE STREETS OF LOS ANGELES ARE CLEANER AND PURER ONCE SWEPT BY MY SCYTHE!
IF YOU'RE NOT GOING TO GIVE ME THE MEDAL I DESERVE--
--THE LEAST YOU COULD DO IS GIVE ME MY PHONE CALL!!
I... UH...
LOOK. I KNOW WE HAVE TO ALLOW SOME COSTUMED CRIMINALS TO OPERATE WITHIN OUR TERRITORY TO KEEP UP APPEARANCES...

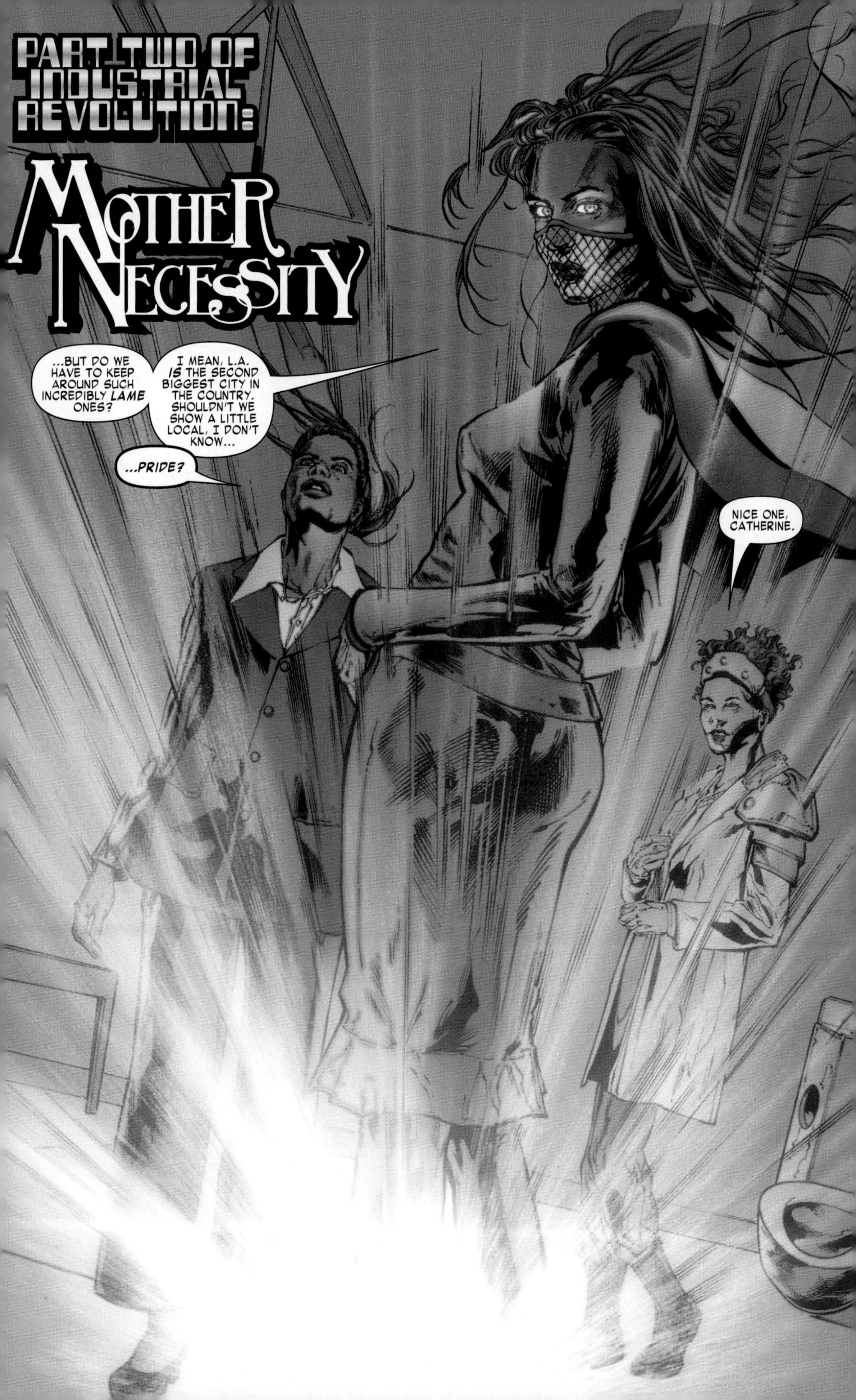
PART TWO OF INDUSTRIAL REVOLUTION:
MOTHER NECESSITY
...BUT DO WE HAVE TO KEEP AROUND SUCH INCREDIBLY LAME ONES?
I MEAN, L.A. IS THE SECOND BIGGEST CITY IN THE COUNTRY. SHOULDN'T WE SHOW A LITTLE LOCAL, I DON'T KNOW...
...PRIDE?
NICE ONE, CATHERINE.

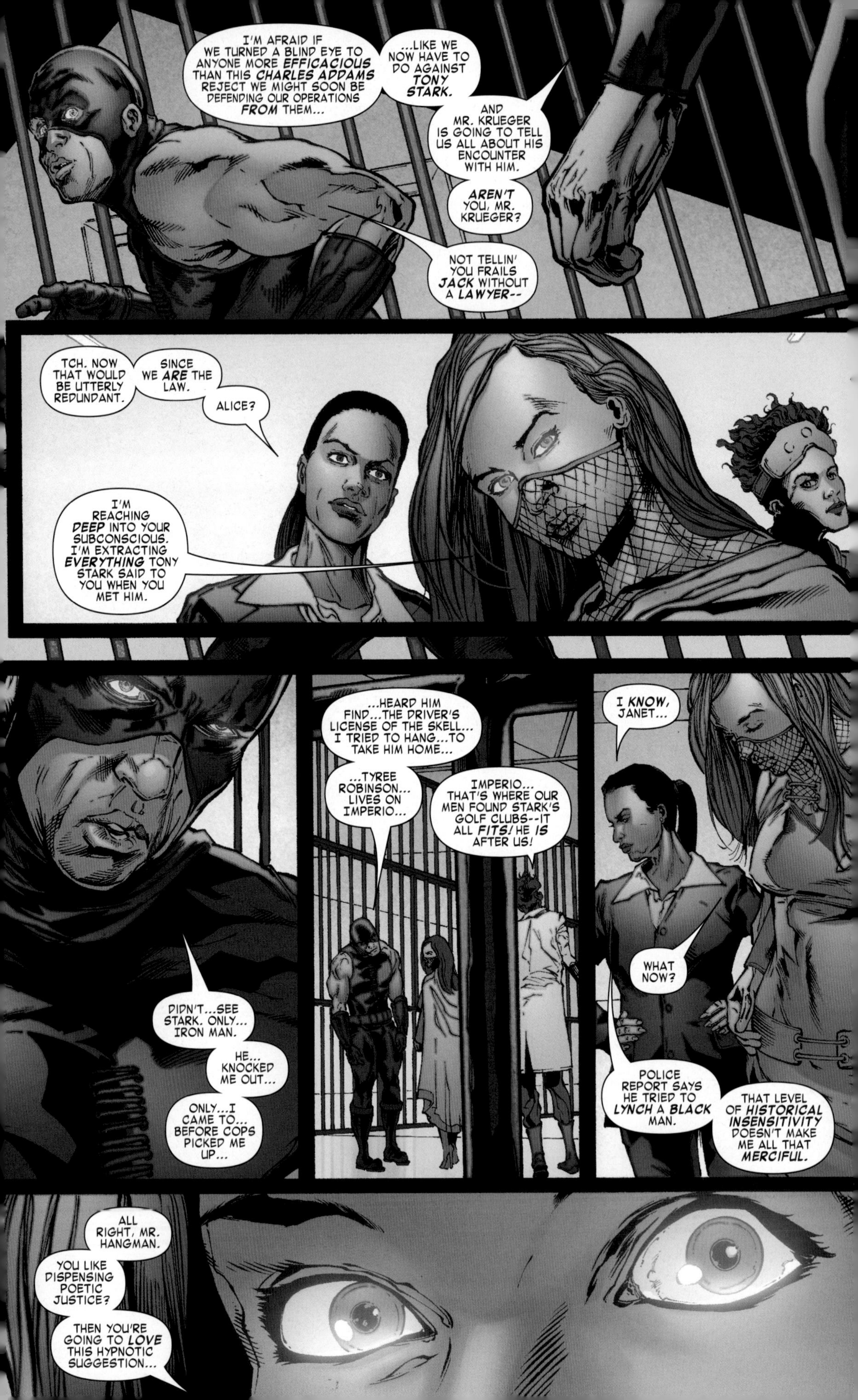

I'M AFRAID IF WE TURNED A BLIND EYE TO ANYONE MORE EFFICACIOUS THAN THIS CHARLES ADDAMS REJECT WE MIGHT SOON BE DEFENDING OUR OPERATIONS FROM THEM...
...LIKE WE NOW HAVE TO DO AGAINST TONY STARK.
AND MR. KRUEGER IS GOING TO TELL US ALL ABOUT HIS ENCOUNTER WITH HIM.
AREN'T YOU, MR. KRUEGER?
NOT TELLIN' YOU FRAILS JACK WITHOUT A LAWYER--
TCH. NOW THAT WOULD BE UTTERLY REDUNDANT.
SINCE WE ARE THE LAW.
ALICE?
I'M REACHING DEEP INTO YOUR SUBCONSCIOUS. I'M EXTRACTING EVERYTHING TONY STARK SAID TO YOU WHEN YOU MET HIM.
DIDN'T...SEE STARK. ONLY... IRON MAN.
HE... KNOCKED ME OUT...
ONLY...I CAME TO... BEFORE COPS PICKED ME UP...
...HEARD HIM FIND...THE DRIVER'S LICENSE OF THE SKELL... I TRIED TO HANG...TO TAKE HIM HOME...
...TYREE ROBINSON... LIVES ON IMPERIO...
IMPERIO... THAT'S WHERE OUR MEN FOUND STARK'S GOLF CLUBS--IT ALL FITS! HE IS AFTER US!
I KNOW, JANET...
WHAT NOW?
POLICE REPORT SAYS HE TRIED TO LYNCH A BLACK MAN.
THAT LEVEL OF HISTORICAL INSENSITIVITY DOESN'T MAKE ME ALL THAT MERCIFUL.
ALL RIGHT, MR. HANGMAN.
YOU LIKE DISPENSING POETIC JUSTICE?
THEN YOU'RE GOING TO LOVE THIS HYPNOTIC SUGGESTION...

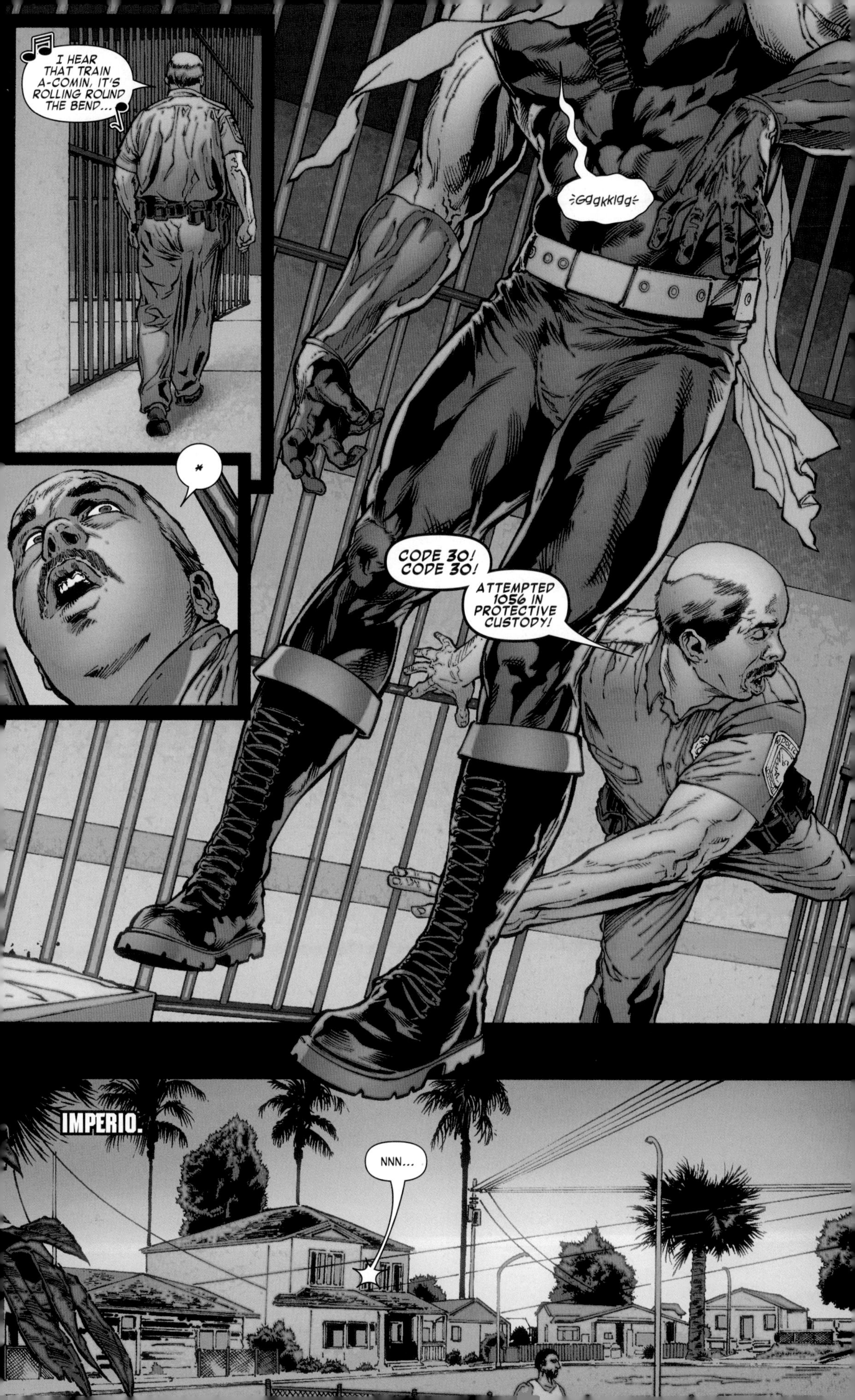
I HEAR THAT TRAIN A-COMIN, IT'S ROLLING ROUND THE BEND...
GGGKKLGG
*
CODE 30! CODE 30!
ATTEMPTED 1056 IN PROTECTIVE CUSTODY!
IMPERIO.
NNN...

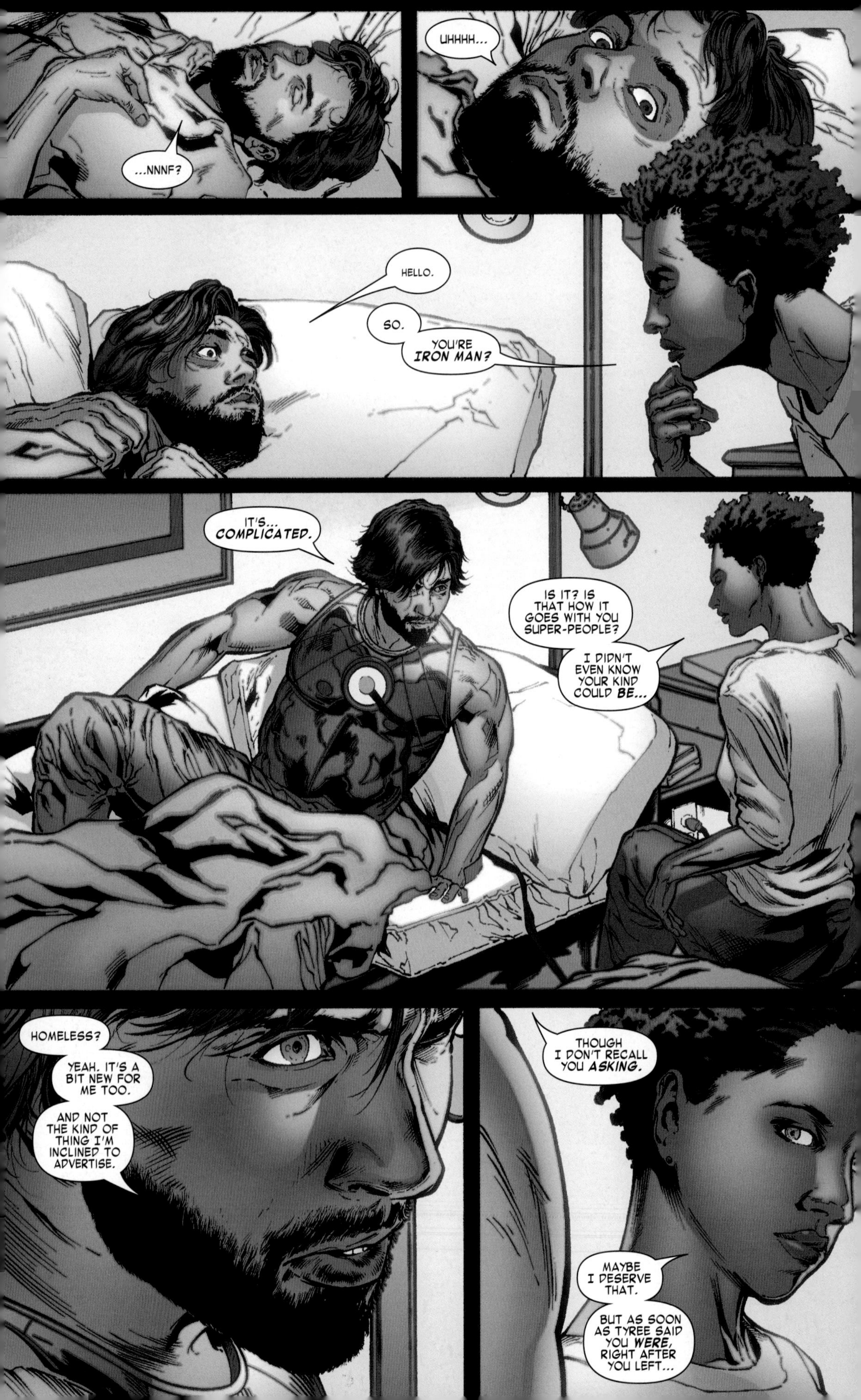
...NNNF?
UHHHH...
HELLO.
SO.
YOU'RE IRON MAN?
IT'S... COMPLICATED.
IS IT? IS THAT HOW IT GOES WITH YOU SUPER-PEOPLE?
I DIDN'T EVEN KNOW YOUR KIND COULD BE...
HOMELESS?
YEAH. IT'S A BIT NEW FOR ME TOO.
AND NOT THE KIND OF THING I'M INCLINED TO ADVERTISE.
THOUGH I DON'T RECALL YOU ASKING.
MAYBE I DESERVE THAT.
BUT AS SOON AS TYREE SAID YOU WERE, RIGHT AFTER YOU LEFT...

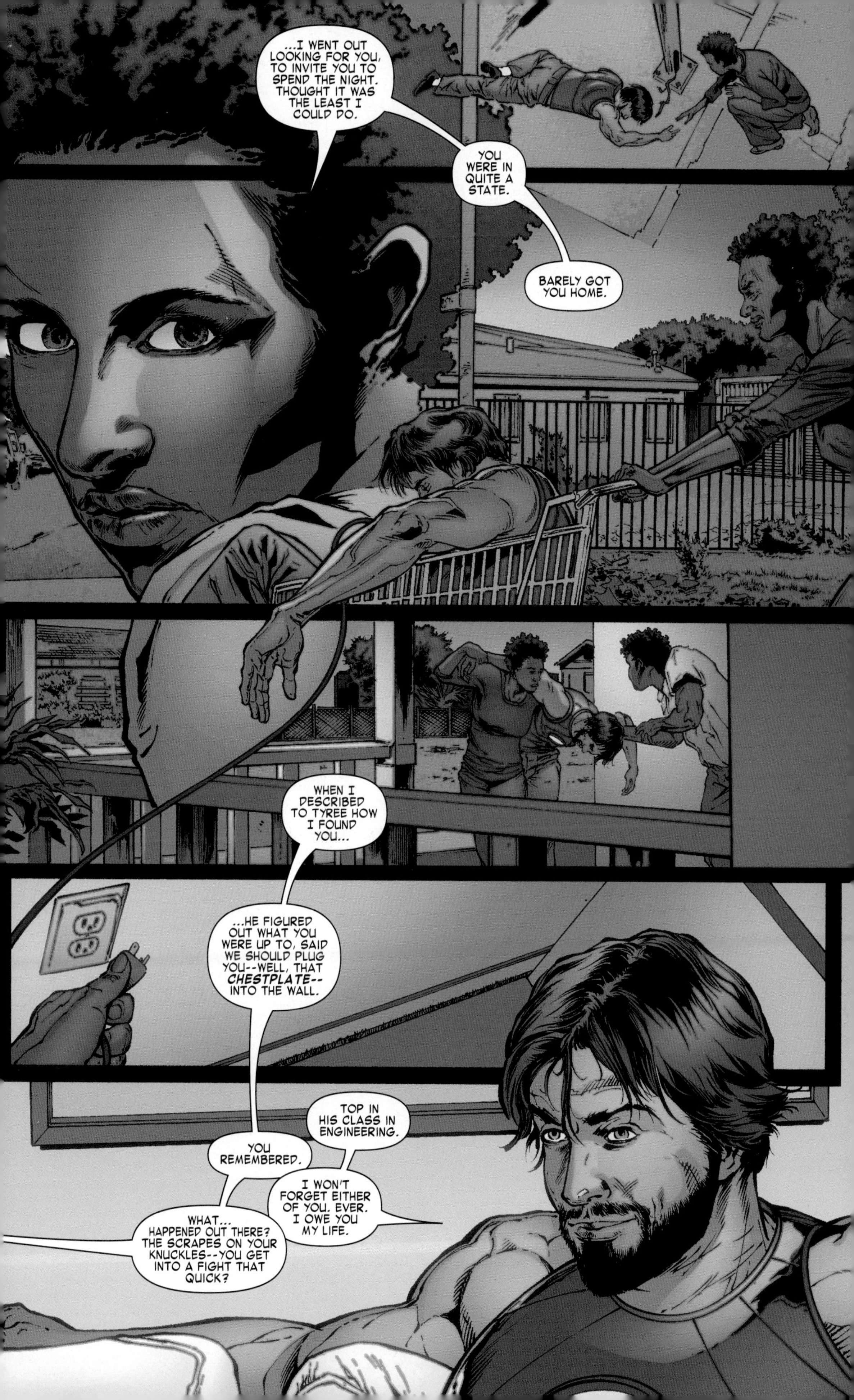
...I WENT OUT LOOKING FOR YOU, TO INVITE YOU TO SPEND THE NIGHT. THOUGHT IT WAS THE LEAST I COULD DO.
YOU WERE IN QUITE A STATE.
BARELY GOT YOU HOME.
WHEN I DESCRIBED TO TYREE HOW I FOUND YOU...
...HE FIGURED OUT WHAT YOU WERE UP TO, SAID WE SHOULD PLUG YOU--WELL, THAT CHESTPLATE-- INTO THE WALL.
TOP IN HIS CLASS IN ENGINEERING.
YOU REMEMBERED.
I WON'T FORGET EITHER OF YOU. EVER. I OWE YOU MY LIFE.
WHAT... HAPPENED OUT THERE? THE SCRAPES ON YOUR KNUCKLES--YOU GET INTO A FIGHT THAT QUICK?

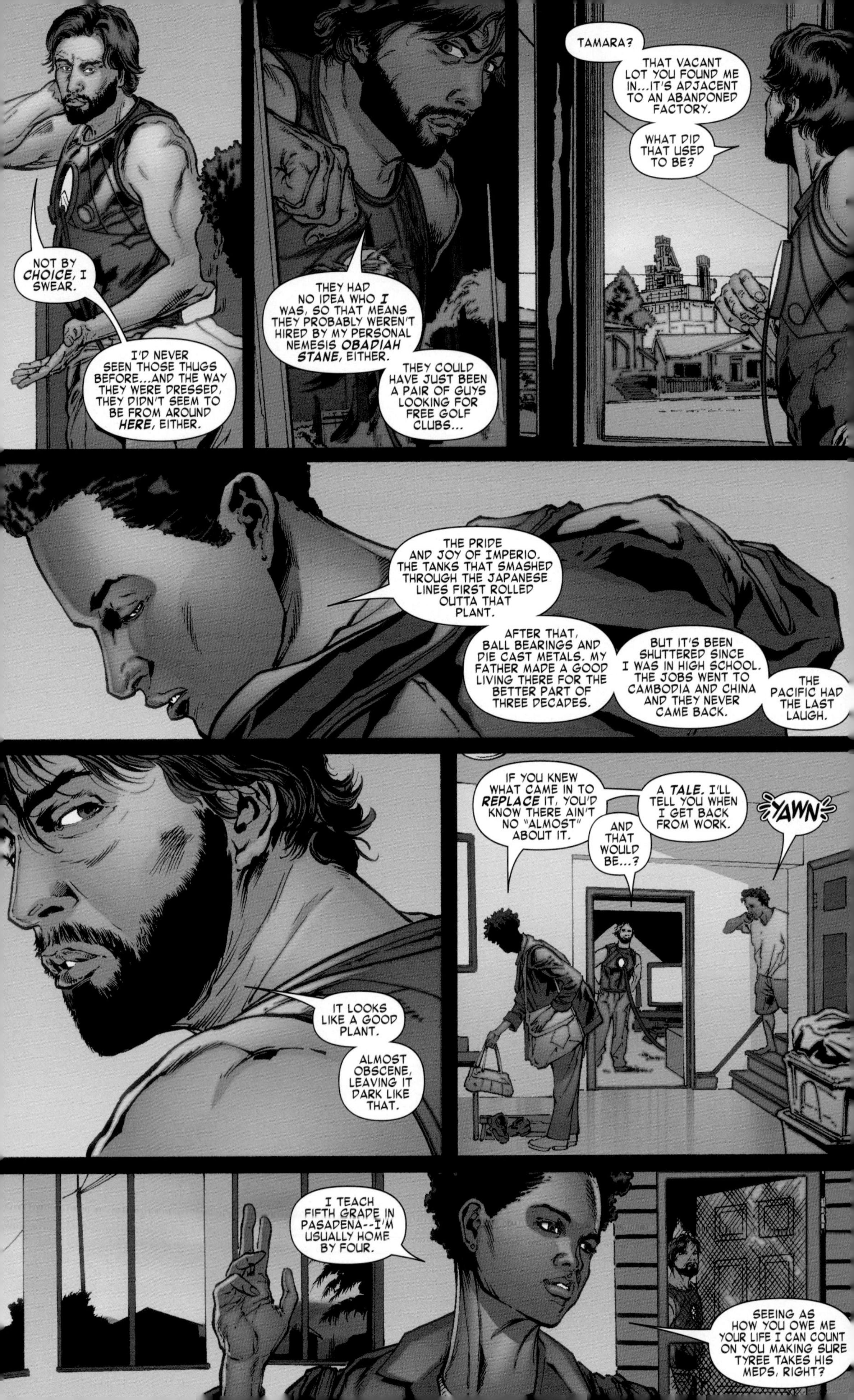
NOT BY *CHOICE*, I SWEAR.
I'D NEVER SEEN THOSE THUGS BEFORE...AND THE WAY THEY WERE DRESSED, THEY DIDN'T SEEM TO BE FROM AROUND *HERE*, EITHER.
THEY HAD NO IDEA WHO *I* WAS, SO THAT MEANS THEY PROBABLY WEREN'T HIRED BY MY PERSONAL NEMESIS *OBADIAH STANE*, EITHER.
THEY COULD HAVE JUST BEEN A PAIR OF GUYS LOOKING FOR FREE GOLF CLUBS...
TAMARA?
THAT VACANT LOT YOU FOUND ME IN...IT'S ADJACENT TO AN ABANDONED FACTORY.
WHAT DID THAT USED TO BE?
THE PRIDE AND JOY OF IMPERIO. THE TANKS THAT SMASHED THROUGH THE JAPANESE LINES FIRST ROLLED OUTTA THAT PLANT.
AFTER THAT, BALL BEARINGS AND DIE CAST METALS. MY FATHER MADE A GOOD LIVING THERE FOR THE BETTER PART OF THREE DECADES.
BUT IT'S BEEN SHUTTERED SINCE I WAS IN HIGH SCHOOL. THE JOBS WENT TO CAMBODIA AND CHINA AND THEY NEVER CAME BACK.
THE PACIFIC HAD THE LAST LAUGH.
IT LOOKS LIKE A GOOD PLANT.
ALMOST OBSCENE, LEAVING IT DARK LIKE THAT.
IF YOU KNEW WHAT CAME IN TO *REPLACE* IT, YOU'D KNOW THERE AIN'T NO "ALMOST" ABOUT IT.
AND THAT WOULD BE...?
A *TALE*. I'LL TELL YOU WHEN I GET BACK FROM WORK.
YAWN
I TEACH FIFTH GRADE IN PASADENA--I'M USUALLY HOME BY FOUR.
SEEING AS HOW YOU OWE ME YOUR LIFE I CAN COUNT ON YOU MAKING SURE TYREE TAKES HIS MEDS, RIGHT?

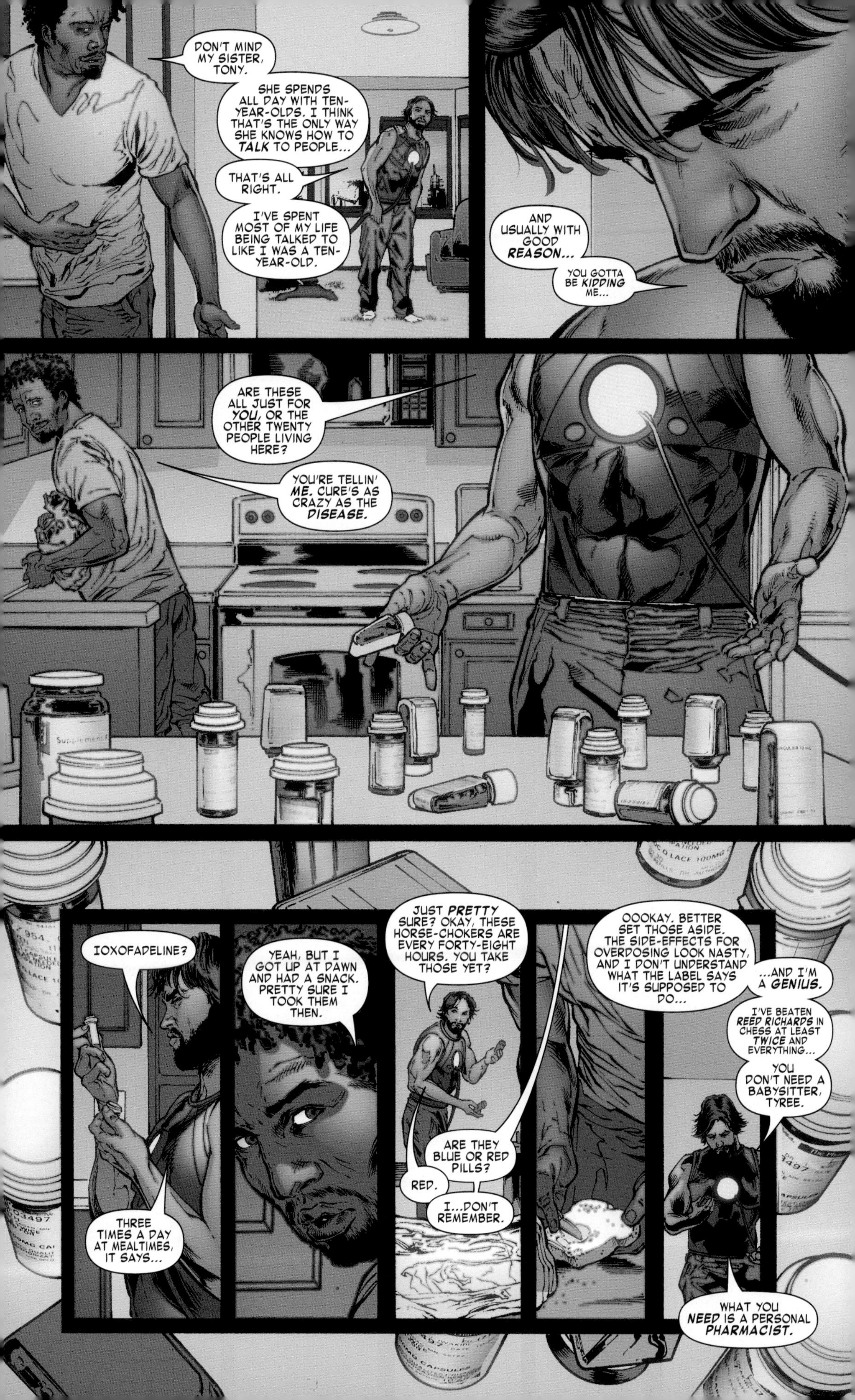
DON'T MIND MY SISTER, TONY.
SHE SPENDS ALL DAY WITH TEN-YEAR-OLDS. I THINK THAT'S THE ONLY WAY SHE KNOWS HOW TO TALK TO PEOPLE...
THAT'S ALL RIGHT.
I'VE SPENT MOST OF MY LIFE BEING TALKED TO LIKE I WAS A TEN-YEAR-OLD.
AND USUALLY WITH GOOD REASON...
YOU GOTTA BE KIDDING ME...
ARE THESE ALL JUST FOR YOU, OR THE OTHER TWENTY PEOPLE LIVING HERE?
YOU'RE TELLIN' ME. CURE'S AS CRAZY AS THE DISEASE.
IOXOFADELINE?
THREE TIMES A DAY AT MEALTIMES, IT SAYS...
YEAH, BUT I GOT UP AT DAWN AND HAD A SNACK. PRETTY SURE I TOOK THEM THEN.
JUST PRETTY SURE? OKAY, THESE HORSE-CHOKERS ARE EVERY FORTY-EIGHT HOURS. YOU TAKE THOSE YET?
ARE THEY BLUE OR RED PILLS?
RED.
I...DON'T REMEMBER.
OOOKAY. BETTER SET THOSE ASIDE. THE SIDE-EFFECTS FOR OVERDOSING LOOK NASTY, AND I DON'T UNDERSTAND WHAT THE LABEL SAYS IT'S SUPPOSED TO DO...
...AND I'M A GENIUS.
I'VE BEATEN REED RICHARDS IN CHESS AT LEAST TWICE AND EVERYTHING...
YOU DON'T NEED A BABYSITTER, TYREE.
WHAT YOU NEED IS A PERSONAL PHARMACIST.

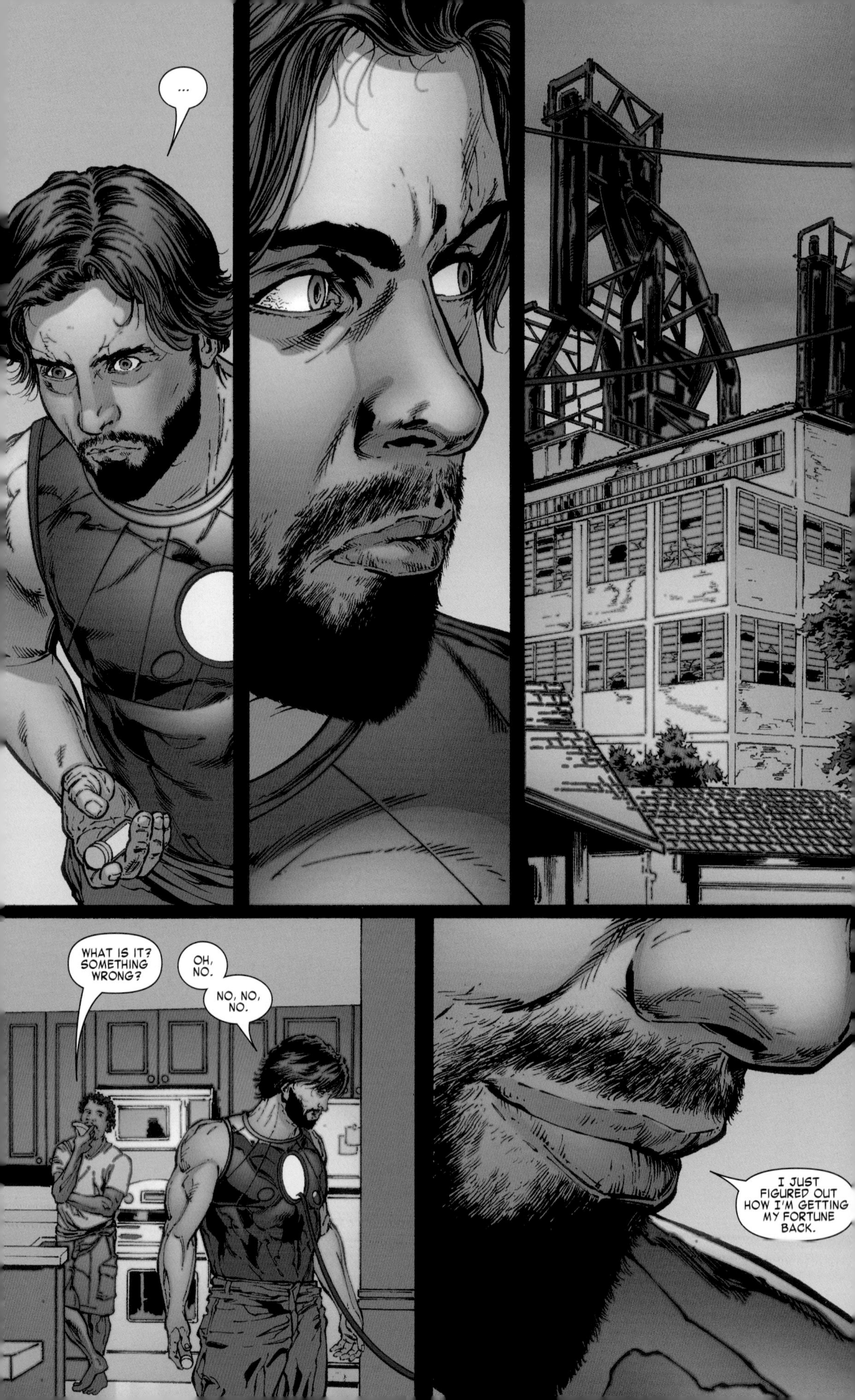
...
WHAT IS IT? SOMETHING WRONG?
OH, NO.
NO, NO, NO.
I JUST FIGURED OUT HOW I'M GETTING MY FORTUNE BACK.

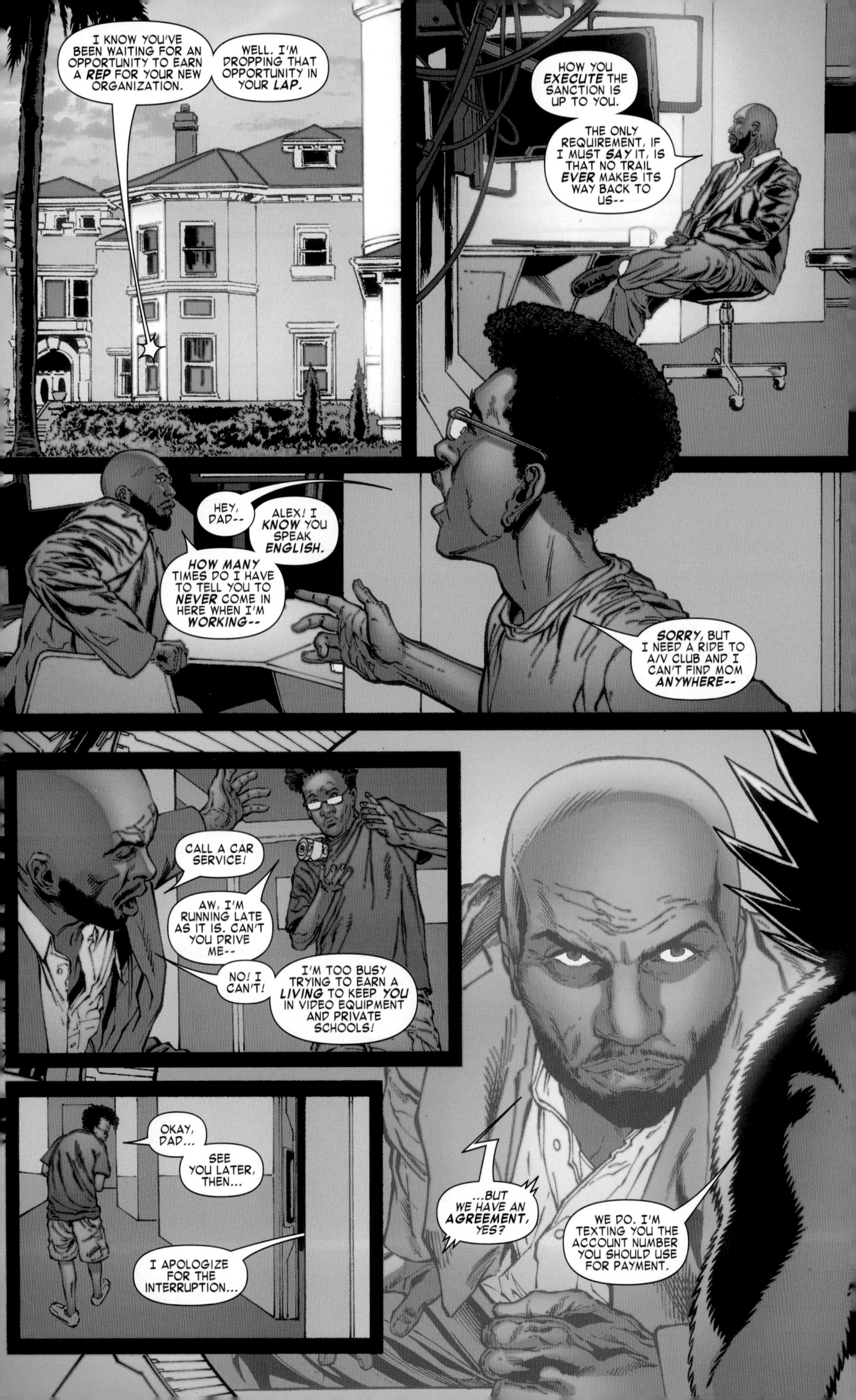
I KNOW YOU'VE BEEN WAITING FOR AN OPPORTUNITY TO EARN A REP FOR YOUR NEW ORGANIZATION.
WELL. I'M DROPPING THAT OPPORTUNITY IN YOUR LAP.
HOW YOU EXECUTE THE SANCTION IS UP TO YOU.
THE ONLY REQUIREMENT, IF I MUST SAY IT, IS THAT NO TRAIL EVER MAKES ITS WAY BACK TO US--
HEY, DAD--
ALEX! I KNOW YOU SPEAK ENGLISH.
HOW MANY TIMES DO I HAVE TO TELL YOU TO NEVER COME IN HERE WHEN I'M WORKING--
SORRY, BUT I NEED A RIDE TO A/V CLUB AND I CAN'T FIND MOM ANYWHERE--
CALL A CAR SERVICE!
AW, I'M RUNNING LATE AS IT IS. CAN'T YOU DRIVE ME--
NO! I CAN'T!
I'M TOO BUSY TRYING TO EARN A LIVING TO KEEP YOU IN VIDEO EQUIPMENT AND PRIVATE SCHOOLS!
OKAY, DAD...
SEE YOU LATER, THEN...
I APOLOGIZE FOR THE INTERRUPTION...
...BUT WE HAVE AN AGREEMENT, YES?
WE DO. I'M TEXTING YOU THE ACCOUNT NUMBER YOU SHOULD USE FOR PAYMENT.

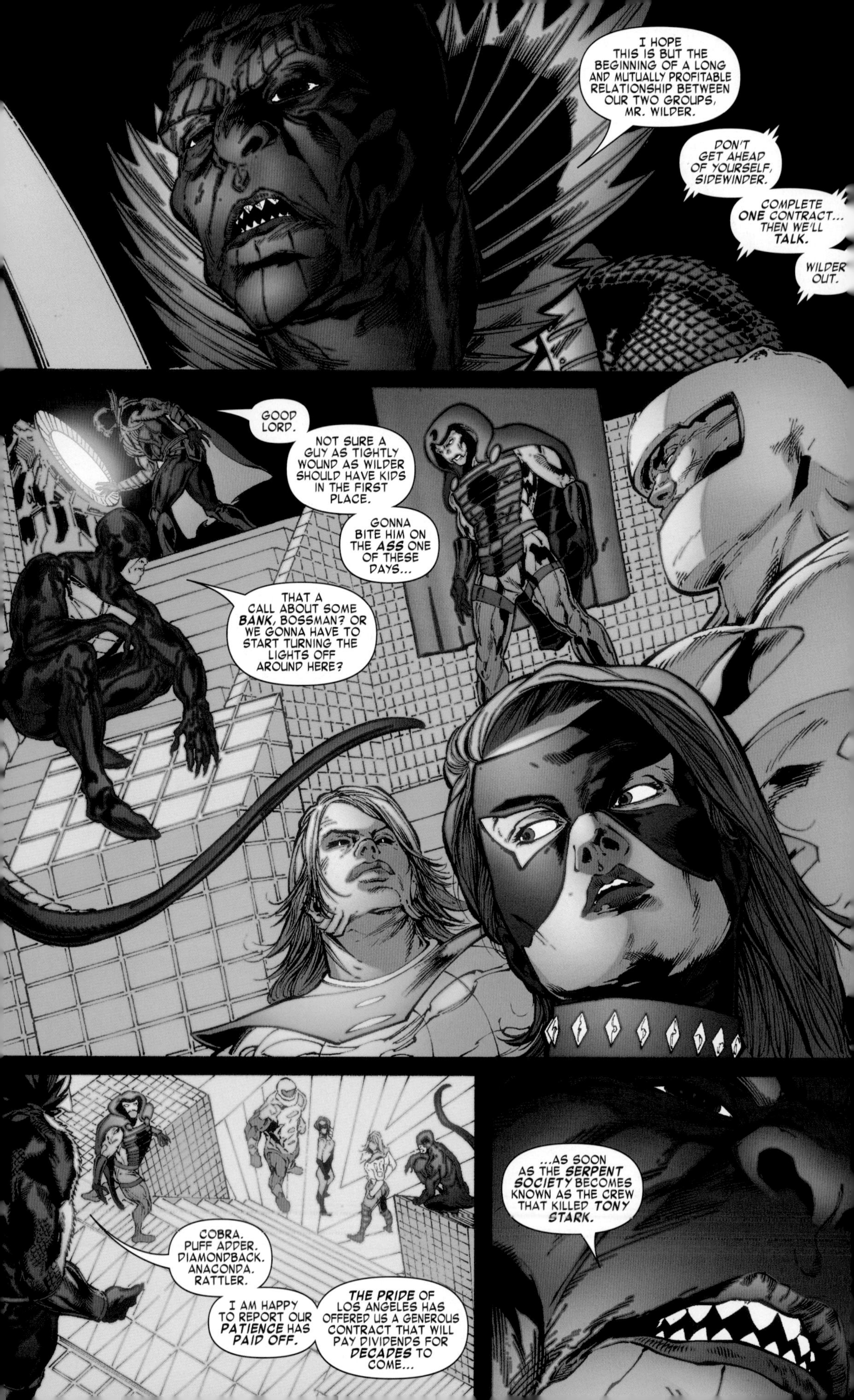
I HOPE THIS IS BUT THE BEGINNING OF A LONG AND MUTUALLY PROFITABLE RELATIONSHIP BETWEEN OUR TWO GROUPS, MR. WILDER.
DON'T GET AHEAD OF YOURSELF, SIDEWINDER.
COMPLETE ONE CONTRACT... THEN WE'LL TALK.
WILDER OUT.
GOOD LORD.
NOT SURE A GUY AS TIGHTLY WOUND AS WILDER SHOULD HAVE KIDS IN THE FIRST PLACE.
GONNA BITE HIM ON THE ASS ONE OF THESE DAYS...
THAT A CALL ABOUT SOME BANK, BOSSMAN? OR WE GONNA HAVE TO START TURNING THE LIGHTS OFF AROUND HERE?
COBRA. PUFF ADDER. DIAMONDBACK. ANACONDA. RATTLER.
I AM HAPPY TO REPORT OUR PATIENCE HAS PAID OFF.
THE PRIDE OF LOS ANGELES HAS OFFERED US A GENEROUS CONTRACT THAT WILL PAY DIVIDENDS FOR DECADES TO COME...
...AS SOON AS THE SERPENT SOCIETY BECOMES KNOWN AS THE CREW THAT KILLED TONY STARK.

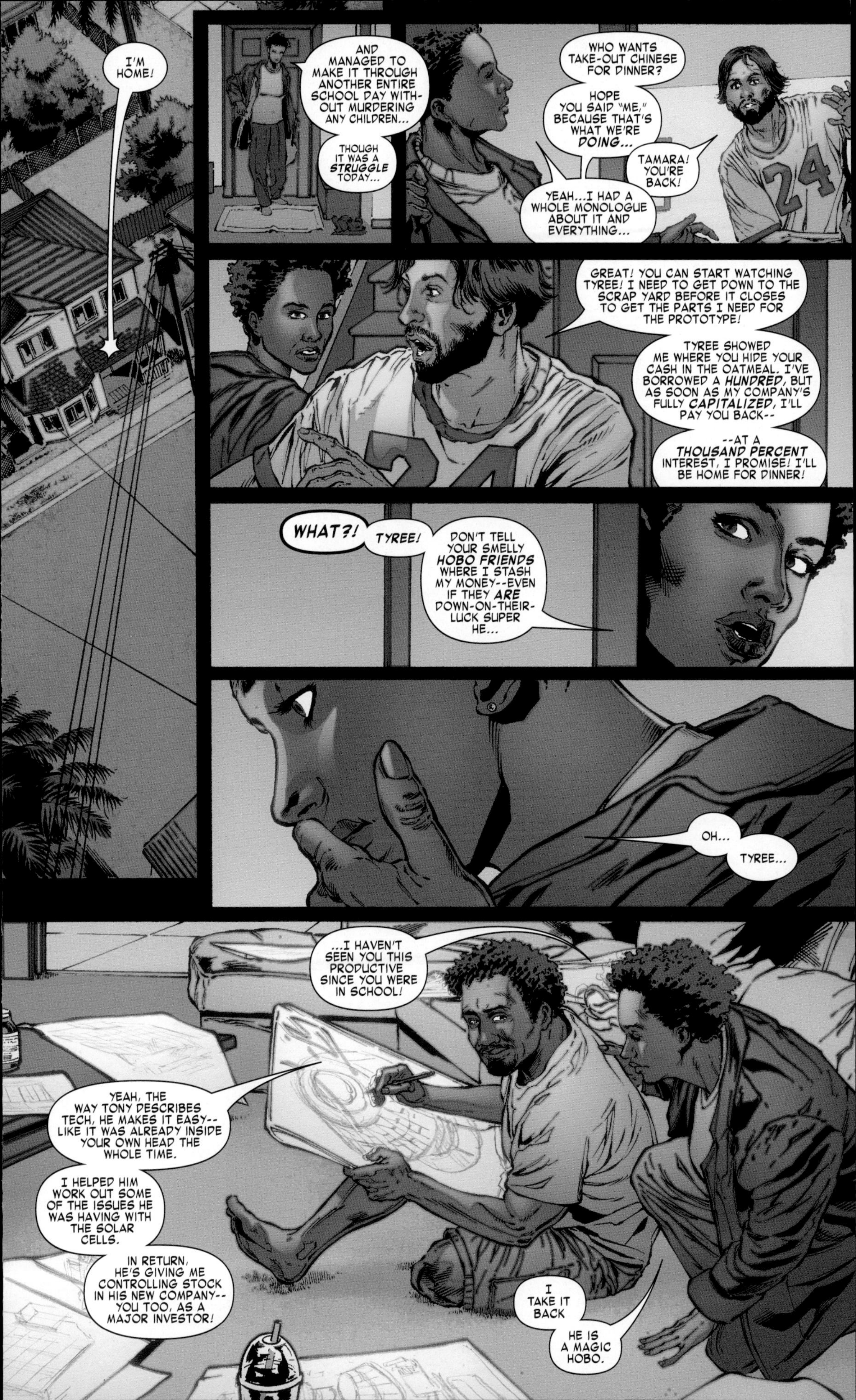
I'M HOME!
AND MANAGED TO MAKE IT THROUGH ANOTHER ENTIRE SCHOOL DAY WITH-OUT MURDERING ANY CHILDREN...
THOUGH IT WAS A STRUGGLE TODAY...
WHO WANTS TAKE-OUT CHINESE FOR DINNER?
HOPE YOU SAID "ME," BECAUSE THAT'S WHAT WE'RE DOING...
TAMARA! YOU'RE BACK!
YEAH...I HAD A WHOLE MONOLOGUE ABOUT IT AND EVERYTHING...
GREAT! YOU CAN START WATCHING TYREE! I NEED TO GET DOWN TO THE SCRAP YARD BEFORE IT CLOSES TO GET THE PARTS I NEED FOR THE PROTOTYPE!
TYREE SHOWED ME WHERE YOU HIDE YOUR CASH IN THE OATMEAL. I'VE BORROWED A HUNDRED, BUT AS SOON AS MY COMPANY'S FULLY CAPITALIZED, I'LL PAY YOU BACK--
--AT A THOUSAND PERCENT INTEREST, I PROMISE! I'LL BE HOME FOR DINNER!
WHAT?!
TYREE!
DON'T TELL YOUR SMELLY HOBO FRIENDS WHERE I STASH MY MONEY--EVEN IF THEY ARE DOWN-ON-THEIR-LUCK SUPER HE...
OH...
TYREE...
...I HAVEN'T SEEN YOU THIS PRODUCTIVE SINCE YOU WERE IN SCHOOL!
YEAH, THE WAY TONY DESCRIBES TECH, HE MAKES IT EASY--LIKE IT WAS ALREADY INSIDE YOUR OWN HEAD THE WHOLE TIME.
I HELPED HIM WORK OUT SOME OF THE ISSUES HE WAS HAVING WITH THE SOLAR CELLS.
IN RETURN, HE'S GIVING ME CONTROLLING STOCK IN HIS NEW COMPANY--YOU TOO, AS A MAJOR INVESTOR!
I TAKE IT BACK
HE IS A MAGIC HOBO.

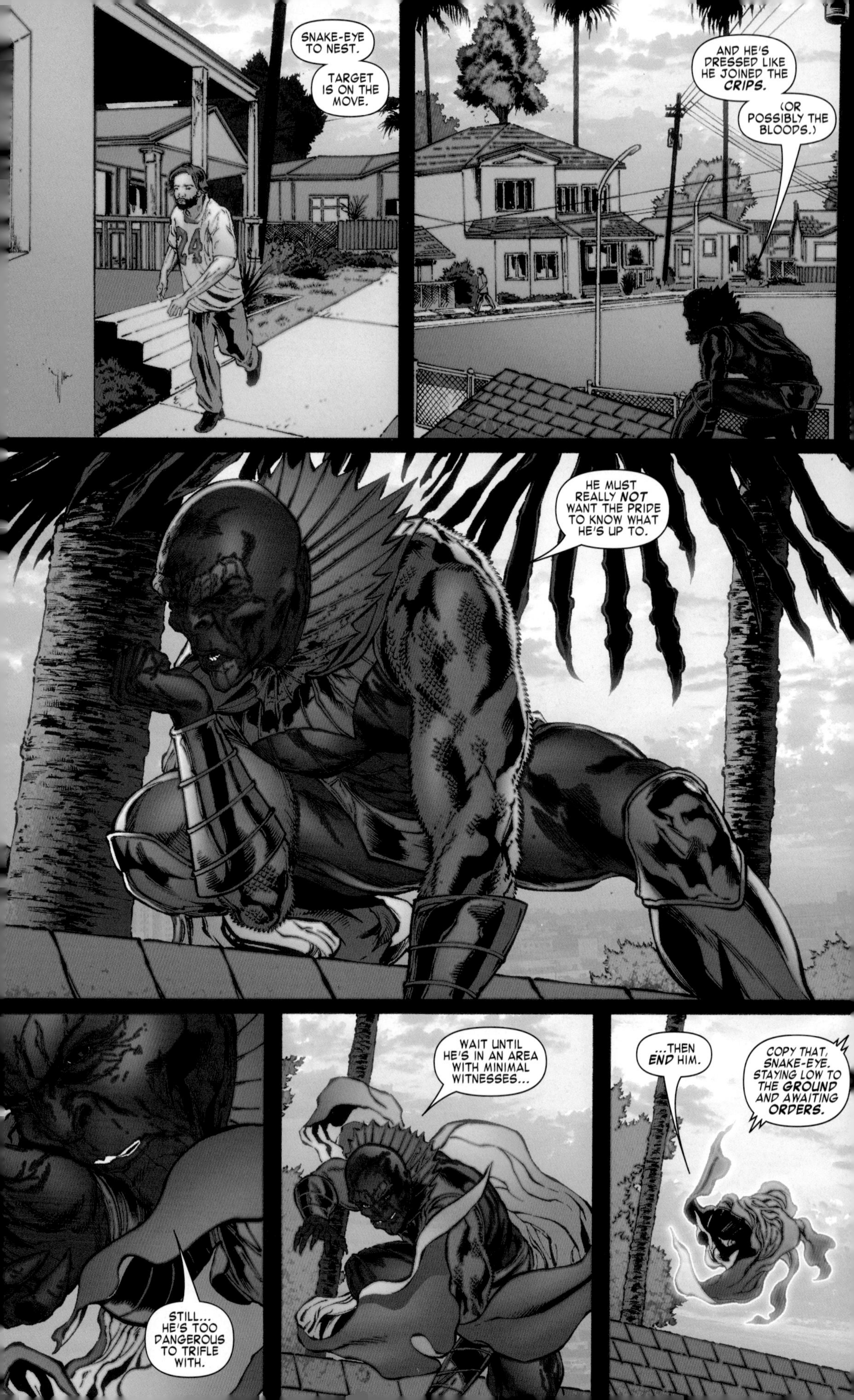
SNAKE-EYE TO NEST.
TARGET IS ON THE MOVE.
AND HE'S DRESSED LIKE HE JOINED THE CRIPS.
(OR POSSIBLY THE BLOODS.)
HE MUST REALLY NOT WANT THE PRIDE TO KNOW WHAT HE'S UP TO.
STILL... HE'S TOO DANGEROUS TO TRIFLE WITH.
WAIT UNTIL HE'S IN AN AREA WITH MINIMAL WITNESSES...
...THEN END HIM.
COPY THAT, SNAKE-EYE. STAYING LOW TO THE GROUND AND AWAITING ORDERS.

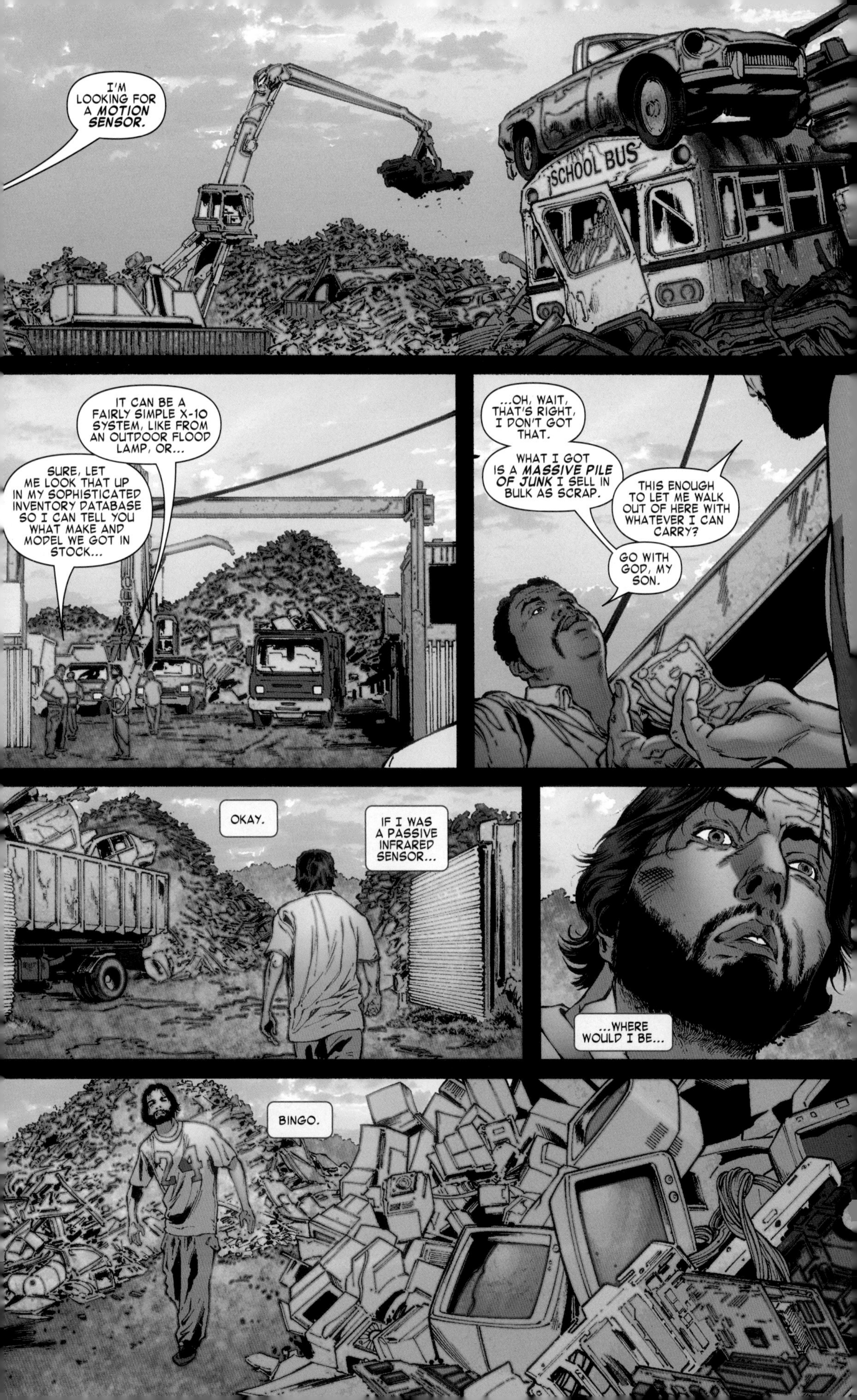
I'M LOOKING FOR A MOTION SENSOR.
IT CAN BE A FAIRLY SIMPLE X-10 SYSTEM, LIKE FROM AN OUTDOOR FLOOD LAMP, OR...
SURE, LET ME LOOK THAT UP IN MY SOPHISTICATED INVENTORY DATABASE SO I CAN TELL YOU WHAT MAKE AND MODEL WE GOT IN STOCK...
...OH, WAIT, THAT'S RIGHT, I DON'T GOT THAT.
WHAT I GOT IS A MASSIVE PILE OF JUNK I SELL IN BULK AS SCRAP.
THIS ENOUGH TO LET ME WALK OUT OF HERE WITH WHATEVER I CAN CARRY?
GO WITH GOD, MY SON.
OKAY.
IF I WAS A PASSIVE INFRARED SENSOR...
...WHERE WOULD I BE...
BINGO.

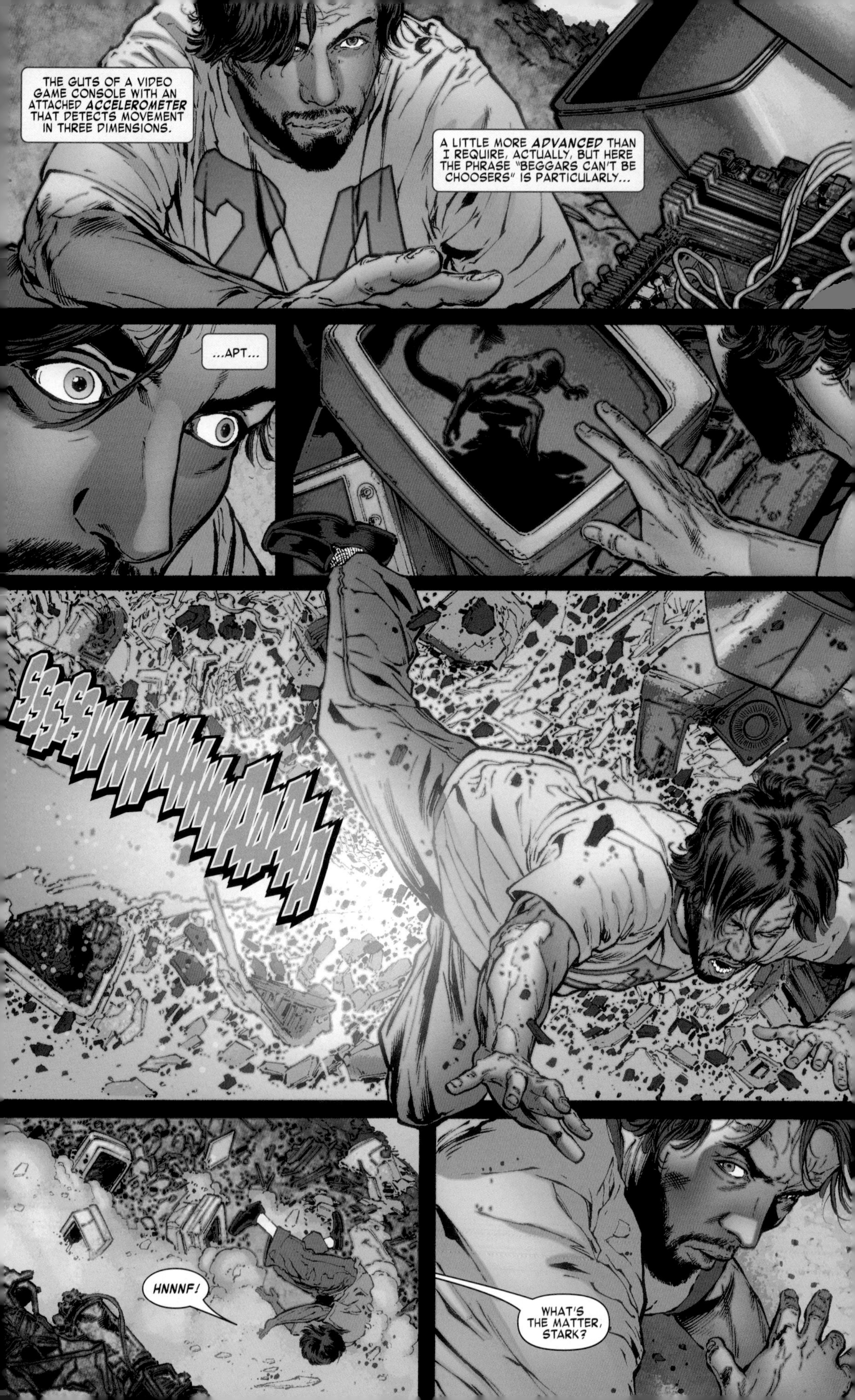
THE GUTS OF A VIDEO GAME CONSOLE WITH AN ATTACHED *ACCELEROMETER* THAT DETECTS MOVEMENT IN THREE DIMENSIONS.
A LITTLE MORE *ADVANCED* THAN I REQUIRE, ACTUALLY, BUT HERE THE PHRASE "BEGGARS CAN'T BE CHOOSERS" IS PARTICULARLY...
...APT...
SSSSHHWHHHHAAAAA
HNNNF!
WHAT'S THE MATTER, STARK?

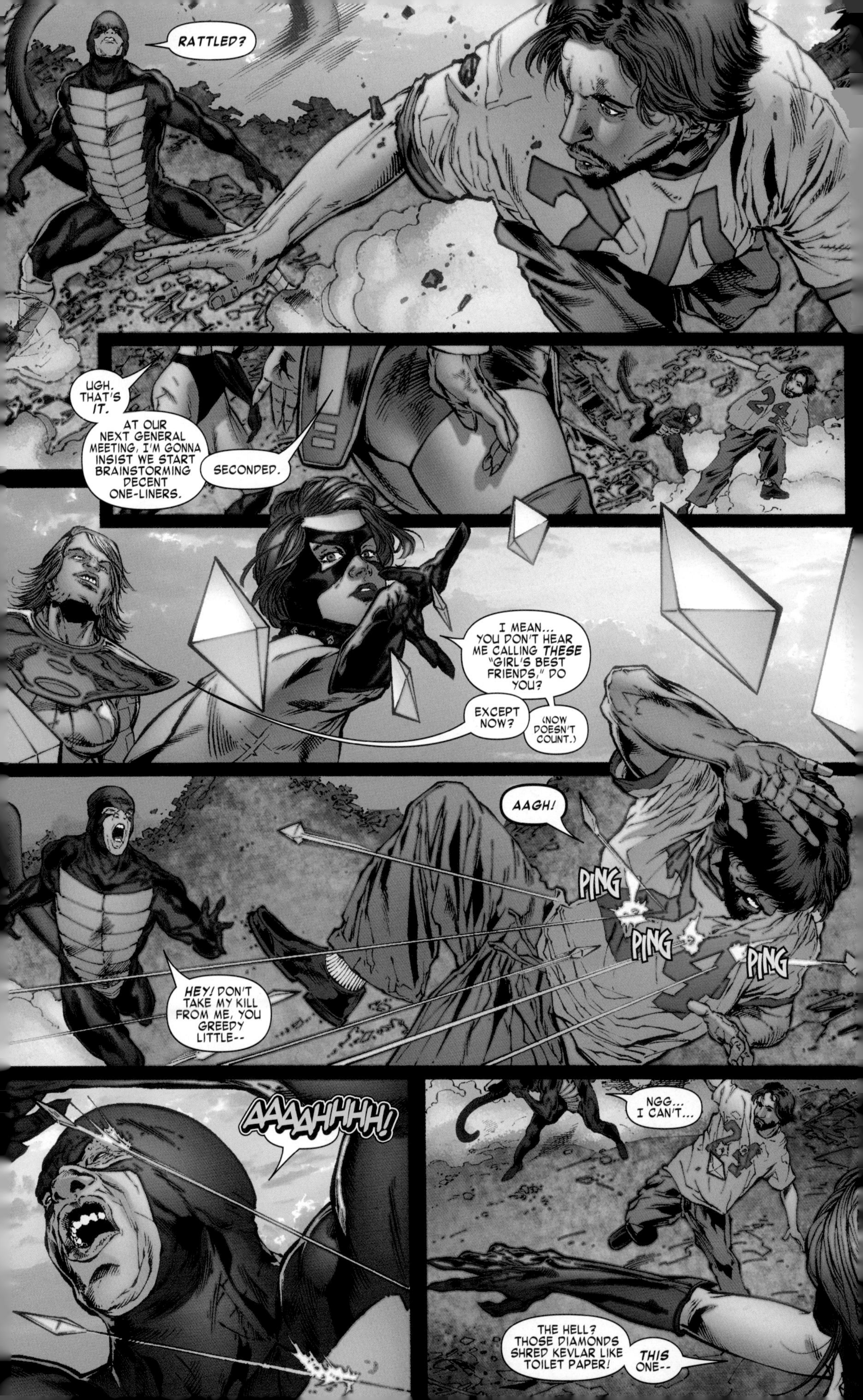
RATTLED?
UGH. THAT'S IT.
AT OUR NEXT GENERAL MEETING, I'M GONNA INSIST WE START BRAINSTORMING DECENT ONE-LINERS.
SECONDED.
I MEAN... YOU DON'T HEAR ME CALLING THESE "GIRL'S BEST FRIENDS," DO YOU?
EXCEPT NOW?
(NOW DOESN'T COUNT.)
AAGH!
PING
PING
PING
HEY! DON'T TAKE MY KILL FROM ME, YOU GREEDY LITTLE--
AAAAHHHH!
NGG... I CAN'T...
THE HELL? THOSE DIAMONDS SHRED KEVLAR LIKE TOILET PAPER!
THIS ONE--

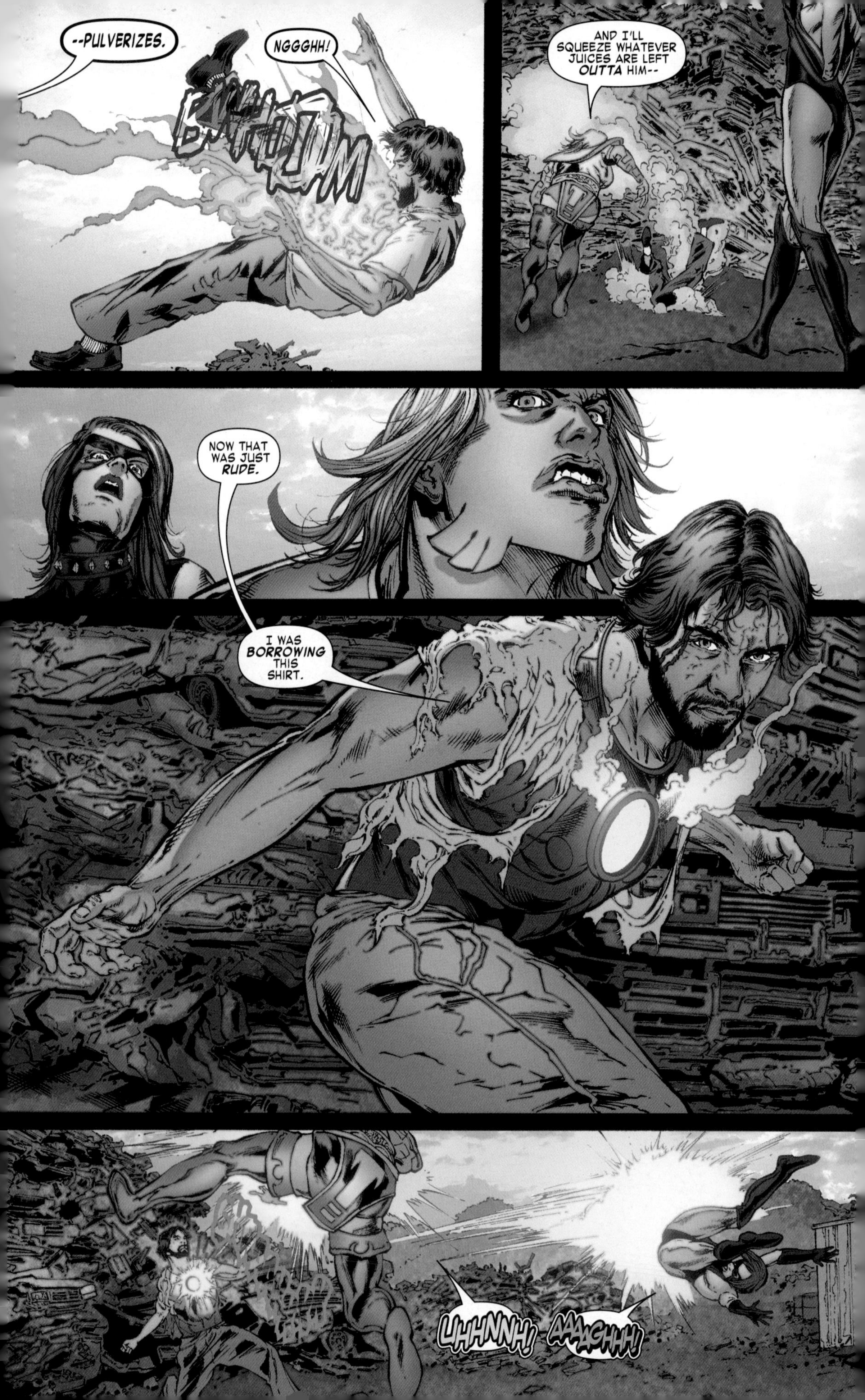
--PULVERIZES.
NGGGHH!
AND I'LL SQUEEZE WHATEVER JUICES ARE LEFT OUTTA HIM--
NOW THAT WAS JUST RUDE.
I WAS BORROWING THIS SHIRT.
UHHNNH!
AAAAGHHH!

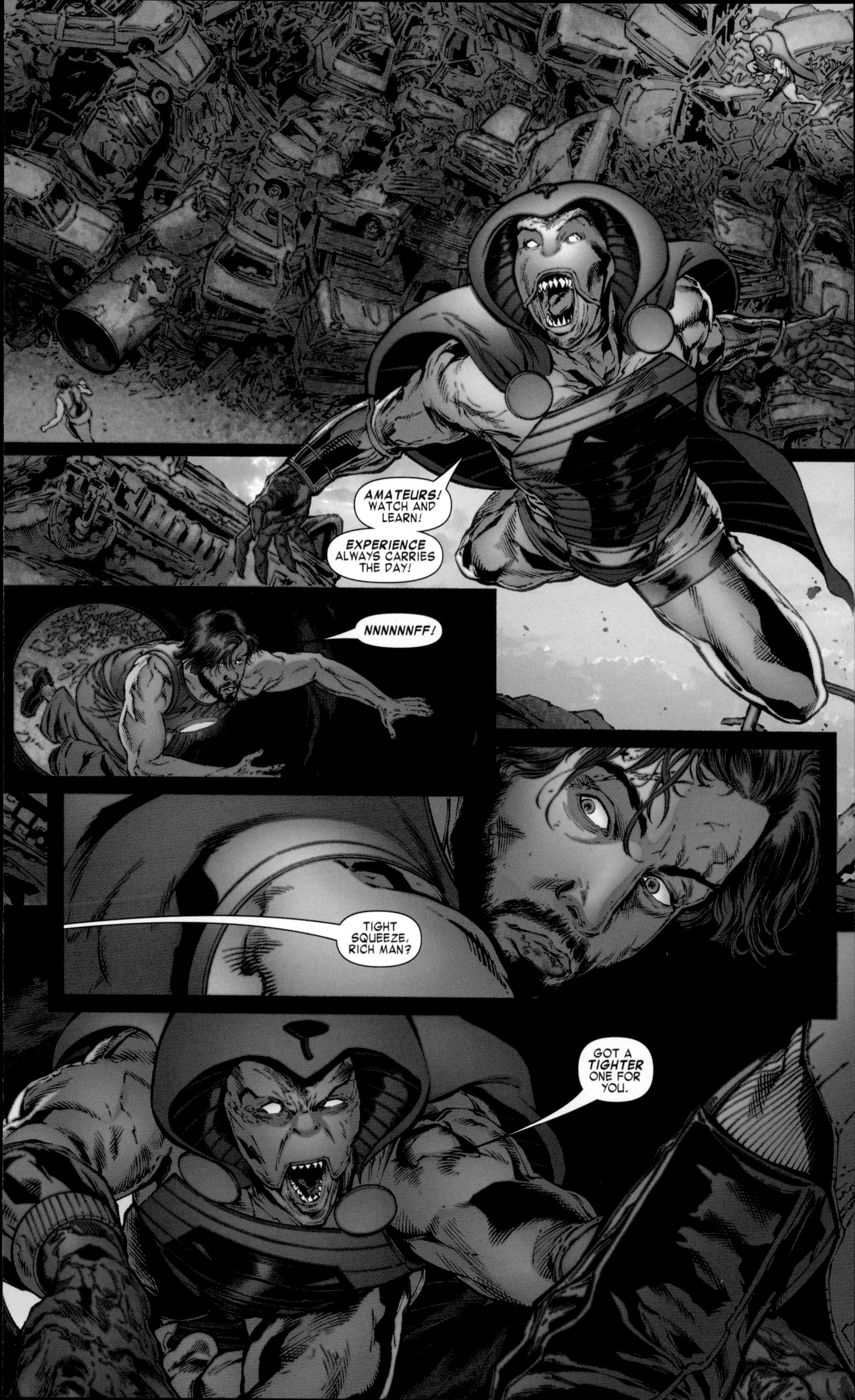
AMATEURS! WATCH AND LEARN!
EXPERIENCE ALWAYS CARRIES THE DAY!
NNNNNNFF!
TIGHT SQUEEZE, RICH MAN?
GOT A TIGHTER ONE FOR YOU.

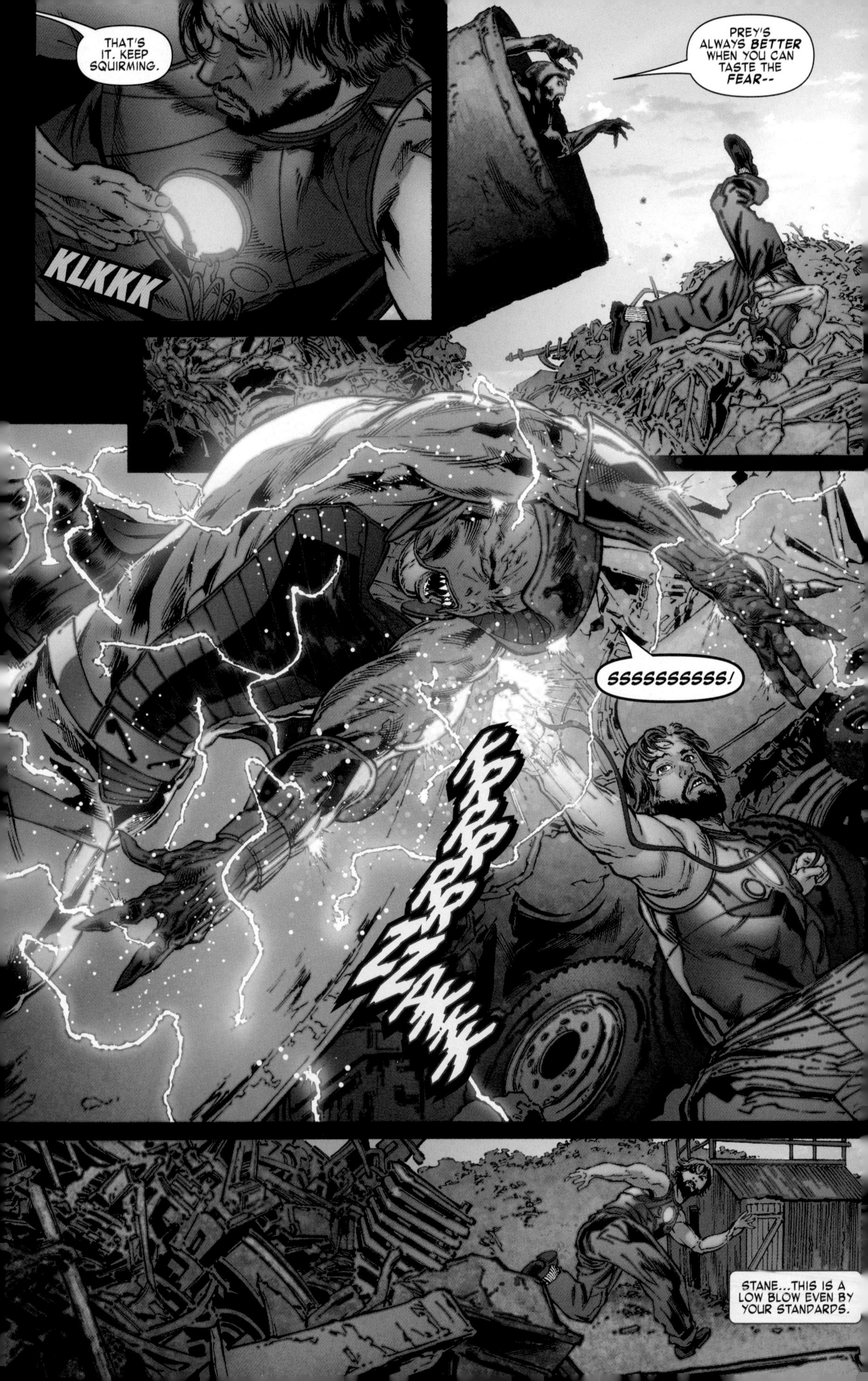
THAT'S IT. KEEP SQUIRMING.
KLKKK
PREY'S ALWAYS BETTER WHEN YOU CAN TASTE THE FEAR--
SSSSSSSSSS!
KRRRRRZZAKK
STANE...THIS IS A LOW BLOW EVEN BY YOUR STANDARDS.

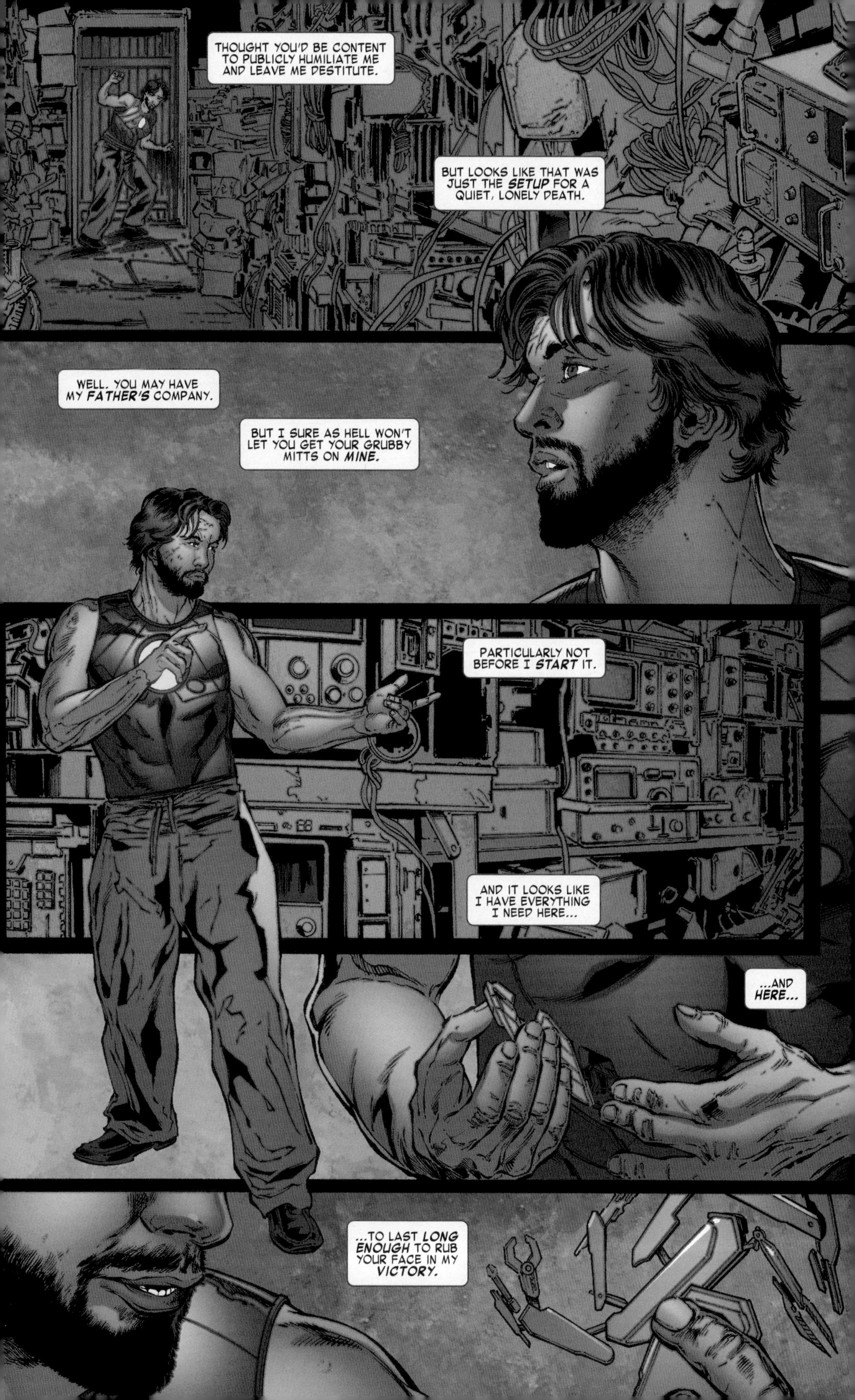
THOUGHT YOU'D BE CONTENT TO PUBLICLY HUMILIATE ME AND LEAVE ME DESTITUTE.
BUT LOOKS LIKE THAT WAS JUST THE SETUP FOR A QUIET, LONELY DEATH.
WELL. YOU MAY HAVE MY FATHER'S COMPANY.
BUT I SURE AS HELL WON'T LET YOU GET YOUR GRUBBY MITTS ON MINE.
PARTICULARLY NOT BEFORE I START IT.
AND IT LOOKS LIKE I HAVE EVERYTHING I NEED HERE...
...AND HERE...
...TO LAST LONG ENOUGH TO RUB YOUR FACE IN MY VICTORY.

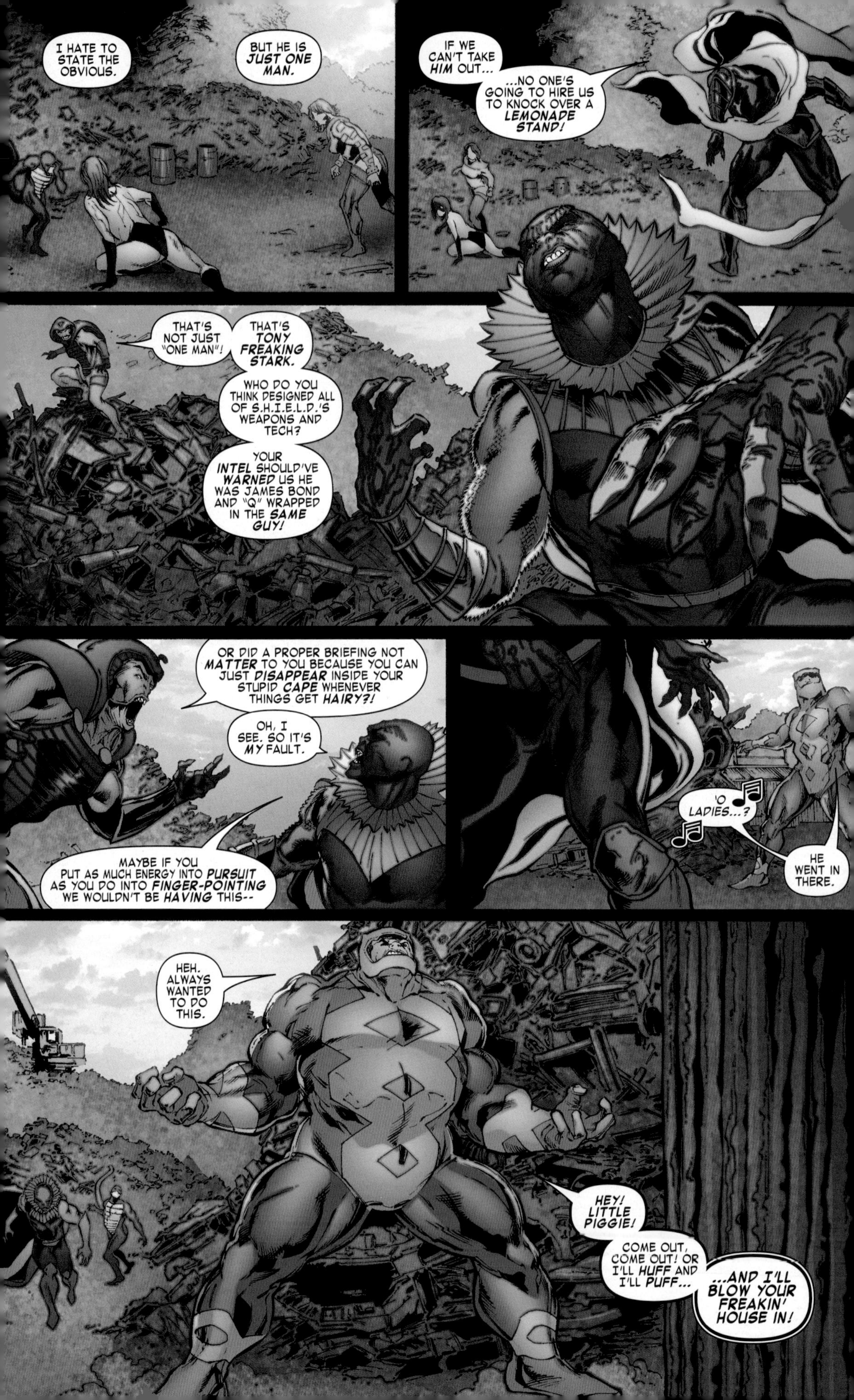

I HATE TO STATE THE OBVIOUS.
BUT HE IS JUST ONE MAN.
IF WE CAN'T TAKE HIM OUT...
...NO ONE'S GOING TO HIRE US TO KNOCK OVER A LEMONADE STAND!
THAT'S NOT JUST "ONE MAN"!
THAT'S TONY FREAKING STARK.
WHO DO YOU THINK DESIGNED ALL OF S.H.I.E.L.D.'S WEAPONS AND TECH?
YOUR INTEL SHOULD'VE WARNED US HE WAS JAMES BOND AND "Q" WRAPPED IN THE SAME GUY!
OR DID A PROPER BRIEFING NOT MATTER TO YOU BECAUSE YOU CAN JUST DISAPPEAR INSIDE YOUR STUPID CAPE WHENEVER THINGS GET HAIRY?!
OH, I SEE. SO IT'S MY FAULT.
MAYBE IF YOU PUT AS MUCH ENERGY INTO PURSUIT AS YOU DO INTO FINGER-POINTING WE WOULDN'T BE HAVING THIS--
'O LADIES...?
HE WENT IN THERE.
HEH. ALWAYS WANTED TO DO THIS.
HEY! LITTLE PIGGIE!
COME OUT, COME OUT! OR I'LL HUFF AND I'LL PUFF...
...AND I'LL BLOW YOUR FREAKIN' HOUSE IN!

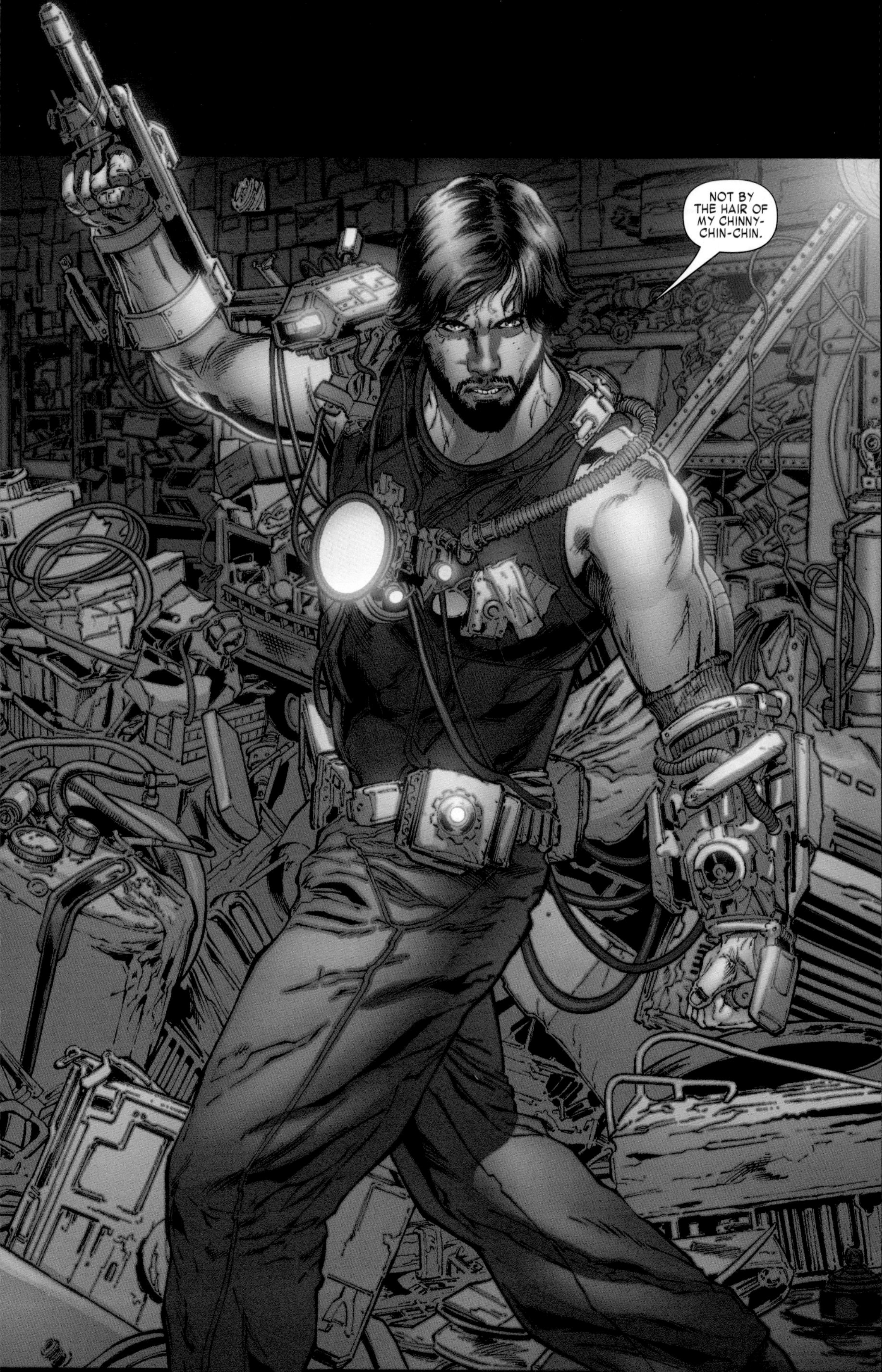
NOT BY THE HAIR OF MY CHINNY-CHIN-CHIN.

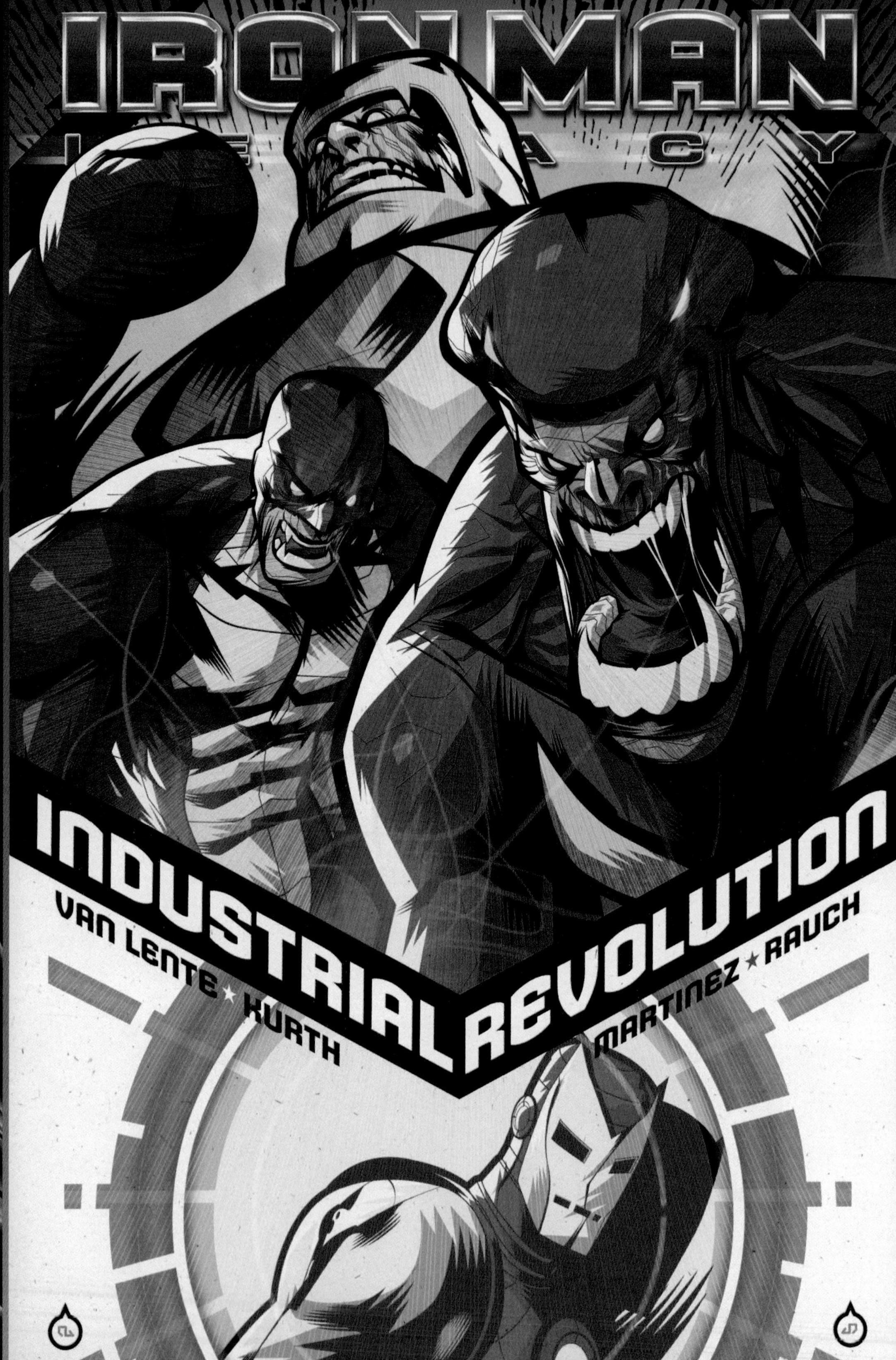
IRON MAN
LEGACY
INDUSTRIAL REVOLUTION
VAN LENTE ★ KURTH
MARTINEZ ★ RAUCH

IRON MAN LEGACY 8

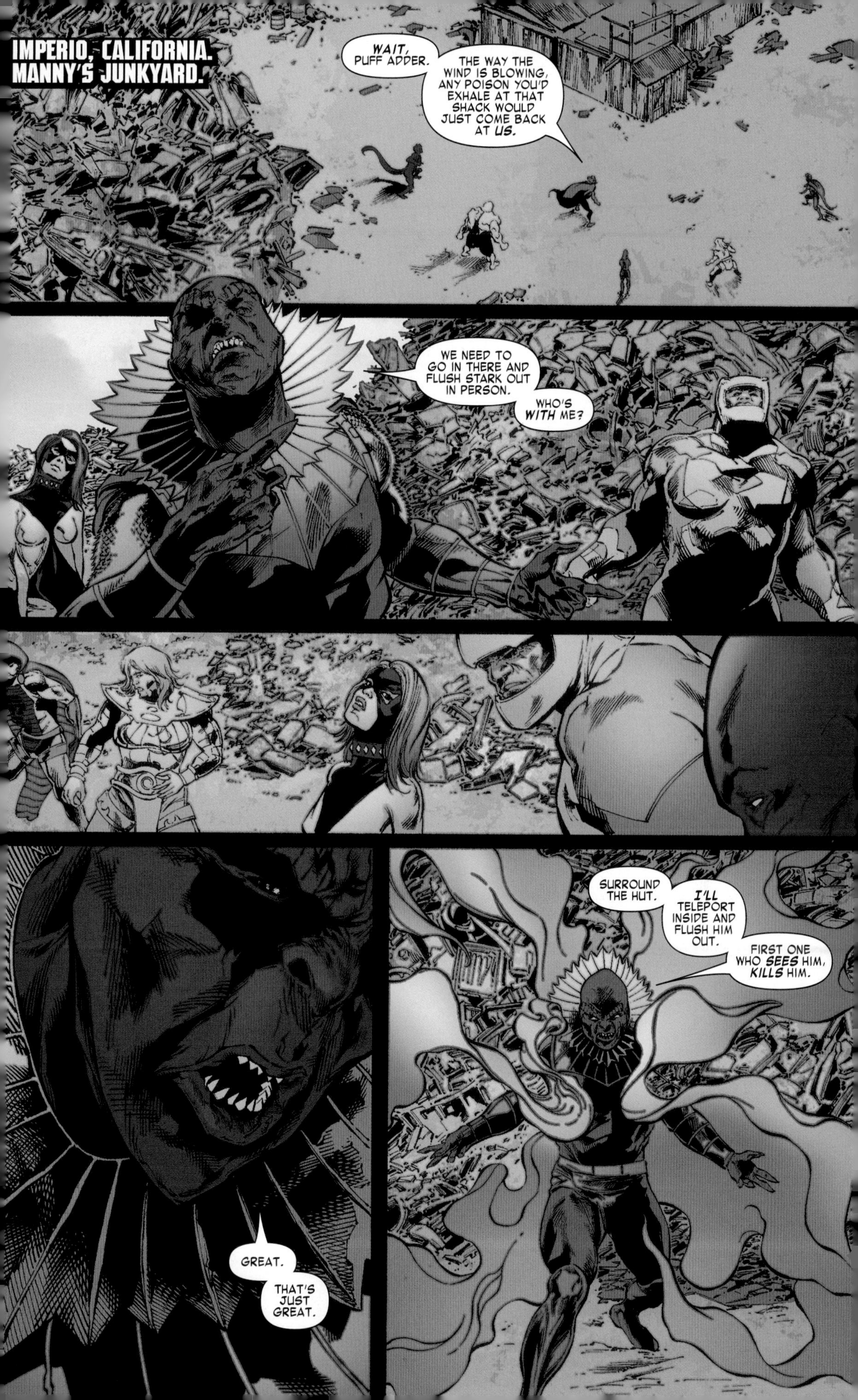
IMPERIO, CALIFORNIA. MANNY'S JUNKYARD.
WAIT, PUFF ADDER.
THE WAY THE WIND IS BLOWING, ANY POISON YOU'D EXHALE AT THAT SHACK WOULD JUST COME BACK AT US.
WE NEED TO GO IN THERE AND FLUSH STARK OUT IN PERSON.
WHO'S WITH ME?
GREAT.
THAT'S JUST GREAT.
SURROUND THE HUT.
I'LL TELEPORT INSIDE AND FLUSH HIM OUT.
FIRST ONE WHO SEES HIM, KILLS HIM.

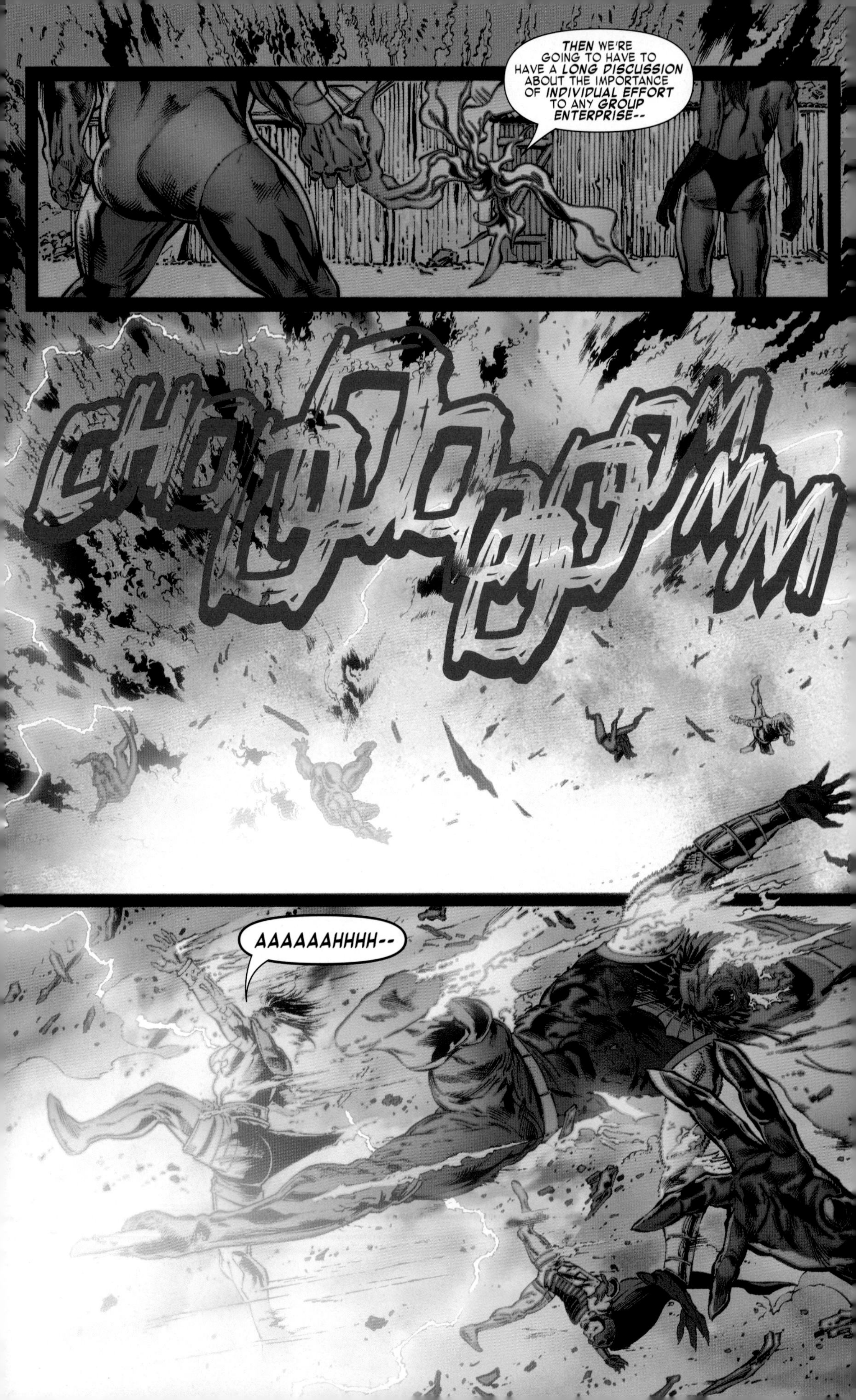
THEN WE'RE GOING TO HAVE TO HAVE A LONG DISCUSSION ABOUT THE IMPORTANCE OF INDIVIDUAL EFFORT TO ANY GROUP ENTERPRISE--
AAAAAAHHHH--

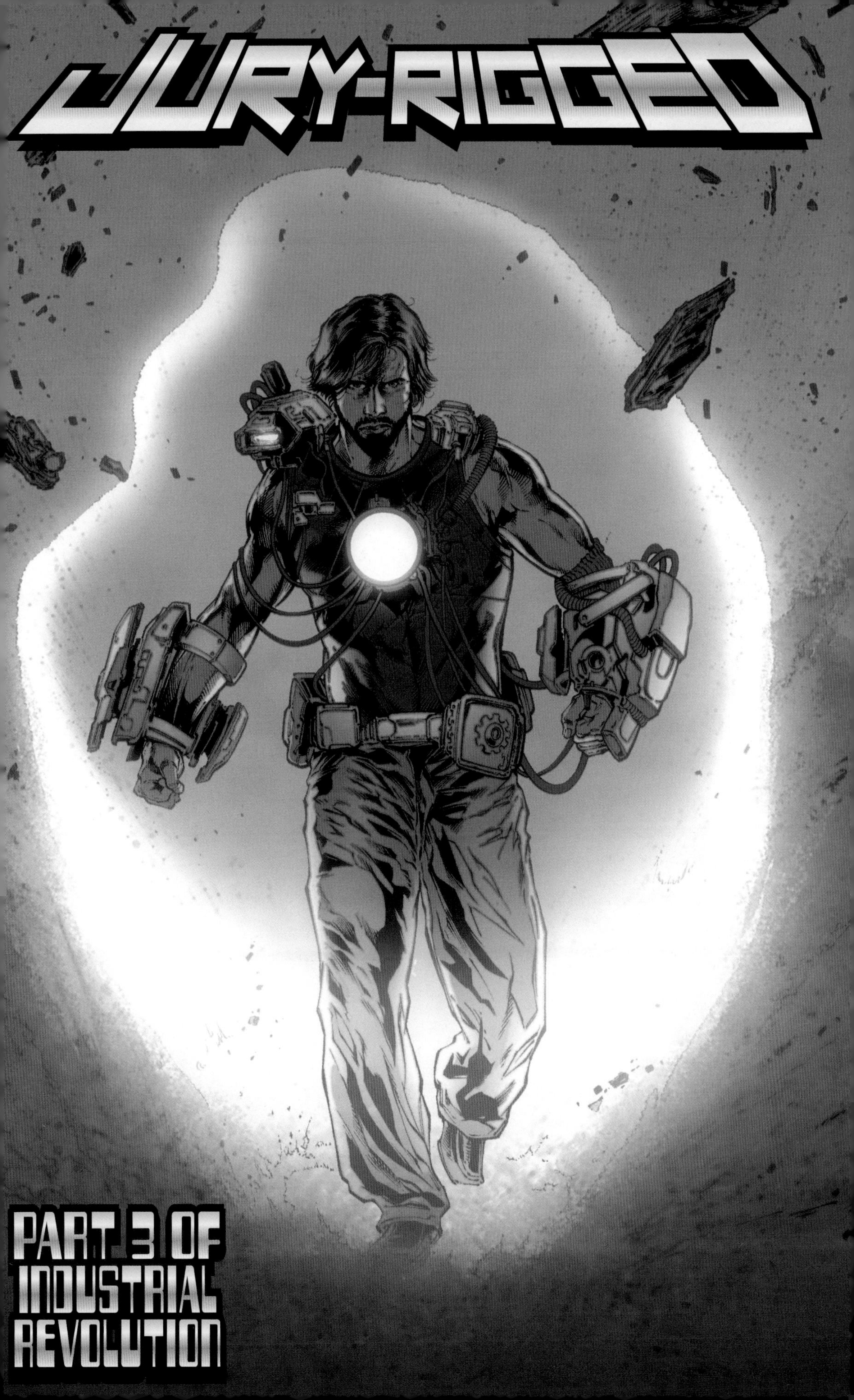
JURY-RIGGED
PART 3 OF
INDUSTRIAL
REVOLUTION

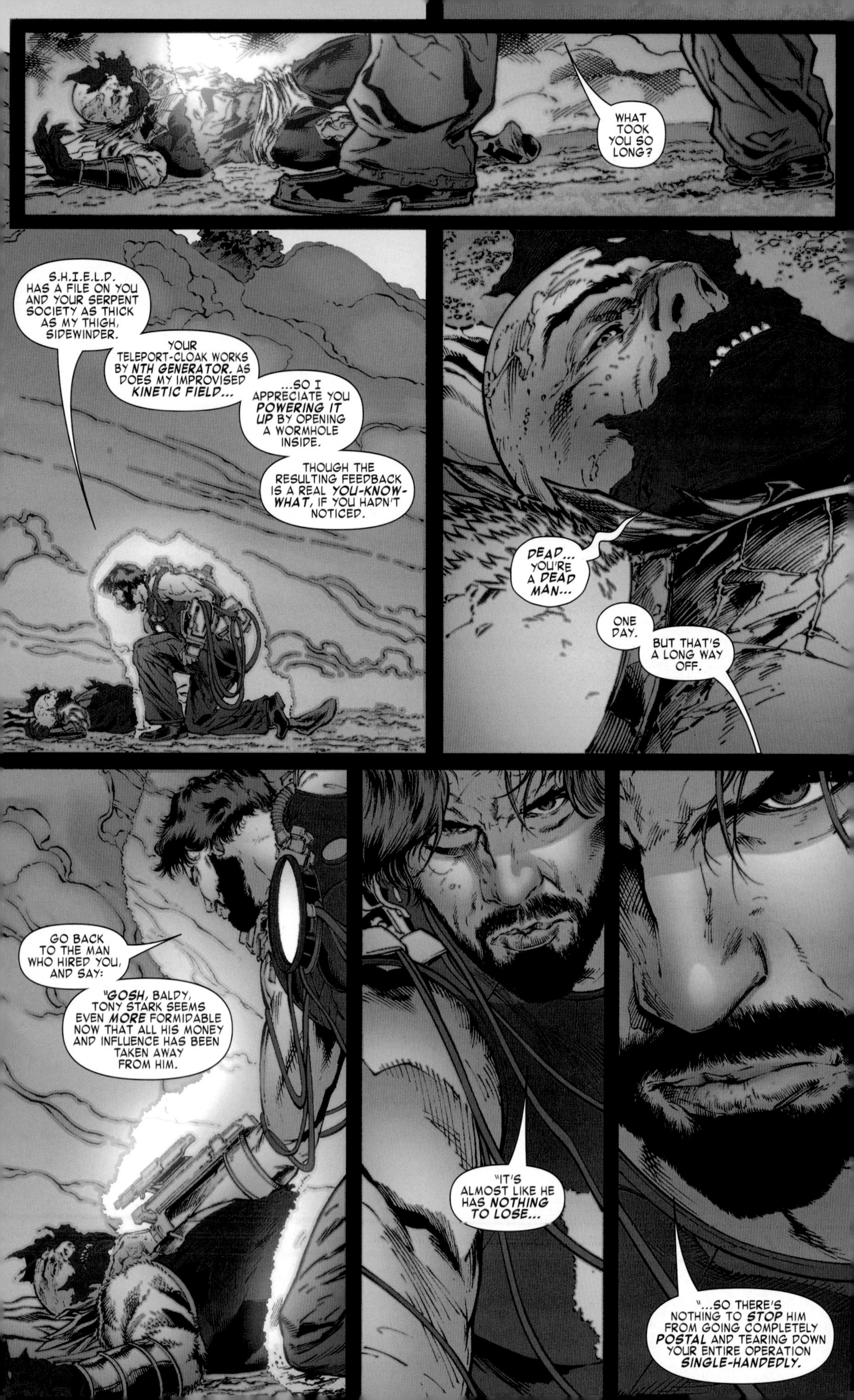
WHAT TOOK YOU SO LONG?
S.H.I.E.L.D. HAS A FILE ON YOU AND YOUR SERPENT SOCIETY AS THICK AS MY THIGH, SIDEWINDER.
YOUR TELEPORT-CLOAK WORKS BY NTH GENERATOR. AS DOES MY IMPROVISED KINETIC FIELD...
...SO I APPRECIATE YOU POWERING IT UP BY OPENING A WORMHOLE INSIDE.
THOUGH THE RESULTING FEEDBACK IS A REAL YOU-KNOW-WHAT, IF YOU HADN'T NOTICED.
DEAD... YOU'RE A DEAD MAN...
ONE DAY.
BUT THAT'S A LONG WAY OFF.
GO BACK TO THE MAN WHO HIRED YOU, AND SAY:
"GOSH, BALDY, TONY STARK SEEMS EVEN MORE FORMIDABLE NOW THAT ALL HIS MONEY AND INFLUENCE HAS BEEN TAKEN AWAY FROM HIM.
"IT'S ALMOST LIKE HE HAS NOTHING TO LOSE...
"...SO THERE'S NOTHING TO STOP HIM FROM GOING COMPLETELY POSTAL AND TEARING DOWN YOUR ENTIRE OPERATION SINGLE-HANDEDLY.

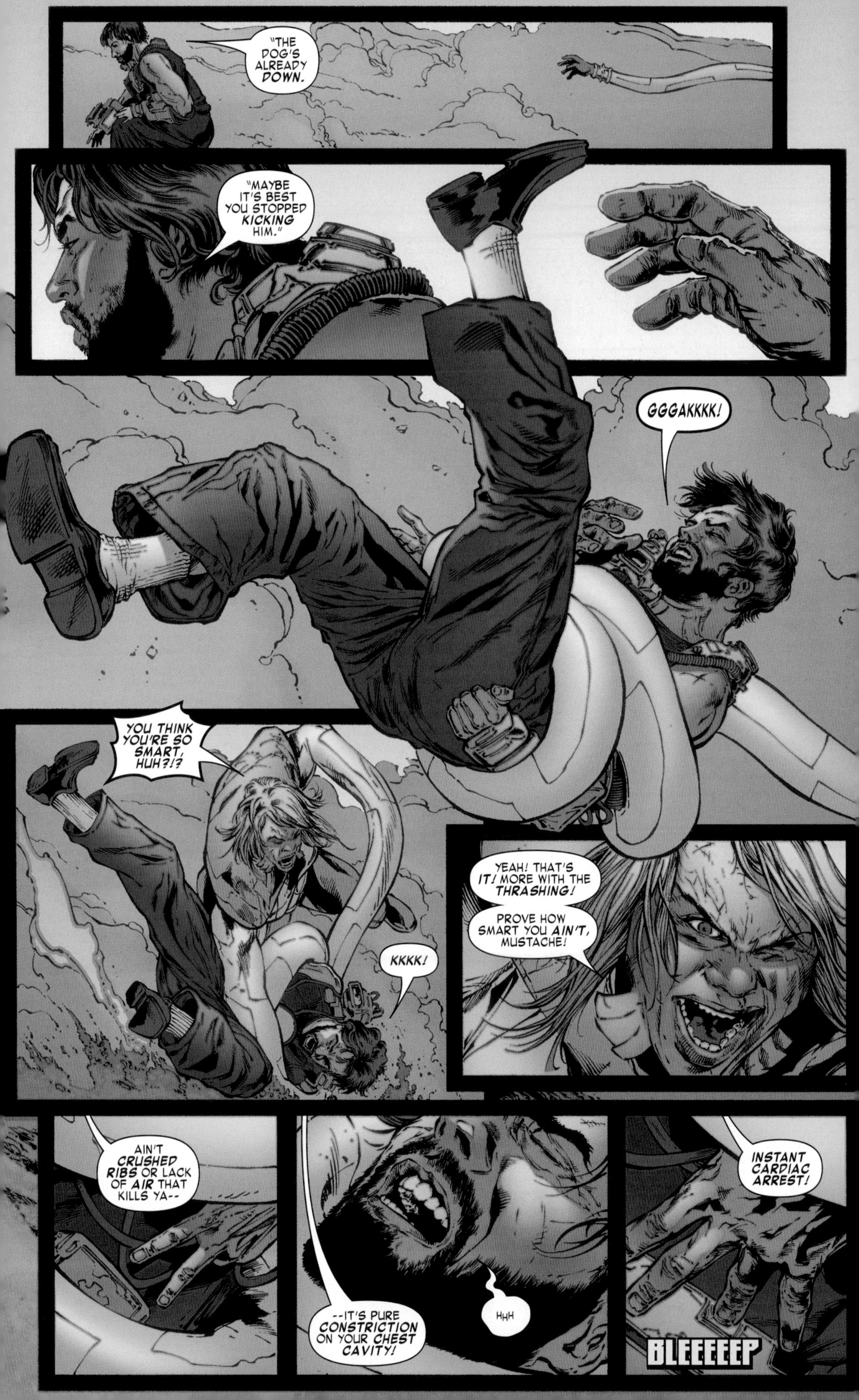
"THE DOG'S ALREADY DOWN.
"MAYBE IT'S BEST YOU STOPPED KICKING HIM."
GGGAKKKK!
YOU THINK YOU'RE SO SMART, HUH?!?
KKKK!
YEAH! THAT'S IT! MORE WITH THE THRASHING!
PROVE HOW SMART YOU AIN'T, MUSTACHE!
AIN'T CRUSHED RIBS OR LACK OF AIR THAT KILLS YA--
--IT'S PURE CONSTRICTION ON YOUR CHEST CAVITY!
HHH
INSTANT CARDIAC ARREST!
BLEEEEEP

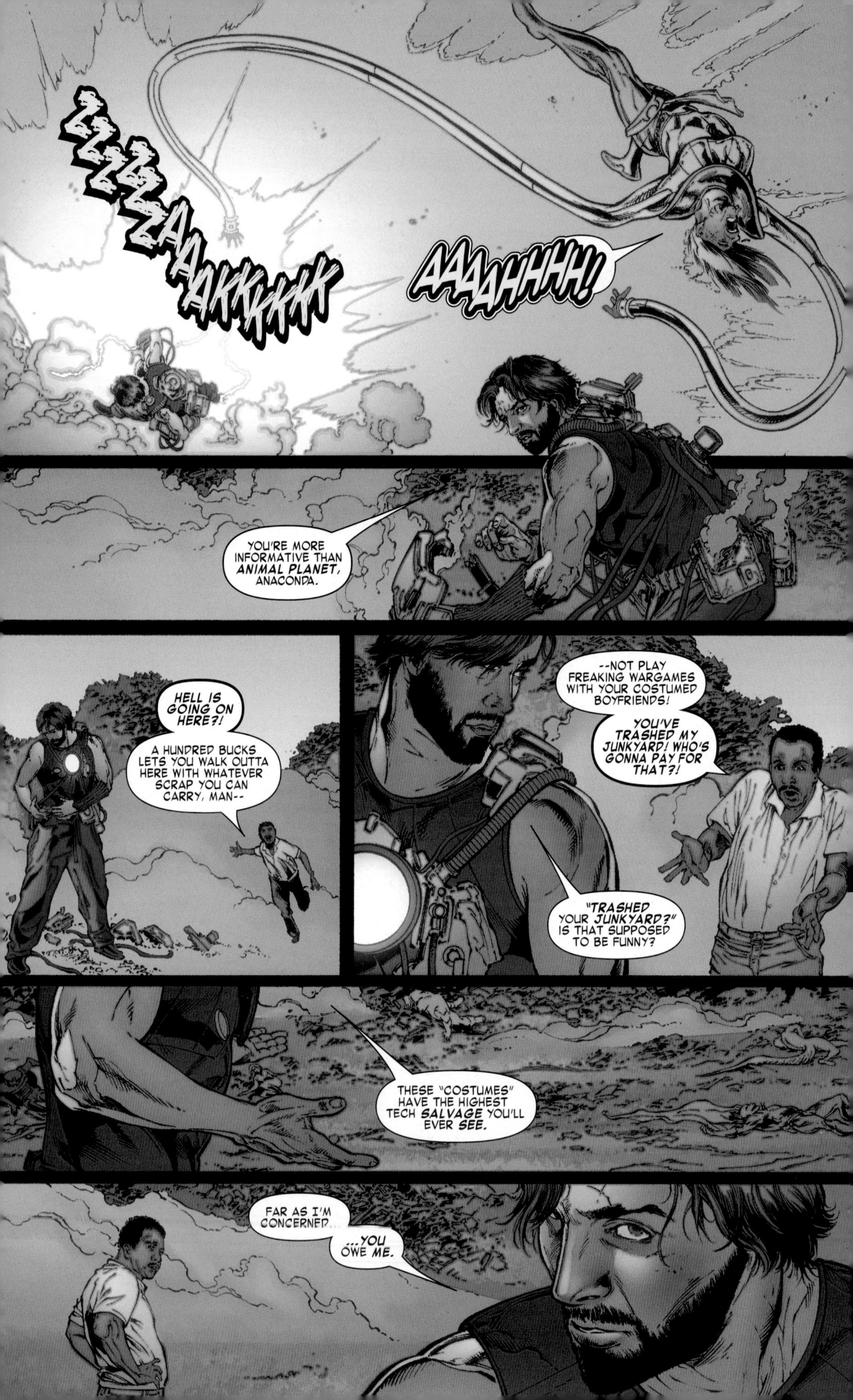
ZZZZZAAAAKKKKKKK
AAAAHHHH!
YOU'RE MORE INFORMATIVE THAN ANIMAL PLANET, ANACONDA.
HELL IS GOING ON HERE?!
A HUNDRED BUCKS LETS YOU WALK OUTTA HERE WITH WHATEVER SCRAP YOU CAN CARRY, MAN--
--NOT PLAY FREAKING WARGAMES WITH YOUR COSTUMED BOYFRIENDS!
YOU'VE TRASHED MY JUNKYARD! WHO'S GONNA PAY FOR THAT?!
"TRASHED YOUR JUNKYARD?" IS THAT SUPPOSED TO BE FUNNY?
THESE "COSTUMES" HAVE THE HIGHEST TECH SALVAGE YOU'LL EVER SEE.
FAR AS I'M CONCERNED...
...YOU OWE ME.

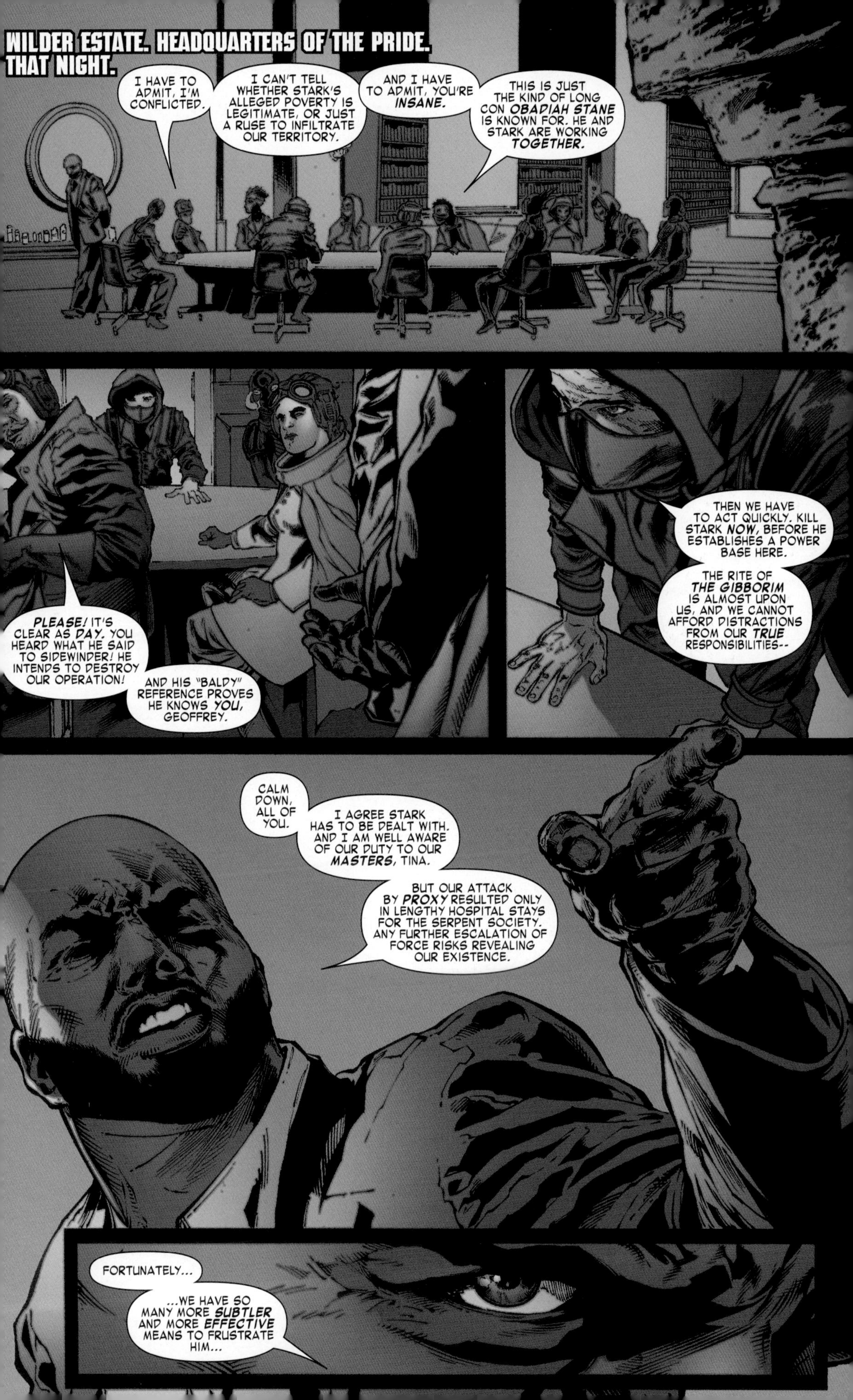
WILDER ESTATE. HEADQUARTERS OF THE PRIDE. THAT NIGHT.
I HAVE TO ADMIT, I'M CONFLICTED.
I CAN'T TELL WHETHER STARK'S ALLEGED POVERTY IS LEGITIMATE, OR JUST A RUSE TO INFILTRATE OUR TERRITORY.
AND I HAVE TO ADMIT, YOU'RE INSANE.
THIS IS JUST THE KIND OF LONG CON OBADIAH STANE IS KNOWN FOR. HE AND STARK ARE WORKING TOGETHER.
PLEASE! IT'S CLEAR AS DAY. YOU HEARD WHAT HE SAID TO SIDEWINDER! HE INTENDS TO DESTROY OUR OPERATION!
AND HIS "BALDY" REFERENCE PROVES HE KNOWS YOU, GEOFFREY.
THEN WE HAVE TO ACT QUICKLY. KILL STARK NOW, BEFORE HE ESTABLISHES A POWER BASE HERE.
THE RITE OF THE GIBBORIM IS ALMOST UPON US, AND WE CANNOT AFFORD DISTRACTIONS FROM OUR TRUE RESPONSIBILITIES--
CALM DOWN, ALL OF YOU.
I AGREE STARK HAS TO BE DEALT WITH. AND I AM WELL AWARE OF OUR DUTY TO OUR MASTERS, TINA.
BUT OUR ATTACK BY PROXY RESULTED ONLY IN LENGTHY HOSPITAL STAYS FOR THE SERPENT SOCIETY. ANY FURTHER ESCALATION OF FORCE RISKS REVEALING OUR EXISTENCE.
FORTUNATELY...
...WE HAVE SO MANY MORE SUBTLER AND MORE EFFECTIVE MEANS TO FRUSTRATE HIM...

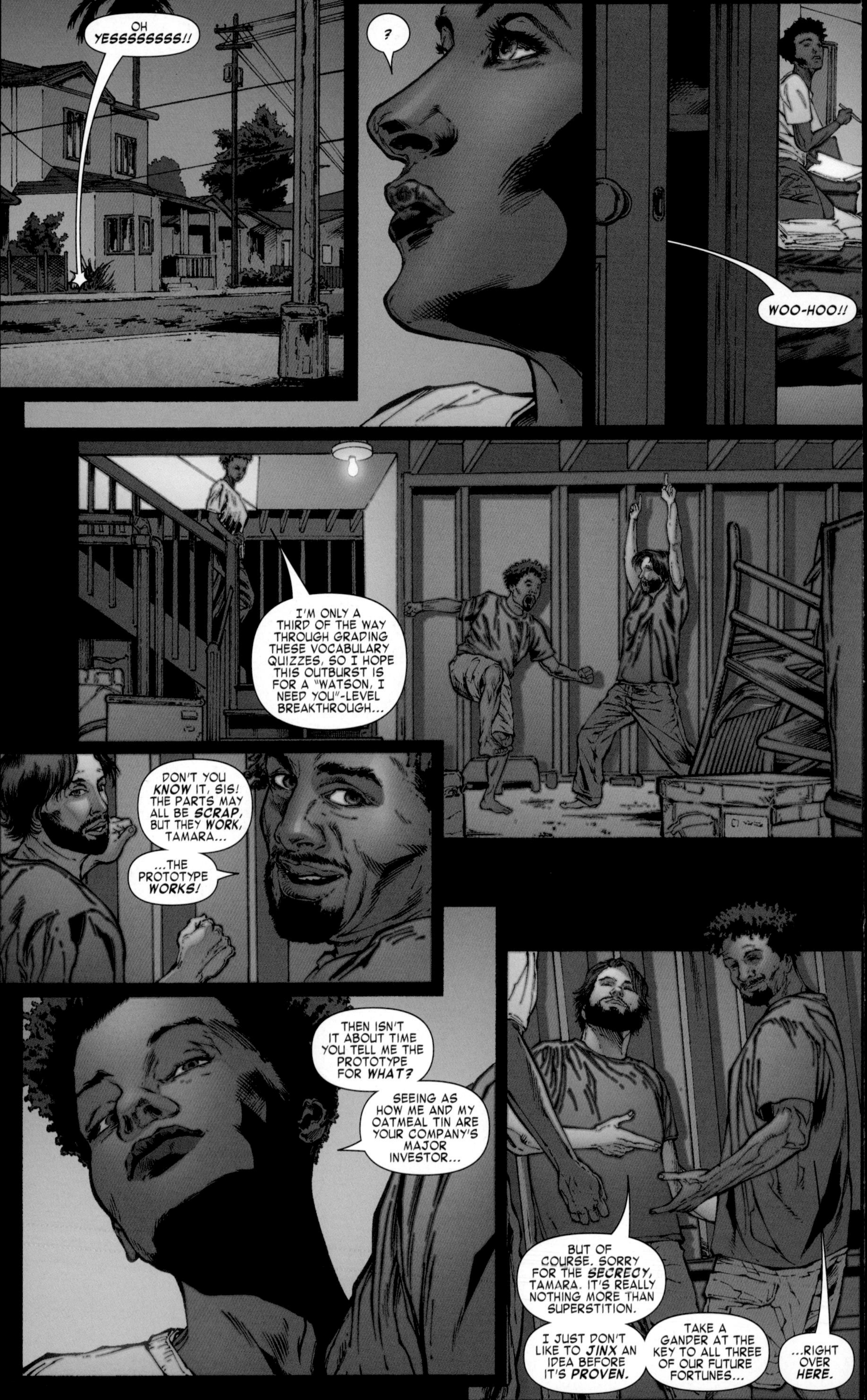

OH YESSSSSSSS!!
?
WOO-HOO!!
I'M ONLY A THIRD OF THE WAY THROUGH GRADING THESE VOCABULARY QUIZZES, SO I HOPE THIS OUTBURST IS FOR A "WATSON, I NEED YOU"-LEVEL BREAKTHROUGH...
DON'T YOU KNOW IT, SIS! THE PARTS MAY ALL BE SCRAP, BUT THEY WORK, TAMARA...
...THE PROTOTYPE WORKS!
THEN ISN'T IT ABOUT TIME YOU TELL ME THE PROTOTYPE FOR WHAT?
SEEING AS HOW ME AND MY OATMEAL TIN ARE YOUR COMPANY'S MAJOR INVESTOR...
BUT OF COURSE. SORRY FOR THE SECRECY, TAMARA. IT'S REALLY NOTHING MORE THAN SUPERSTITION.
I JUST DON'T LIKE TO JINX AN IDEA BEFORE IT'S PROVEN.
TAKE A GANDER AT THE KEY TO ALL THREE OF OUR FUTURE FORTUNES...
...RIGHT OVER HERE.

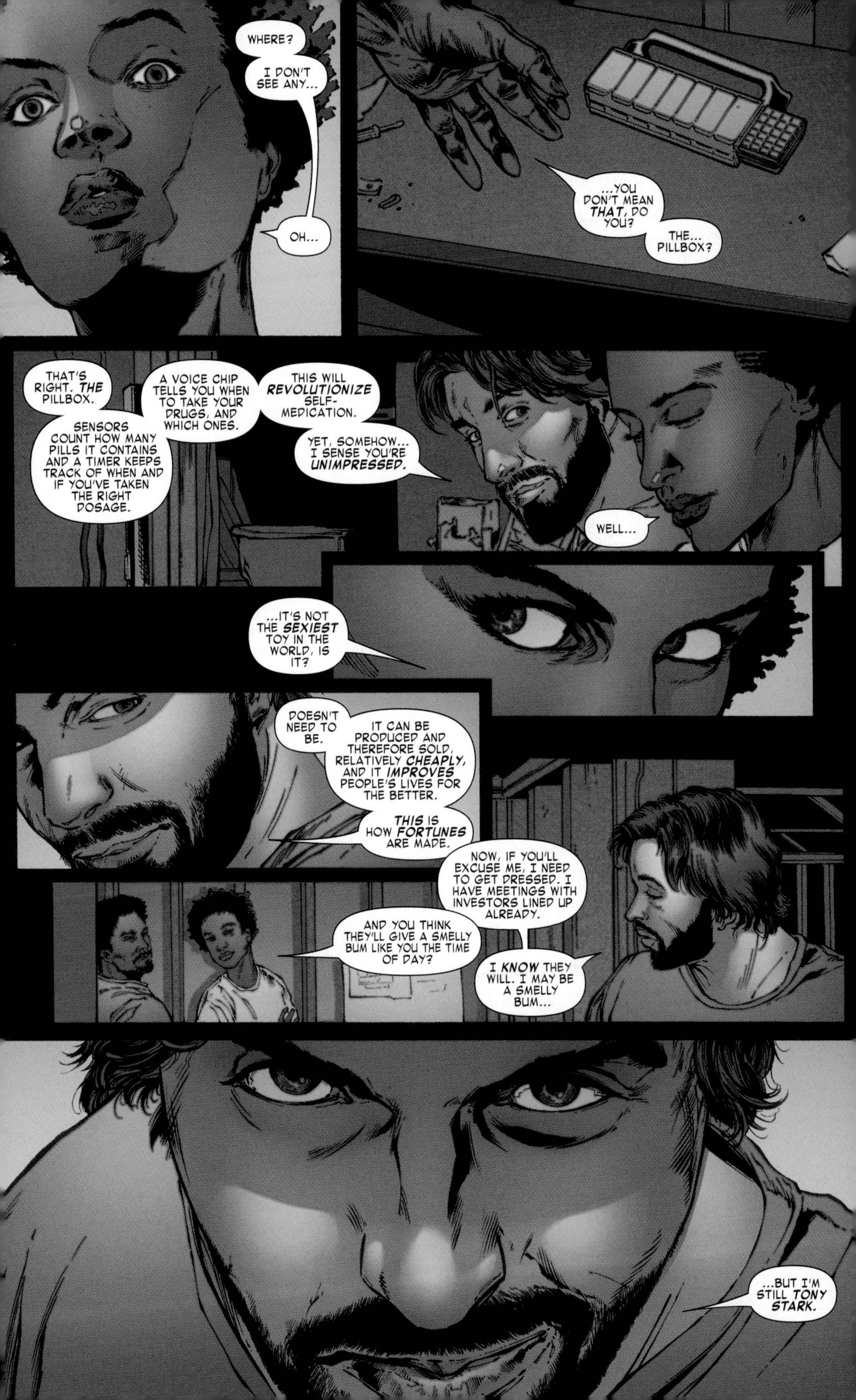
WHERE?
I DON'T SEE ANY...
OH...
...YOU DON'T MEAN THAT, DO YOU?
THE... PILLBOX?
THAT'S RIGHT. THE PILLBOX.
SENSORS COUNT HOW MANY PILLS IT CONTAINS AND A TIMER KEEPS TRACK OF WHEN AND IF YOU'VE TAKEN THE RIGHT DOSAGE.
A VOICE CHIP TELLS YOU WHEN TO TAKE YOUR DRUGS, AND WHICH ONES.
THIS WILL REVOLUTIONIZE SELF-MEDICATION.
YET, SOMEHOW... I SENSE YOU'RE UNIMPRESSED.
WELL...
...IT'S NOT THE SEXIEST TOY IN THE WORLD, IS IT?
DOESN'T NEED TO BE.
IT CAN BE PRODUCED AND THEREFORE SOLD, RELATIVELY CHEAPLY, AND IT IMPROVES PEOPLE'S LIVES FOR THE BETTER.
THIS IS HOW FORTUNES ARE MADE.
NOW, IF YOU'LL EXCUSE ME, I NEED TO GET DRESSED. I HAVE MEETINGS WITH INVESTORS LINED UP ALREADY.
AND YOU THINK THEY'LL GIVE A SMELLY BUM LIKE YOU THE TIME OF DAY?
I KNOW THEY WILL. I MAY BE A SMELLY BUM...
...BUT I'M STILL TONY STARK.

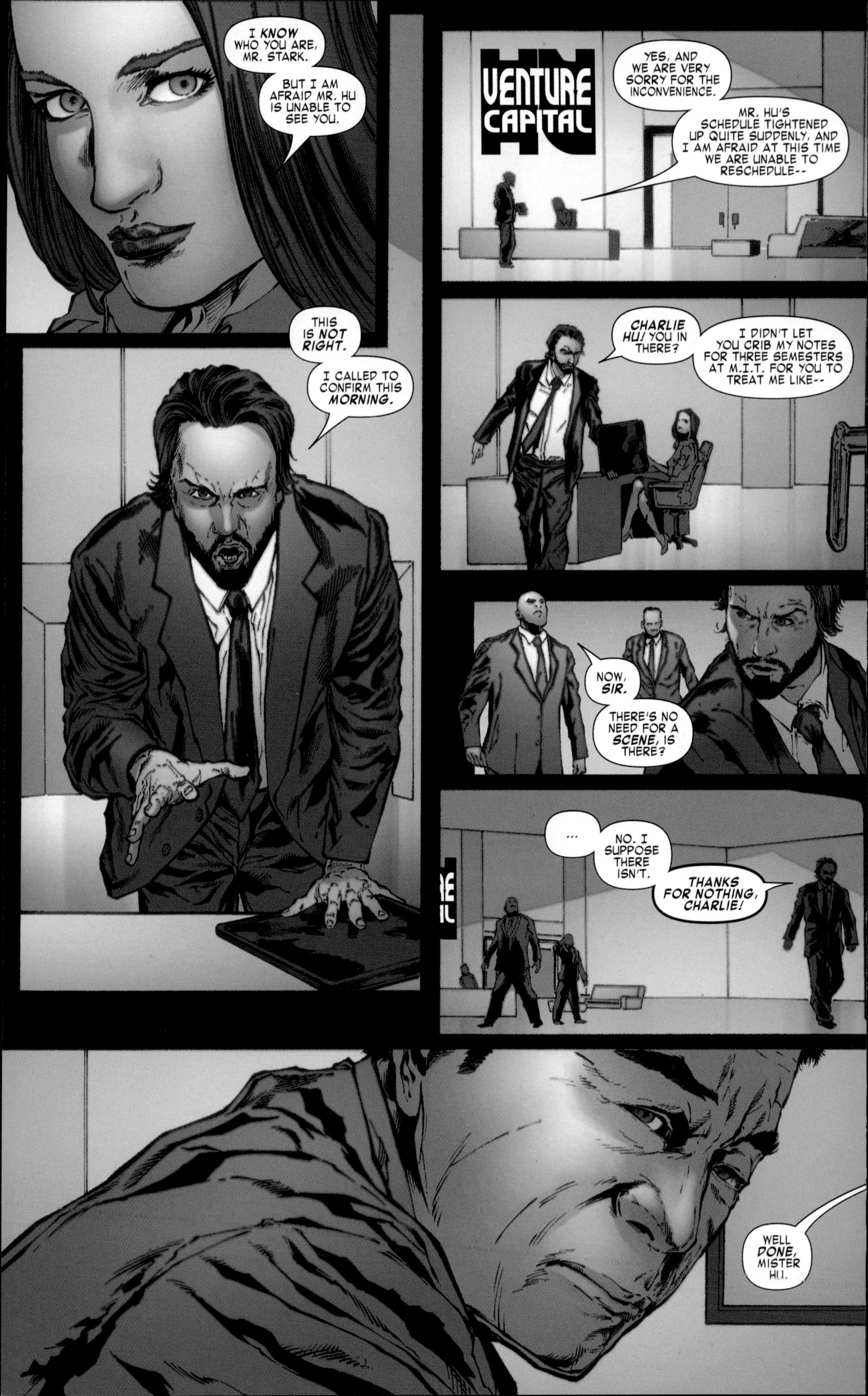
I KNOW WHO YOU ARE, MR. STARK.
BUT I AM AFRAID MR. HU IS UNABLE TO SEE YOU.
VENTURE CAPITAL
YES, AND WE ARE VERY SORRY FOR THE INCONVENIENCE.
MR. HU'S SCHEDULE TIGHTENED UP QUITE SUDDENLY, AND I AM AFRAID AT THIS TIME WE ARE UNABLE TO RESCHEDULE--
THIS IS NOT RIGHT.
I CALLED TO CONFIRM THIS MORNING.
CHARLIE HU! YOU IN THERE?
I DIDN'T LET YOU CRIB MY NOTES FOR THREE SEMESTERS AT M.I.T. FOR YOU TO TREAT ME LIKE--
NOW, SIR.
THERE'S NO NEED FOR A SCENE, IS THERE?
...
NO. I SUPPOSE THERE ISN'T.
THANKS FOR NOTHING, CHARLIE!
WELL DONE, MISTER HU.

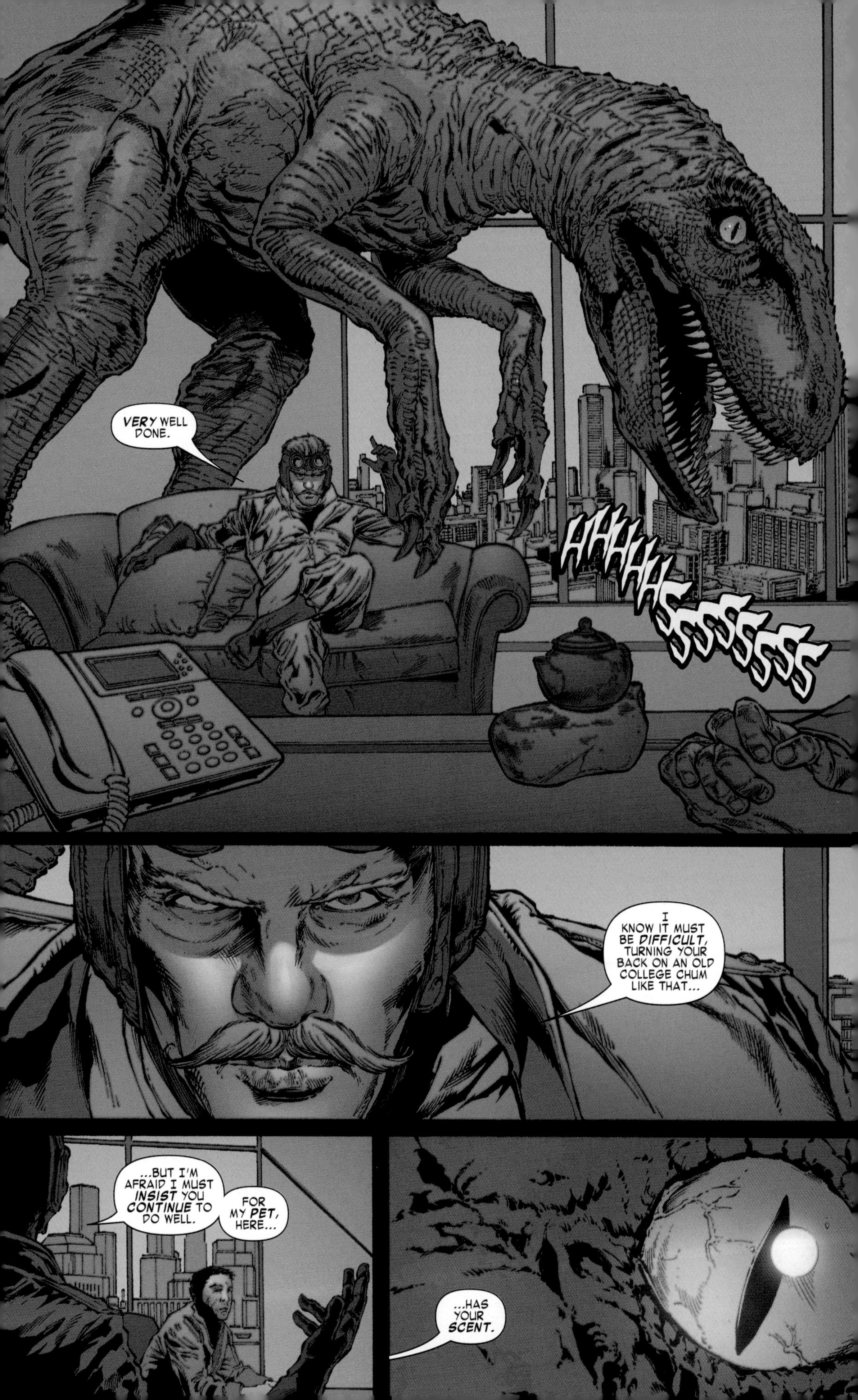
VERY WELL DONE.
HHHHHSSSSSSSSS
I KNOW IT MUST BE DIFFICULT, TURNING YOUR BACK ON AN OLD COLLEGE CHUM LIKE THAT...
...BUT I'M AFRAID I MUST INSIST YOU CONTINUE TO DO WELL.
FOR MY PET, HERE...
...HAS YOUR SCENT.

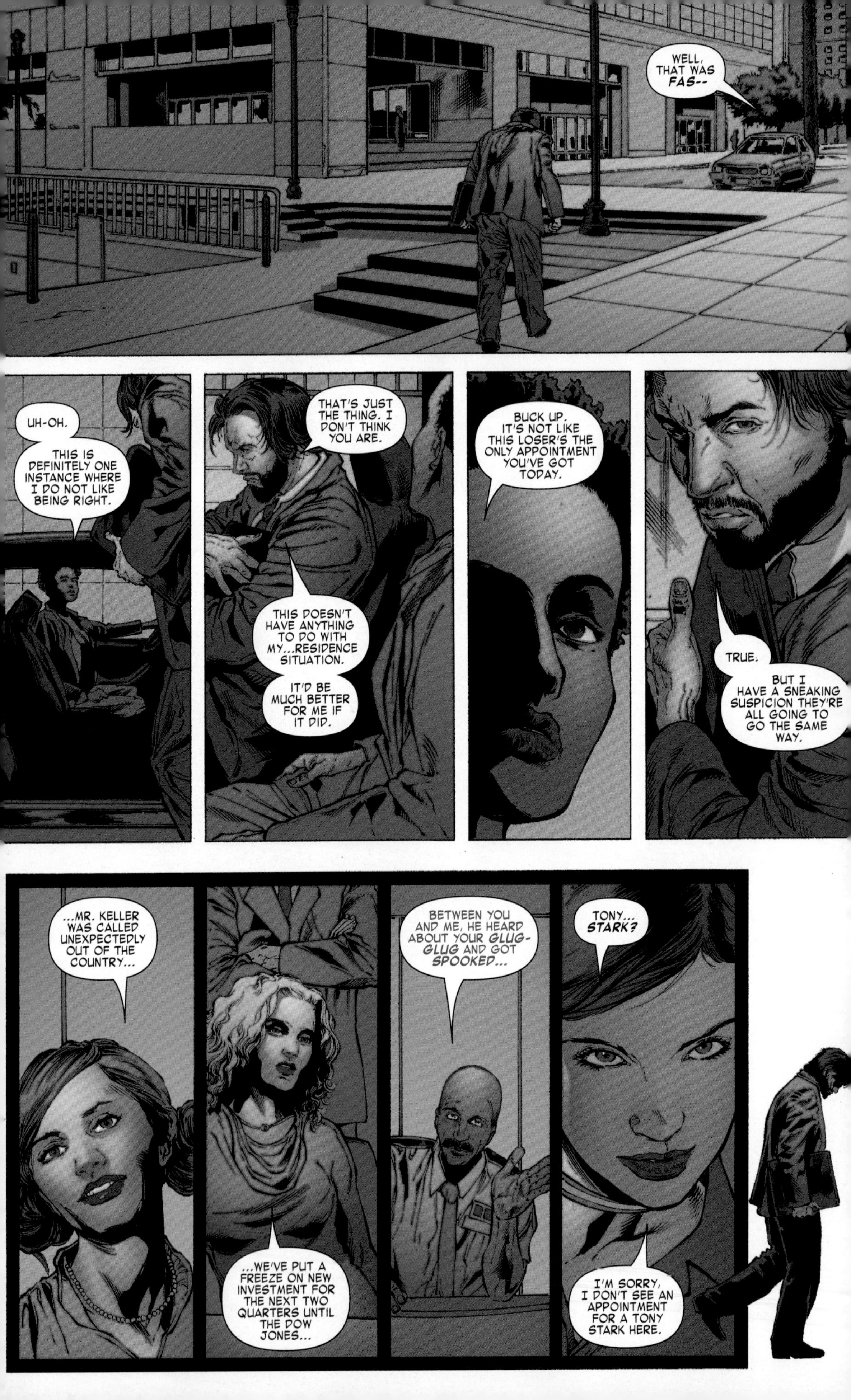
WELL, THAT WAS FAS--
UH-OH.
THIS IS DEFINITELY ONE INSTANCE WHERE I DO NOT LIKE BEING RIGHT.
THAT'S JUST THE THING. I DON'T THINK YOU ARE.
THIS DOESN'T HAVE ANYTHING TO DO WITH MY...RESIDENCE SITUATION.
IT'D BE MUCH BETTER FOR ME IF IT DID.
BUCK UP. IT'S NOT LIKE THIS LOSER'S THE ONLY APPOINTMENT YOU'VE GOT TODAY.
TRUE.
BUT I HAVE A SNEAKING SUSPICION THEY'RE ALL GOING TO GO THE SAME WAY.
...MR. KELLER WAS CALLED UNEXPECTEDLY OUT OF THE COUNTRY...
...WE'VE PUT A FREEZE ON NEW INVESTMENT FOR THE NEXT TWO QUARTERS UNTIL THE DOW JONES...
BETWEEN YOU AND ME, HE HEARD ABOUT YOUR GLUG-GLUG AND GOT SPOOKED...
TONY... STARK?
I'M SORRY, I DON'T SEE AN APPOINTMENT FOR A TONY STARK HERE.

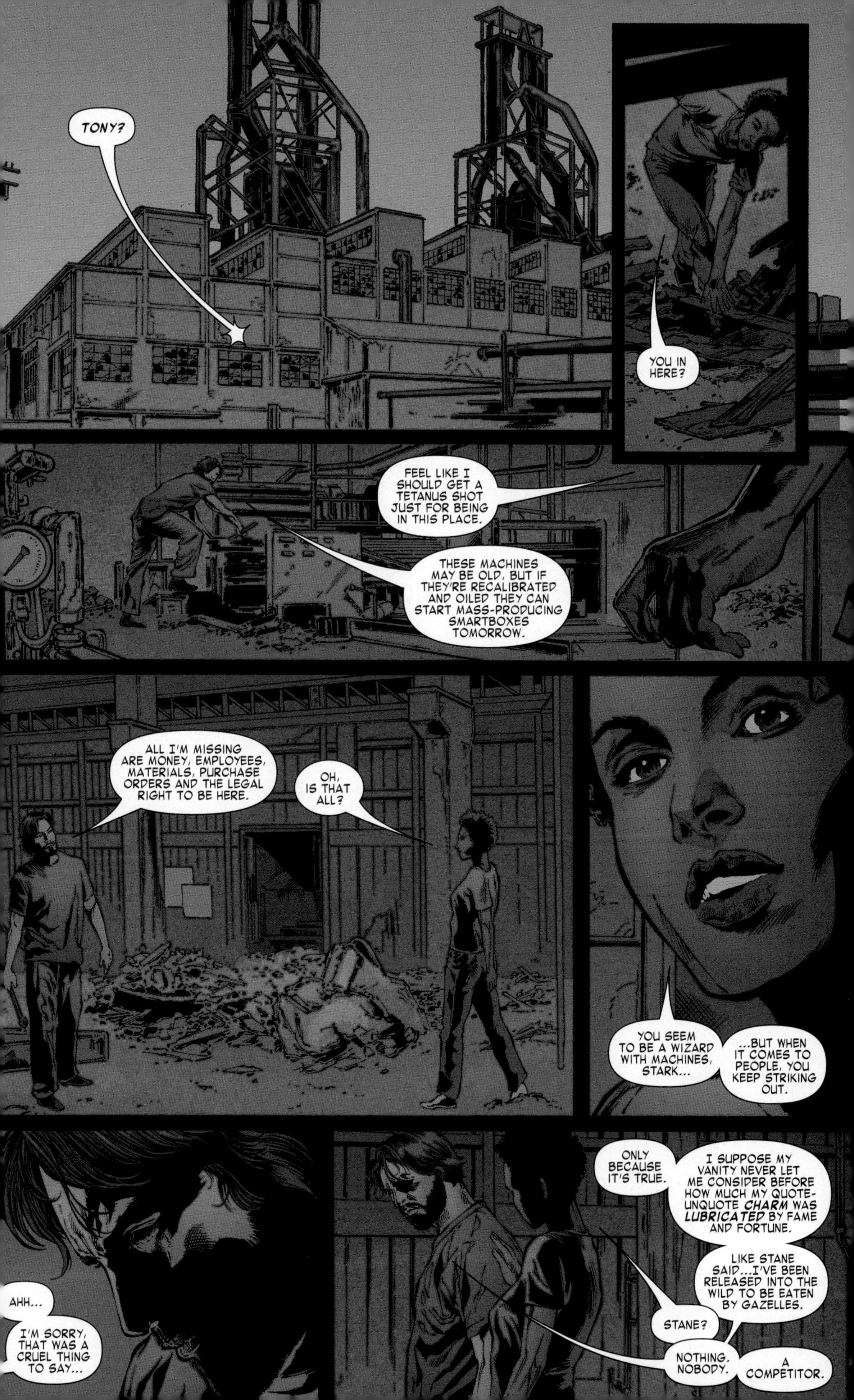
TONY?
YOU IN HERE?
FEEL LIKE I SHOULD GET A TETANUS SHOT JUST FOR BEING IN THIS PLACE.
THESE MACHINES MAY BE OLD, BUT IF THEY'RE RECALIBRATED AND OILED THEY CAN START MASS-PRODUCING SMARTBOXES TOMORROW.
ALL I'M MISSING ARE MONEY, EMPLOYEES, MATERIALS, PURCHASE ORDERS AND THE LEGAL RIGHT TO BE HERE.
OH, IS THAT ALL?
YOU SEEM TO BE A WIZARD WITH MACHINES, STARK...
...BUT WHEN IT COMES TO PEOPLE, YOU KEEP STRIKING OUT.
AHH...
I'M SORRY, THAT WAS A CRUEL THING TO SAY...
ONLY BECAUSE IT'S TRUE.
I SUPPOSE MY VANITY NEVER LET ME CONSIDER BEFORE HOW MUCH MY QUOTE-UNQUOTE *CHARM* WAS *LUBRICATED* BY FAME AND FORTUNE.
LIKE STANE SAID...I'VE BEEN RELEASED INTO THE WILD TO BE EATEN BY GAZELLES.
STANE?
NOTHING. NOBODY.
A COMPETITOR.

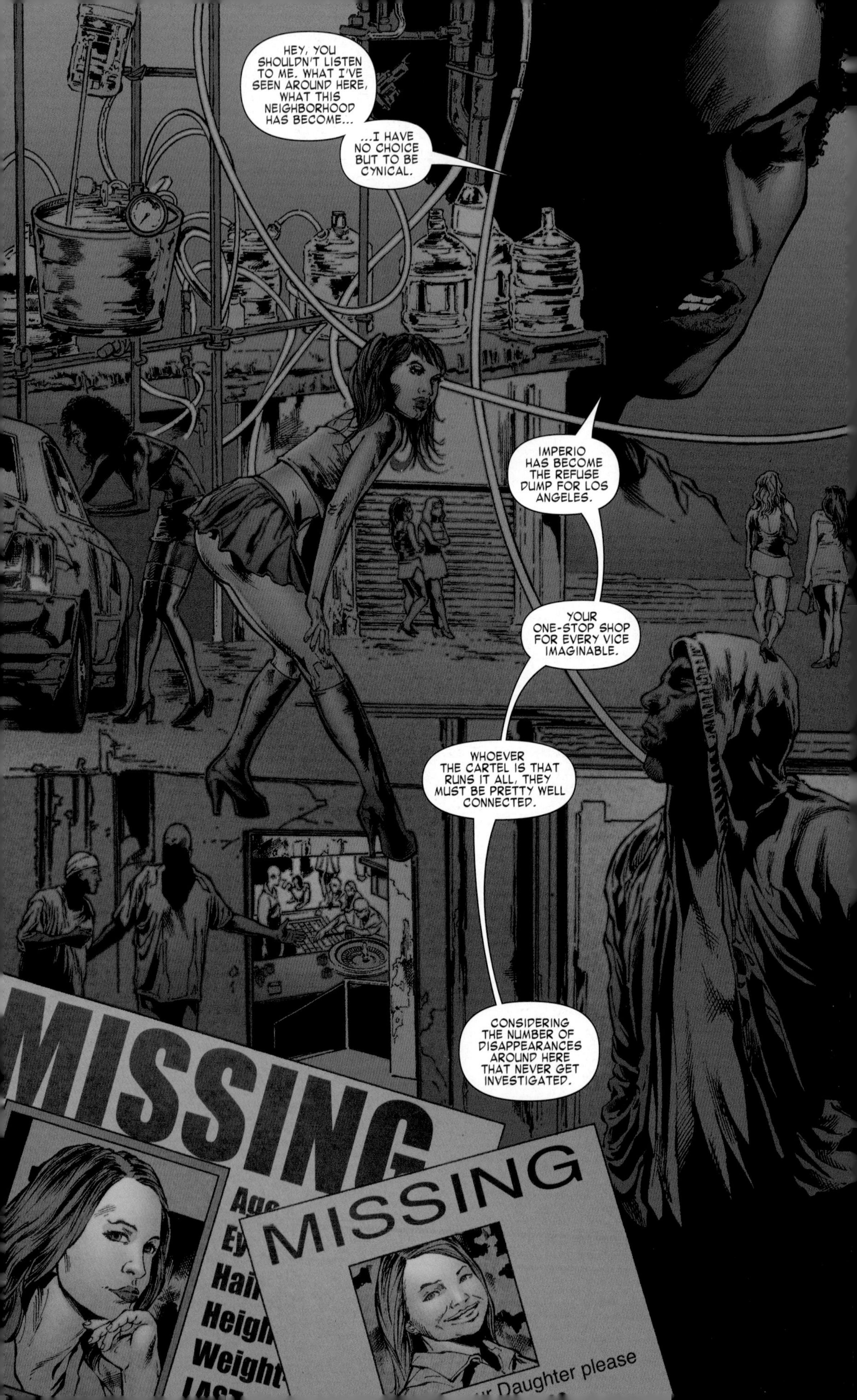
HEY, YOU SHOULDN'T LISTEN TO ME. WHAT I'VE SEEN AROUND HERE, WHAT THIS NEIGHBORHOOD HAS BECOME...
...I HAVE NO CHOICE BUT TO BE CYNICAL.
IMPERIO HAS BECOME THE REFUSE DUMP FOR LOS ANGELES.
YOUR ONE-STOP SHOP FOR EVERY VICE IMAGINABLE.
WHOEVER THE CARTEL IS THAT RUNS IT ALL, THEY MUST BE PRETTY WELL CONNECTED.
CONSIDERING THE NUMBER OF DISAPPEARANCES AROUND HERE THAT NEVER GET INVESTIGATED.
MISSING
Age
Ey
Hai
Heigh
Weight
MISSING
r Daughter please

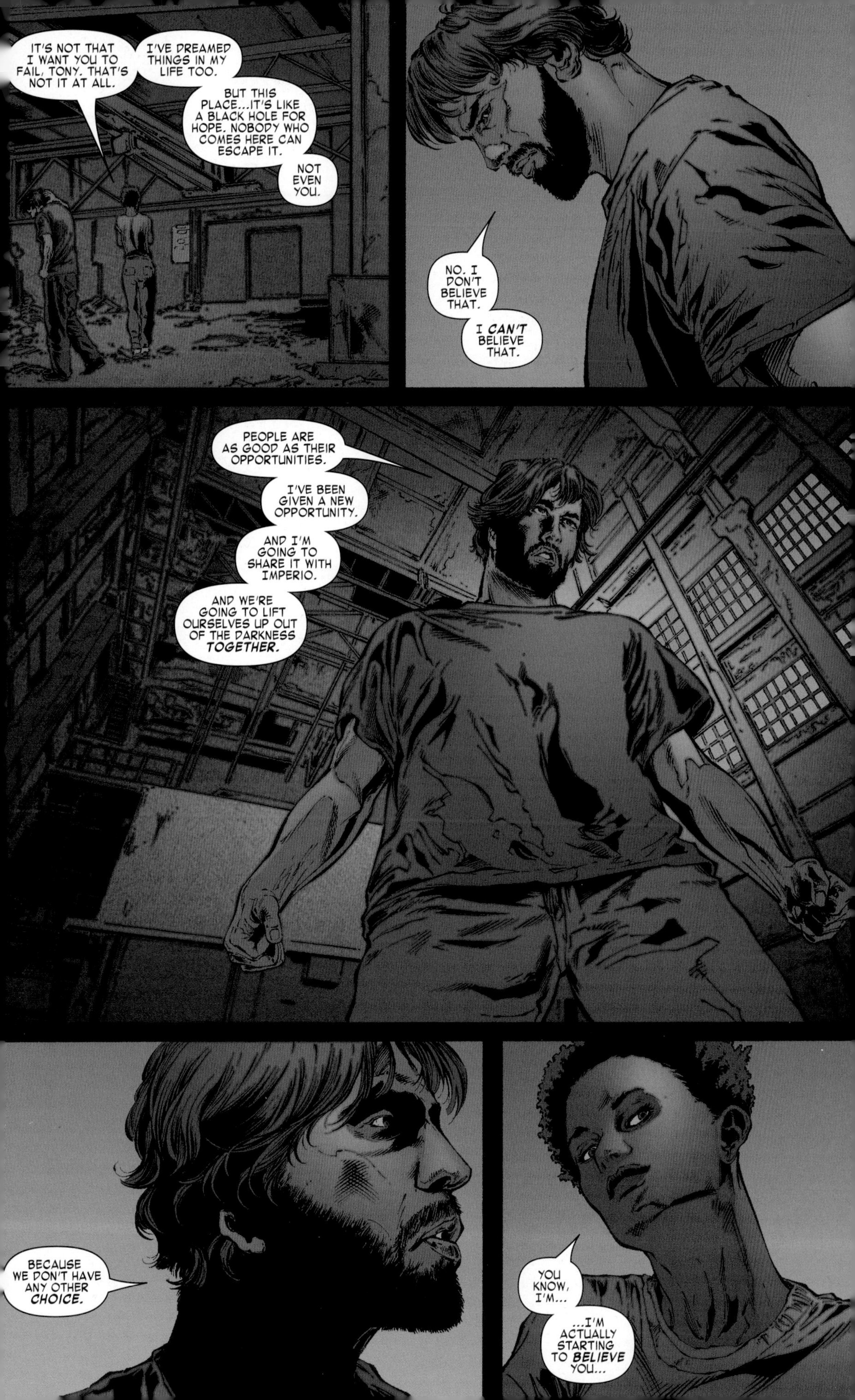
IT'S NOT THAT I WANT YOU TO FAIL, TONY. THAT'S NOT IT AT ALL.
I'VE DREAMED THINGS IN MY LIFE TOO.
BUT THIS PLACE...IT'S LIKE A BLACK HOLE FOR HOPE. NOBODY WHO COMES HERE CAN ESCAPE IT.
NOT EVEN YOU.
NO. I DON'T BELIEVE THAT.
I *CAN'T* BELIEVE THAT.
PEOPLE ARE AS GOOD AS THEIR OPPORTUNITIES.
I'VE BEEN GIVEN A NEW OPPORTUNITY.
AND I'M GOING TO SHARE IT WITH IMPERIO.
AND WE'RE GOING TO LIFT OURSELVES UP OUT OF THE DARKNESS *TOGETHER.*
BECAUSE WE DON'T HAVE ANY OTHER *CHOICE.*
YOU KNOW, I'M...
...I'M ACTUALLY STARTING TO *BELIEVE* YOU...

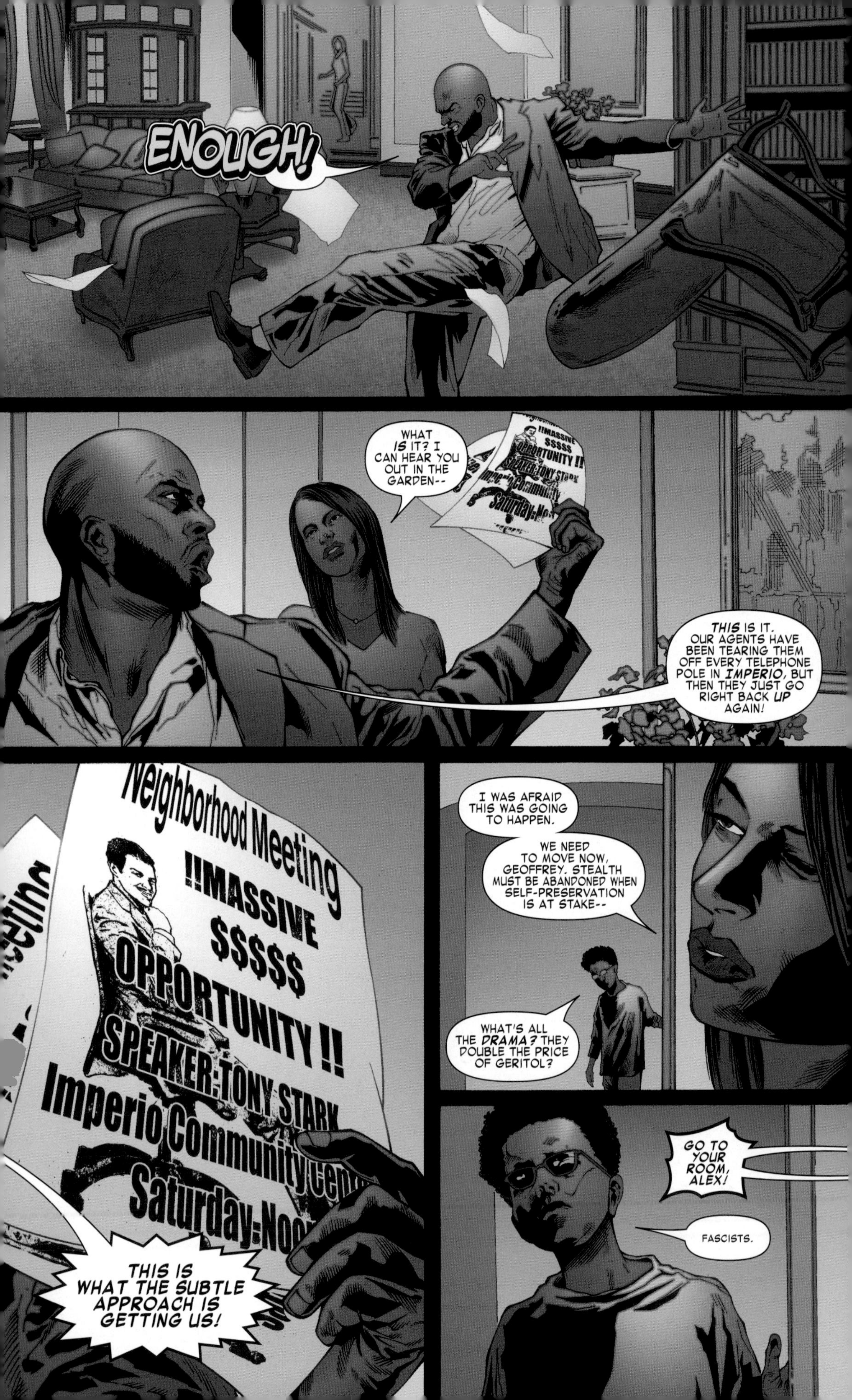
ENOUGH!
WHAT *IS* IT? I CAN HEAR YOU OUT IN THE GARDEN--
THIS IS IT. OUR AGENTS HAVE BEEN TEARING THEM OFF EVERY TELEPHONE POLE IN *IMPERIO*, BUT THEN THEY JUST GO RIGHT BACK *UP* AGAIN!
Neighborhood Meeting
!!MASSIVE
$$$$$
OPPORTUNITY !!
SPEAKER:TONY STARK
Imperio Community Cent
Saturday:Noo
THIS IS WHAT THE SUBTLE APPROACH IS GETTING US!
I WAS AFRAID THIS WAS GOING TO HAPPEN.
WE NEED TO MOVE NOW, GEOFFREY. STEALTH MUST BE ABANDONED WHEN SELF-PRESERVATION IS AT STAKE--
WHAT'S ALL THE *DRAMA?* THEY DOUBLE THE PRICE OF GERITOL?
GO TO YOUR ROOM, ALEX!
FASCISTS.

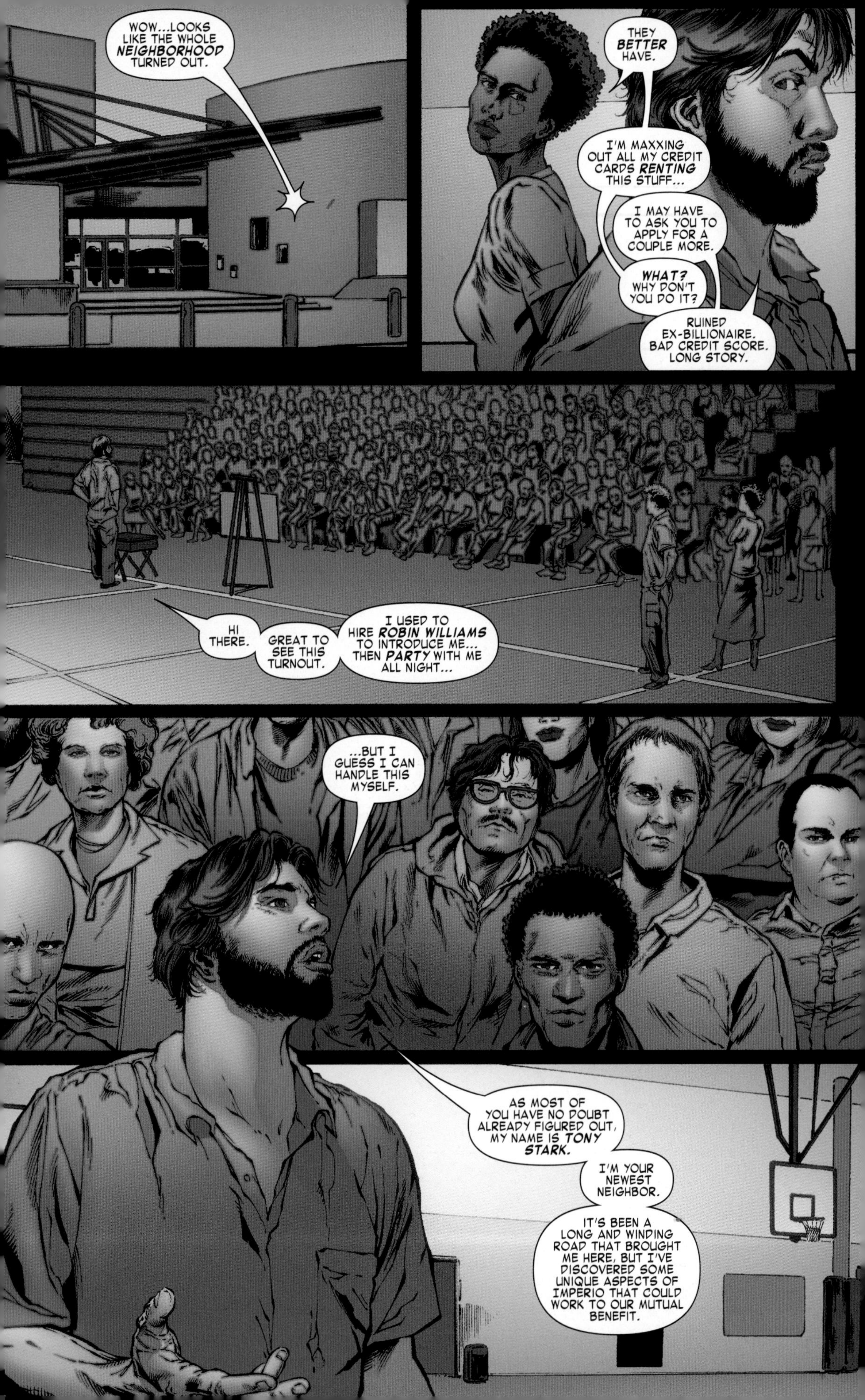
WOW...LOOKS LIKE THE WHOLE NEIGHBORHOOD TURNED OUT.
THEY BETTER HAVE.
I'M MAXXING OUT ALL MY CREDIT CARDS RENTING THIS STUFF...
I MAY HAVE TO ASK YOU TO APPLY FOR A COUPLE MORE.
WHAT? WHY DON'T YOU DO IT?
RUINED EX-BILLIONAIRE. BAD CREDIT SCORE. LONG STORY.
HI THERE.
GREAT TO SEE THIS TURNOUT.
I USED TO HIRE ROBIN WILLIAMS TO INTRODUCE ME... THEN PARTY WITH ME ALL NIGHT...
...BUT I GUESS I CAN HANDLE THIS MYSELF.
AS MOST OF YOU HAVE NO DOUBT ALREADY FIGURED OUT, MY NAME IS TONY STARK.
I'M YOUR NEWEST NEIGHBOR.
IT'S BEEN A LONG AND WINDING ROAD THAT BROUGHT ME HERE, BUT I'VE DISCOVERED SOME UNIQUE ASPECTS OF IMPERIO THAT COULD WORK TO OUR MUTUAL BENEFIT.

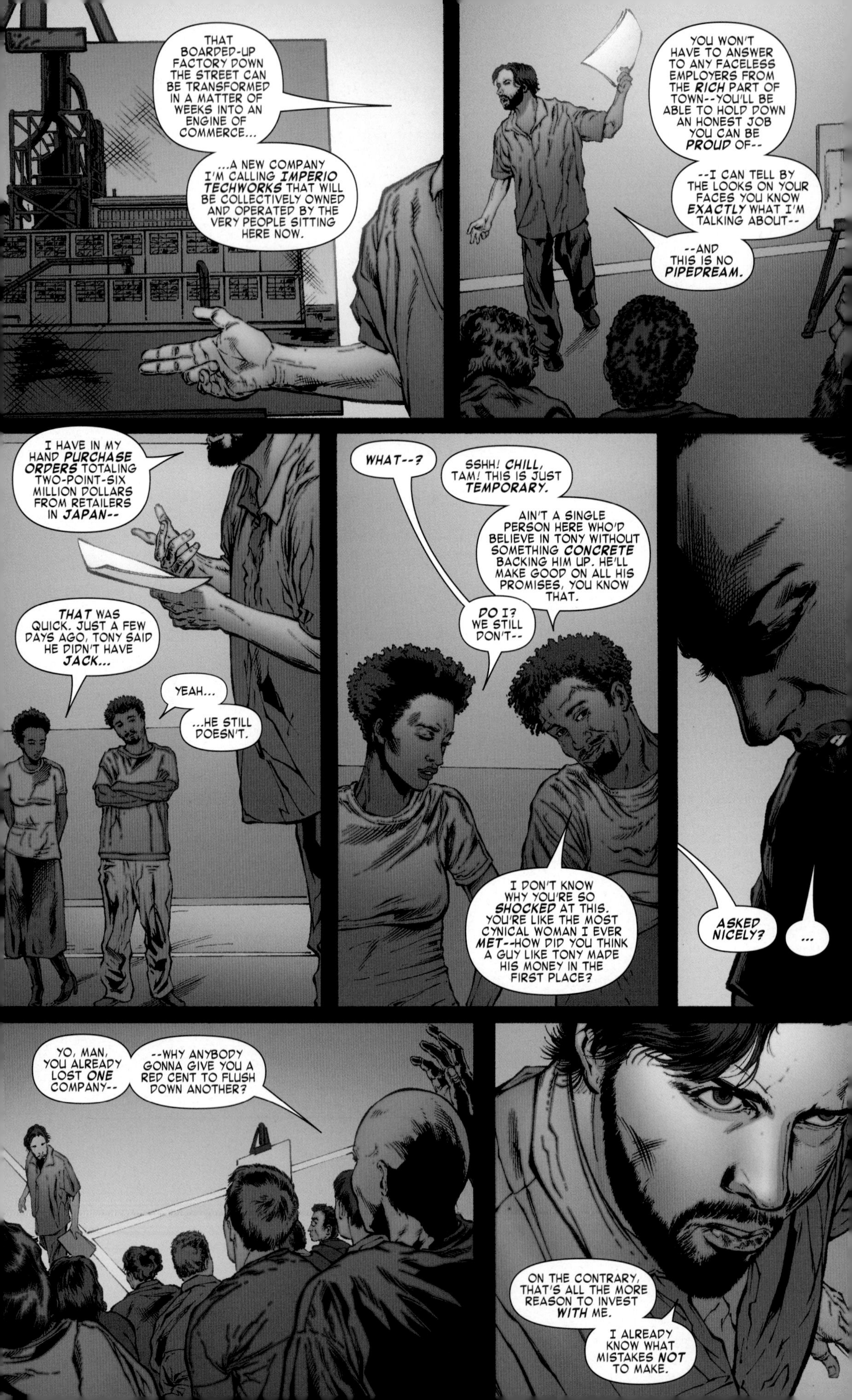
THAT BOARDED-UP FACTORY DOWN THE STREET CAN BE TRANSFORMED IN A MATTER OF WEEKS INTO AN ENGINE OF COMMERCE...
...A NEW COMPANY I'M CALLING IMPERIO TECHWORKS THAT WILL BE COLLECTIVELY OWNED AND OPERATED BY THE VERY PEOPLE SITTING HERE NOW.
YOU WON'T HAVE TO ANSWER TO ANY FACELESS EMPLOYERS FROM THE RICH PART OF TOWN--YOU'LL BE ABLE TO HOLD DOWN AN HONEST JOB YOU CAN BE PROUD OF--
--I CAN TELL BY THE LOOKS ON YOUR FACES YOU KNOW EXACTLY WHAT I'M TALKING ABOUT--
--AND THIS IS NO PIPEDREAM.
I HAVE IN MY HAND PURCHASE ORDERS TOTALING TWO-POINT-SIX MILLION DOLLARS FROM RETAILERS IN JAPAN--
THAT WAS QUICK. JUST A FEW DAYS AGO, TONY SAID HE DIDN'T HAVE JACK...
YEAH...
...HE STILL DOESN'T.
WHAT--?
SSHH! CHILL, TAM! THIS IS JUST TEMPORARY.
AIN'T A SINGLE PERSON HERE WHO'D BELIEVE IN TONY WITHOUT SOMETHING CONCRETE BACKING HIM UP. HE'LL MAKE GOOD ON ALL HIS PROMISES, YOU KNOW THAT.
DO I? WE STILL DON'T--
I DON'T KNOW WHY YOU'RE SO SHOCKED AT THIS. YOU'RE LIKE THE MOST CYNICAL WOMAN I EVER MET--HOW DID YOU THINK A GUY LIKE TONY MADE HIS MONEY IN THE FIRST PLACE?
ASKED NICELY?
...
YO, MAN, YOU ALREADY LOST ONE COMPANY--
--WHY ANYBODY GONNA GIVE YOU A RED CENT TO FLUSH DOWN ANOTHER?
ON THE CONTRARY, THAT'S ALL THE MORE REASON TO INVEST WITH ME.
I ALREADY KNOW WHAT MISTAKES NOT TO MAKE.

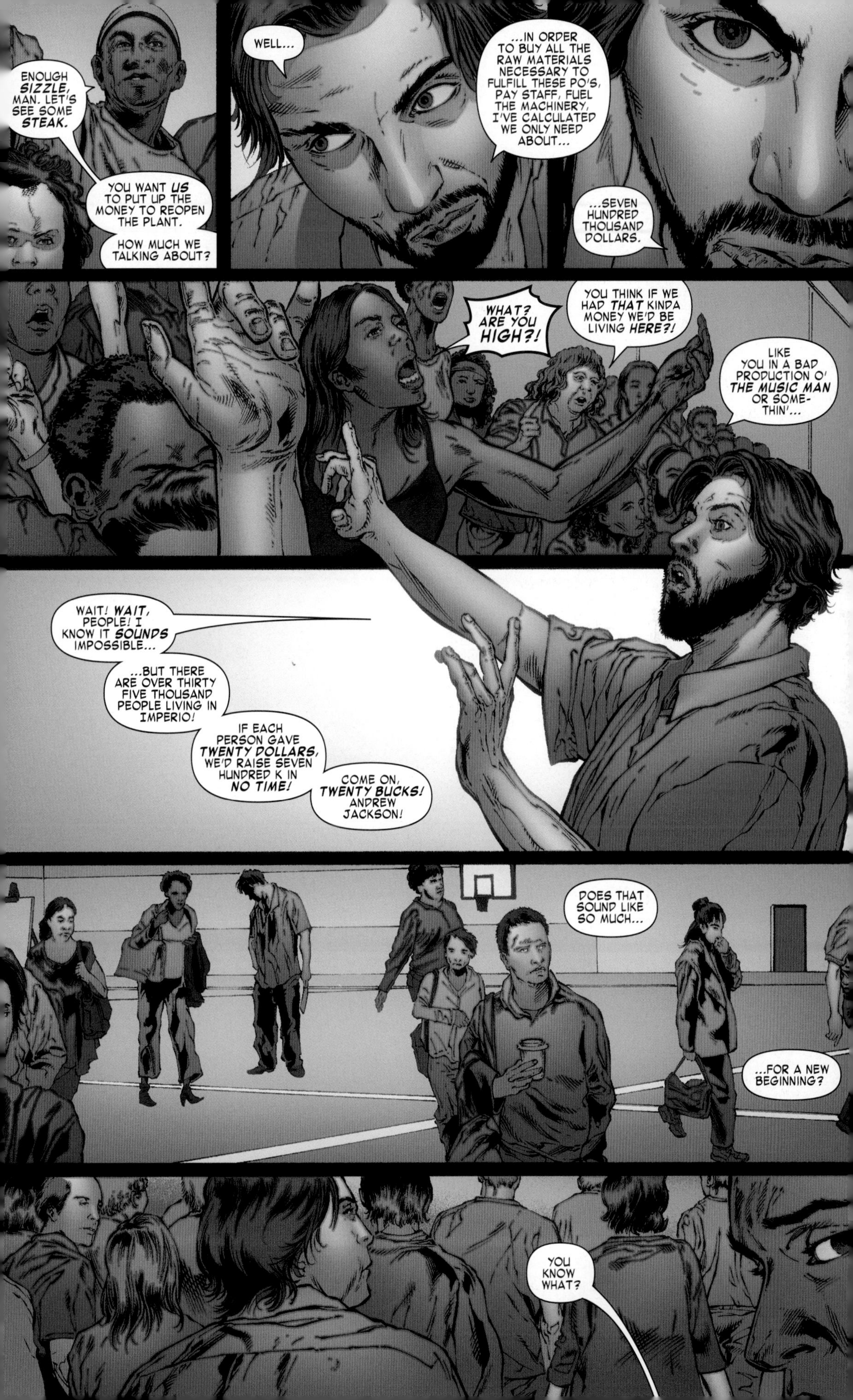
ENOUGH SIZZLE, MAN. LET'S SEE SOME STEAK.
YOU WANT US TO PUT UP THE MONEY TO REOPEN THE PLANT.
HOW MUCH WE TALKING ABOUT?
WELL...
...IN ORDER TO BUY ALL THE RAW MATERIALS NECESSARY TO FULFILL THESE PO'S, PAY STAFF, FUEL THE MACHINERY, I'VE CALCULATED WE ONLY NEED ABOUT...
...SEVEN HUNDRED THOUSAND DOLLARS.
WHAT? ARE YOU HIGH?!
YOU THINK IF WE HAD THAT KINDA MONEY WE'D BE LIVING HERE?!
LIKE YOU IN A BAD PRODUCTION O' THE MUSIC MAN OR SOME-THIN'...
WAIT! WAIT, PEOPLE! I KNOW IT SOUNDS IMPOSSIBLE...
...BUT THERE ARE OVER THIRTY FIVE THOUSAND PEOPLE LIVING IN IMPERIO!
IF EACH PERSON GAVE TWENTY DOLLARS, WE'D RAISE SEVEN HUNDRED K IN NO TIME!
COME ON, TWENTY BUCKS! ANDREW JACKSON!
DOES THAT SOUND LIKE SO MUCH...
...FOR A NEW BEGINNING?
YOU KNOW WHAT?

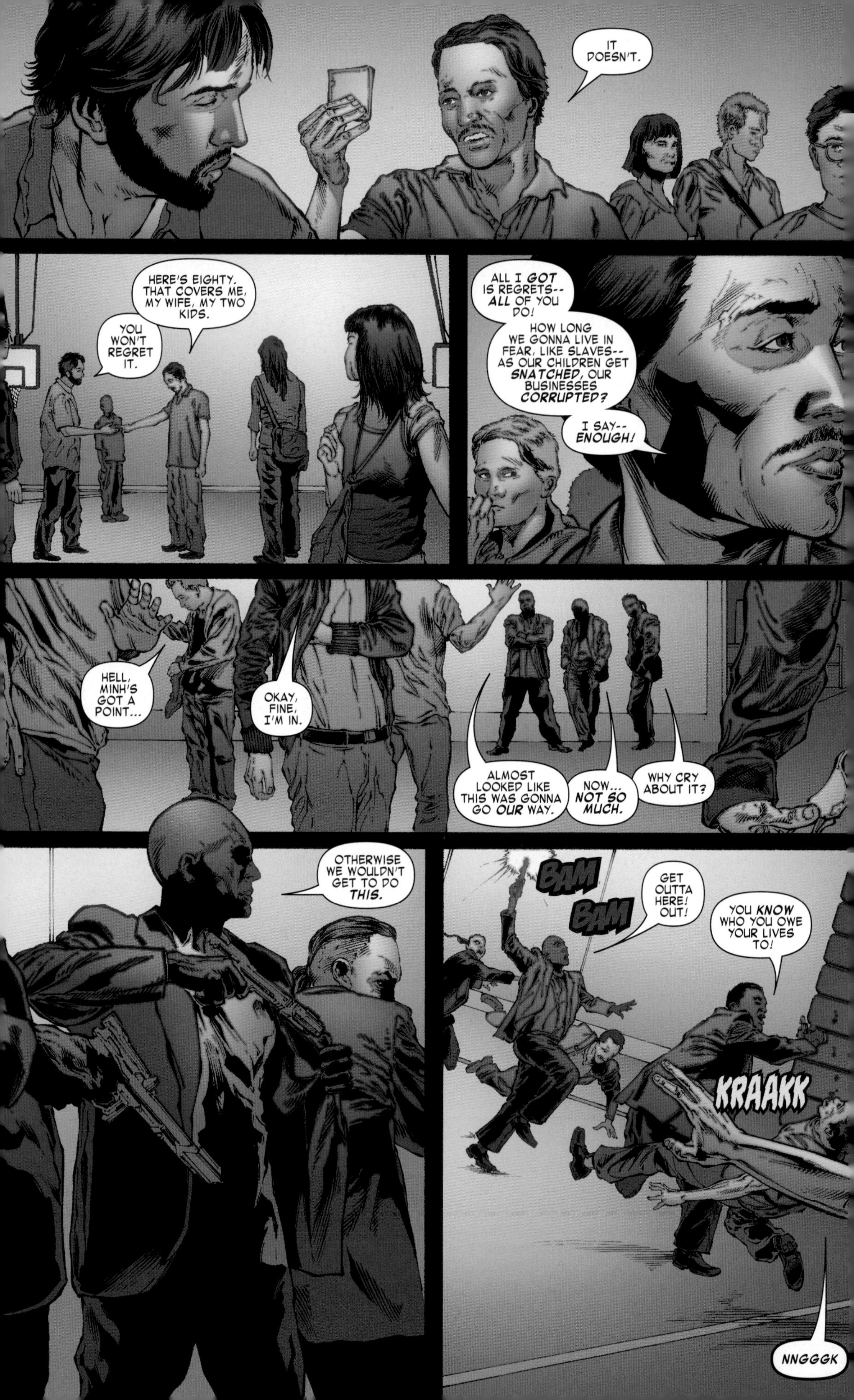
IT DOESN'T.
HERE'S EIGHTY. THAT COVERS ME, MY WIFE, MY TWO KIDS.
YOU WON'T REGRET IT.
ALL I GOT IS REGRETS-- ALL OF YOU DO!
HOW LONG WE GONNA LIVE IN FEAR, LIKE SLAVES-- AS OUR CHILDREN GET SNATCHED, OUR BUSINESSES CORRUPTED?
I SAY-- ENOUGH!
HELL, MINH'S GOT A POINT...
OKAY, FINE, I'M IN.
ALMOST LOOKED LIKE THIS WAS GONNA GO OUR WAY.
NOW... NOT SO MUCH.
WHY CRY ABOUT IT?
OTHERWISE WE WOULDN'T GET TO DO THIS.
BAM
BAM
GET OUTTA HERE! OUT!
YOU KNOW WHO YOU OWE YOUR LIVES TO!
KRAAKK
NNGGGK

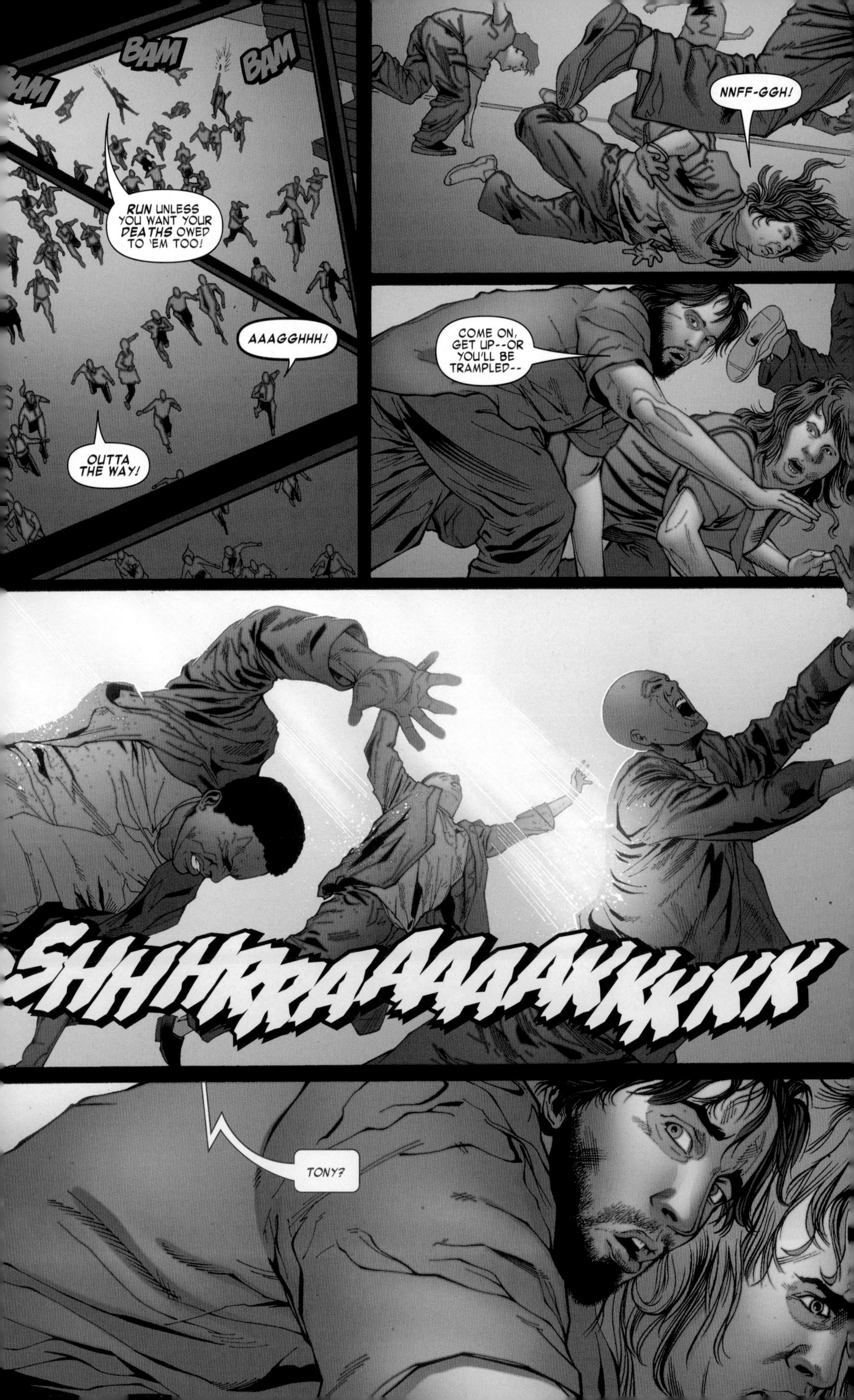
BAM
BAM
BAM
RUN UNLESS YOU WANT YOUR DEATHS OWED TO 'EM TOO!
AAAGGHHH!
OUTTA THE WAY!
NNFF-GGH!
COME ON, GET UP--OR YOU'LL BE TRAMPLED--
SHHHRRAAAAAKKKKK
TONY?

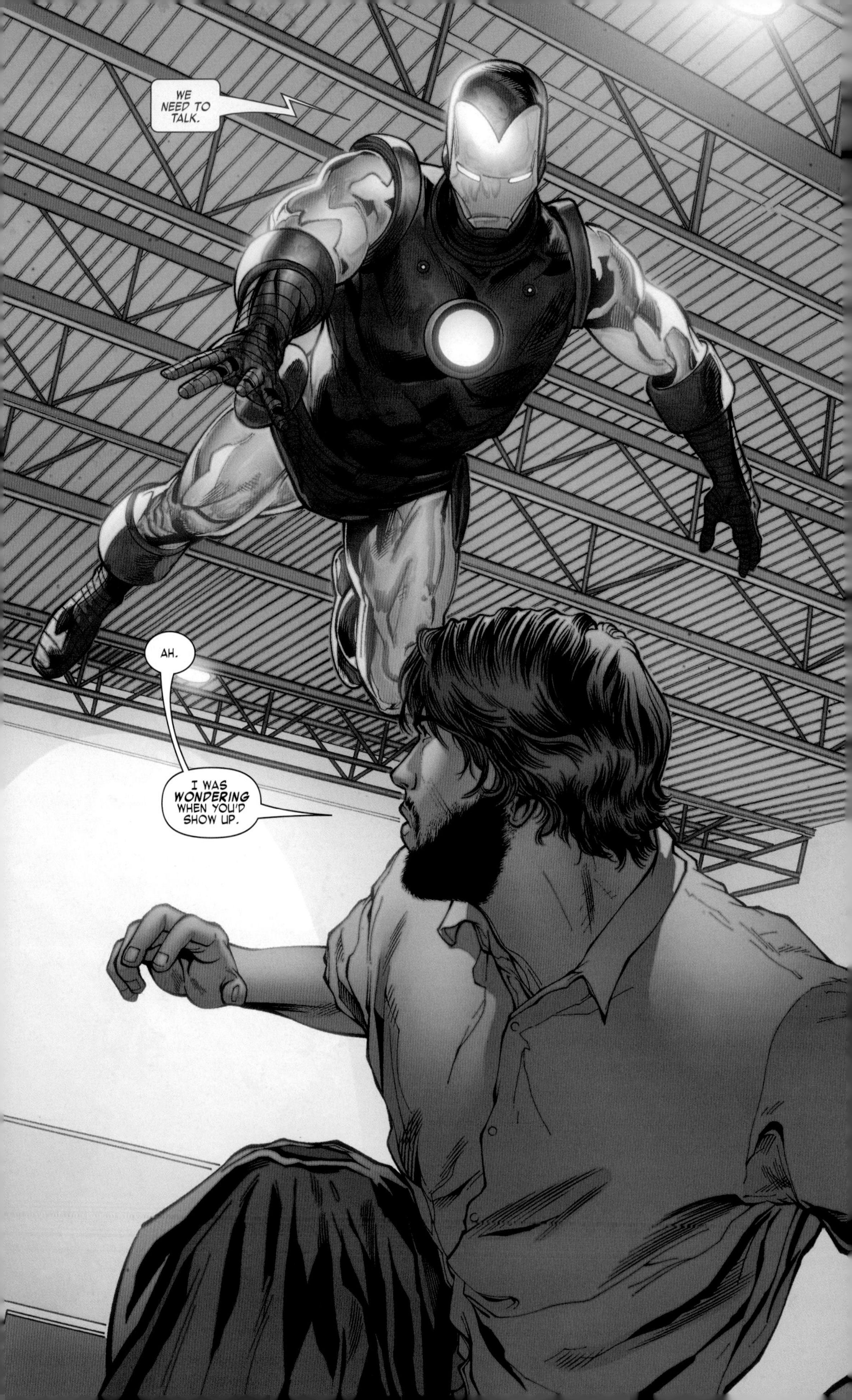
WE NEED TO TALK.
AH.
I WAS WONDERING WHEN YOU'D SHOW UP.

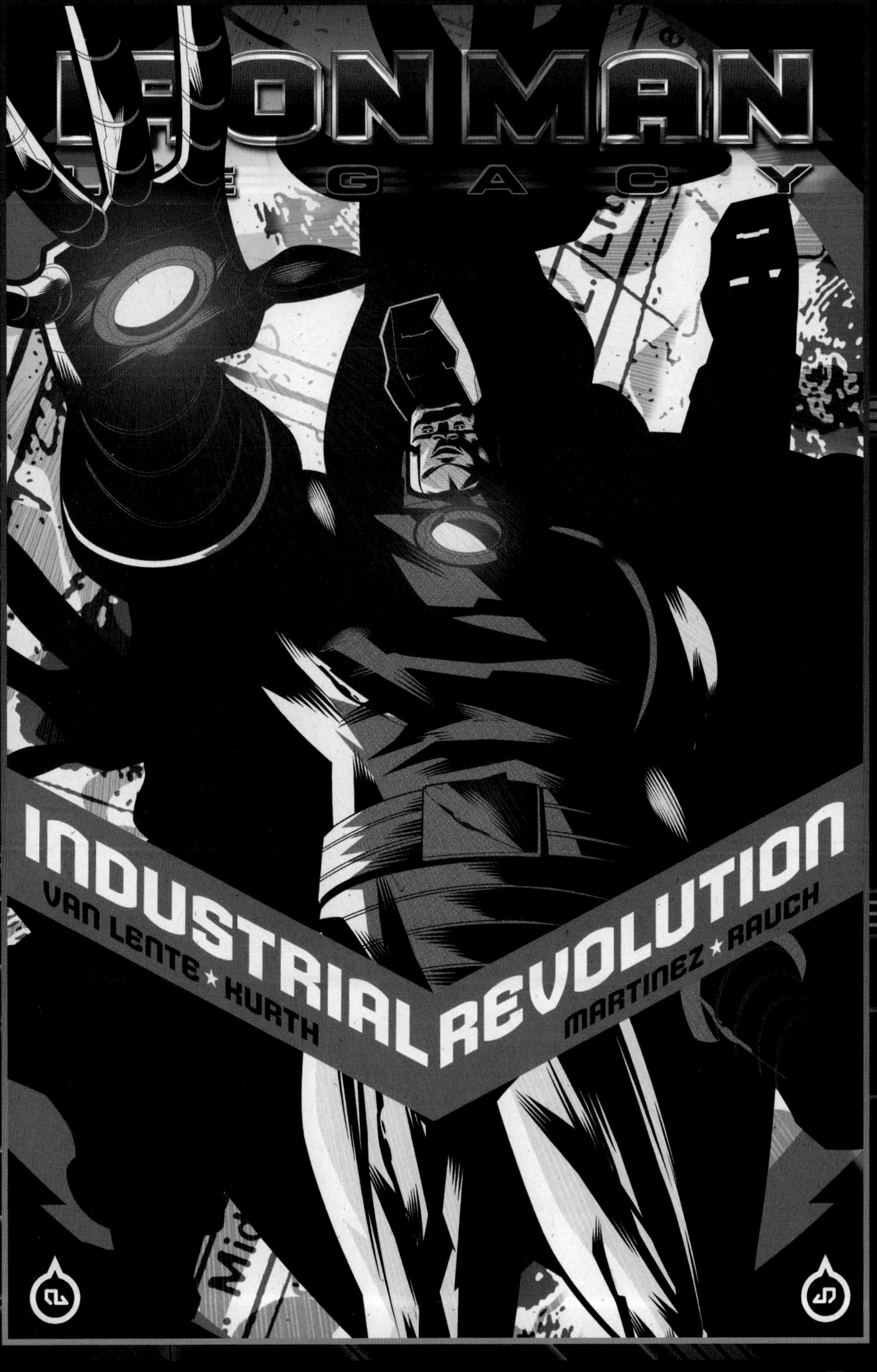

IRON MAN
LEGACY
INDUSTRIAL REVOLUTION
VAN LENTE ★ KURTH
MARTINEZ ★ RAUCH

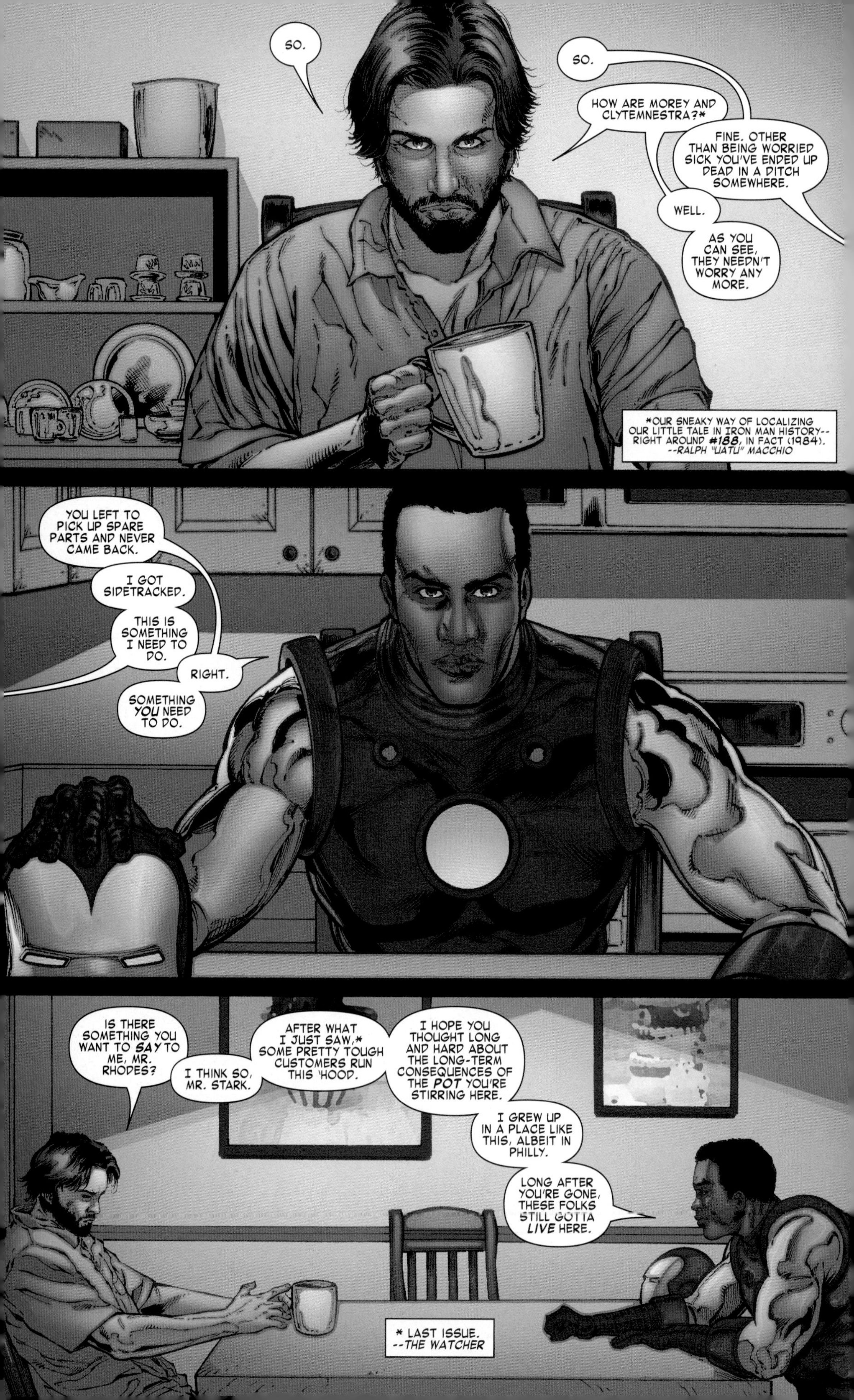
SO.
SO.
HOW ARE MOREY AND CLYTEMNESTRA?*
FINE. OTHER THAN BEING WORRIED SICK YOU'VE ENDED UP DEAD IN A DITCH SOMEWHERE.
WELL.
AS YOU CAN SEE, THEY NEEDN'T WORRY ANY MORE.
*OUR SNEAKY WAY OF LOCALIZING OUR LITTLE TALE IN IRON MAN HISTORY-- RIGHT AROUND #188, IN FACT (1984). --RALPH "UATU" MACCHIO
YOU LEFT TO PICK UP SPARE PARTS AND NEVER CAME BACK.
I GOT SIDETRACKED.
THIS IS SOMETHING I NEED TO DO.
RIGHT.
SOMETHING YOU NEED TO DO.
IS THERE SOMETHING YOU WANT TO SAY TO ME, MR. RHODES?
I THINK SO, MR. STARK.
AFTER WHAT I JUST SAW,* SOME PRETTY TOUGH CUSTOMERS RUN THIS 'HOOD.
I HOPE YOU THOUGHT LONG AND HARD ABOUT THE LONG-TERM CONSEQUENCES OF THE POT YOU'RE STIRRING HERE.
I GREW UP IN A PLACE LIKE THIS, ALBEIT IN PHILLY.
LONG AFTER YOU'RE GONE, THESE FOLKS STILL GOTTA LIVE HERE.
* LAST ISSUE. --THE WATCHER

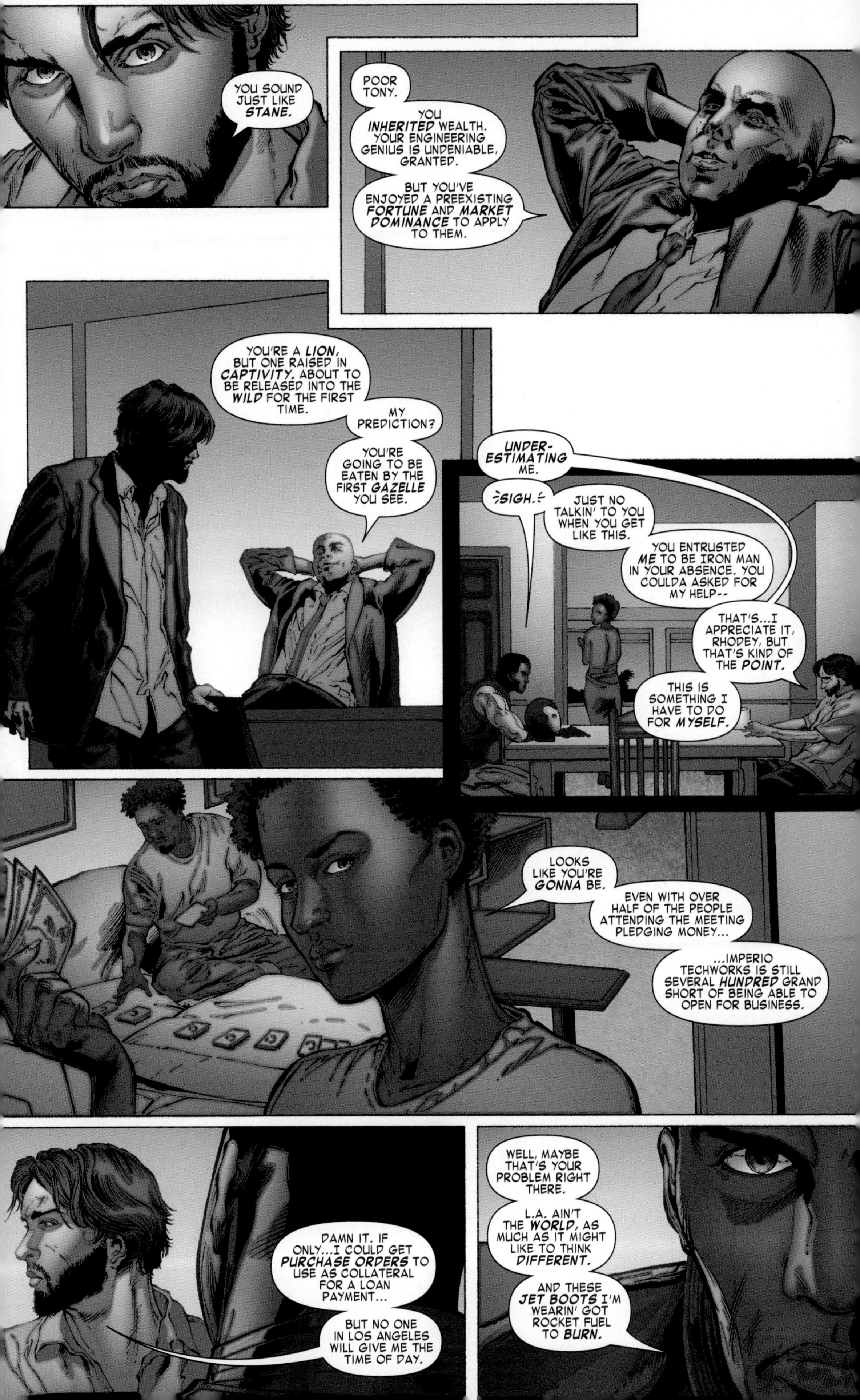
YOU SOUND JUST LIKE STANE.
POOR TONY.
YOU INHERITED WEALTH. YOUR ENGINEERING GENIUS IS UNDENIABLE, GRANTED.
BUT YOU'VE ENJOYED A PREEXISTING FORTUNE AND MARKET DOMINANCE TO APPLY TO THEM.
YOU'RE A LION, BUT ONE RAISED IN CAPTIVITY. ABOUT TO BE RELEASED INTO THE WILD FOR THE FIRST TIME.
MY PREDICTION?
YOU'RE GOING TO BE EATEN BY THE FIRST GAZELLE YOU SEE.
UNDER-ESTIMATING ME.
SIGH.
JUST NO TALKIN' TO YOU WHEN YOU GET LIKE THIS.
YOU ENTRUSTED ME TO BE IRON MAN IN YOUR ABSENCE. YOU COULDA ASKED FOR MY HELP--
THAT'S...I APPRECIATE IT, RHODEY, BUT THAT'S KIND OF THE POINT.
THIS IS SOMETHING I HAVE TO DO FOR MYSELF.
LOOKS LIKE YOU'RE GONNA BE.
EVEN WITH OVER HALF OF THE PEOPLE ATTENDING THE MEETING PLEDGING MONEY...
...IMPERIO TECHWORKS IS STILL SEVERAL HUNDRED GRAND SHORT OF BEING ABLE TO OPEN FOR BUSINESS.
DAMN IT. IF ONLY...I COULD GET PURCHASE ORDERS TO USE AS COLLATERAL FOR A LOAN PAYMENT...
BUT NO ONE IN LOS ANGELES WILL GIVE ME THE TIME OF DAY.
WELL, MAYBE THAT'S YOUR PROBLEM RIGHT THERE.
L.A. AIN'T THE WORLD, AS MUCH AS IT MIGHT LIKE TO THINK DIFFERENT.
AND THESE JET BOOTS I'M WEARIN' GOT ROCKET FUEL TO BURN.

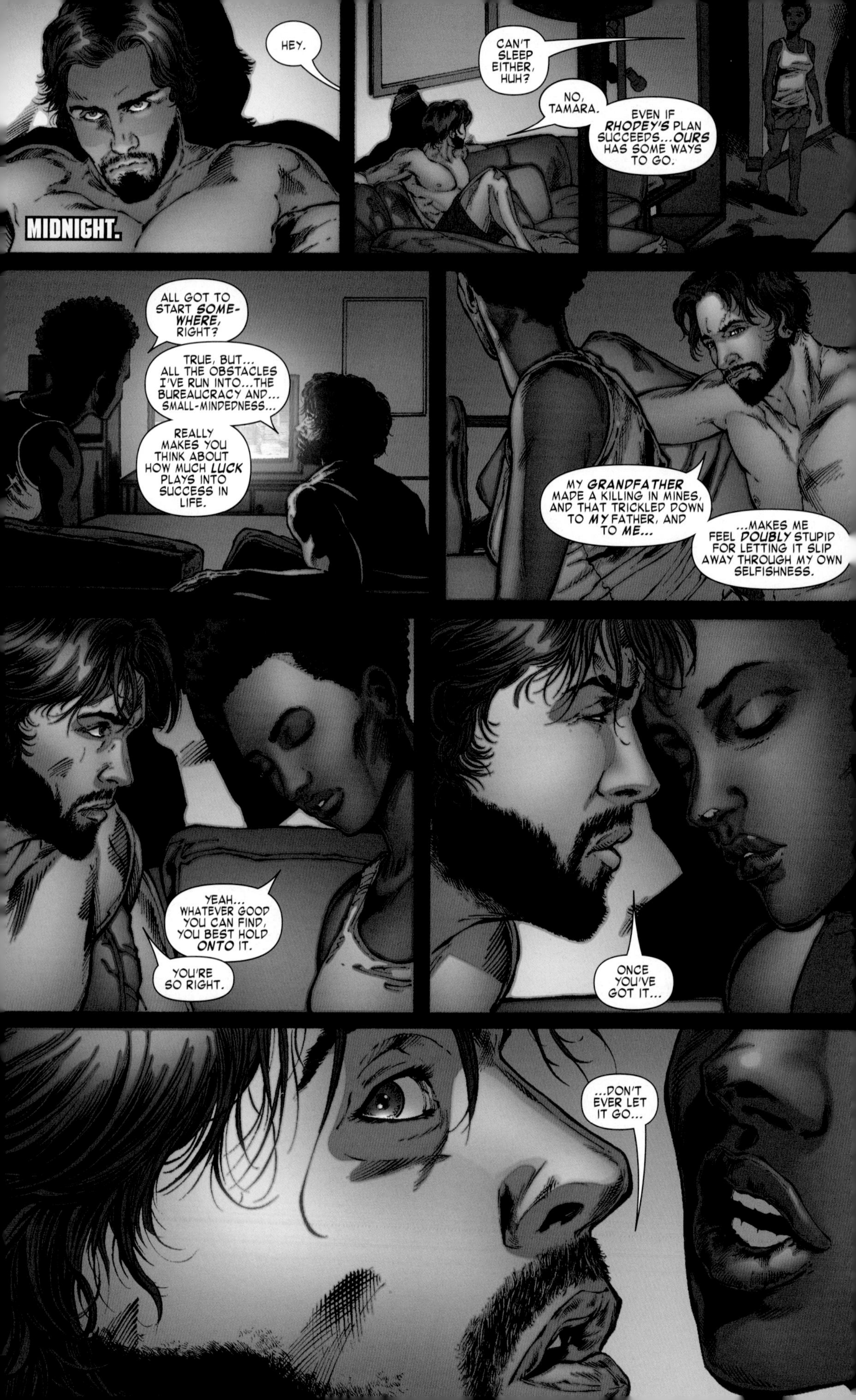
HEY.
MIDNIGHT.
CAN'T SLEEP EITHER, HUH?
NO, TAMARA.
EVEN IF RHODEY'S PLAN SUCCEEDS...OURS HAS SOME WAYS TO GO.
ALL GOT TO START SOME-WHERE, RIGHT?
TRUE, BUT... ALL THE OBSTACLES I'VE RUN INTO...THE BUREAUCRACY AND... SMALL-MINDEDNESS...
REALLY MAKES YOU THINK ABOUT HOW MUCH LUCK PLAYS INTO SUCCESS IN LIFE.
MY GRANDFATHER MADE A KILLING IN MINES, AND THAT TRICKLED DOWN TO MY FATHER, AND TO ME...
...MAKES ME FEEL DOUBLY STUPID FOR LETTING IT SLIP AWAY THROUGH MY OWN SELFISHNESS.
YEAH... WHATEVER GOOD YOU CAN FIND, YOU BEST HOLD ONTO IT.
YOU'RE SO RIGHT.
ONCE YOU'VE GOT IT...
...DON'T EVER LET IT GO...

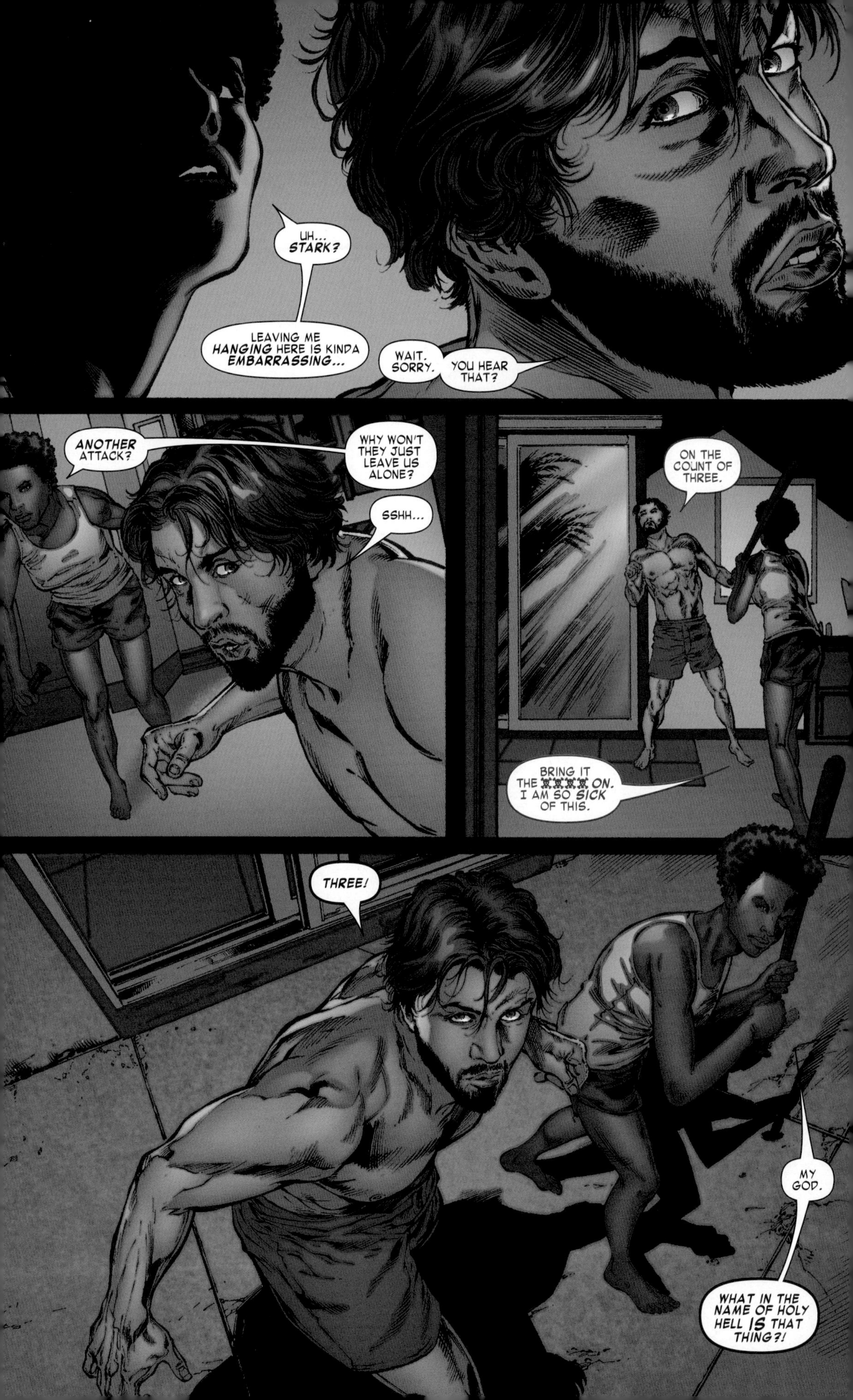
UH... STARK?
LEAVING ME HANGING HERE IS KINDA EMBARRASSING...
WAIT. SORRY.
YOU HEAR THAT?
ANOTHER ATTACK?
WHY WON'T THEY JUST LEAVE US ALONE?
SSHH...
ON THE COUNT OF THREE.
BRING IT THE ☠☠☠☠ ON. I AM SO SICK OF THIS.
THREE!
MY GOD.
WHAT IN THE NAME OF HOLY HELL IS THAT THING?!

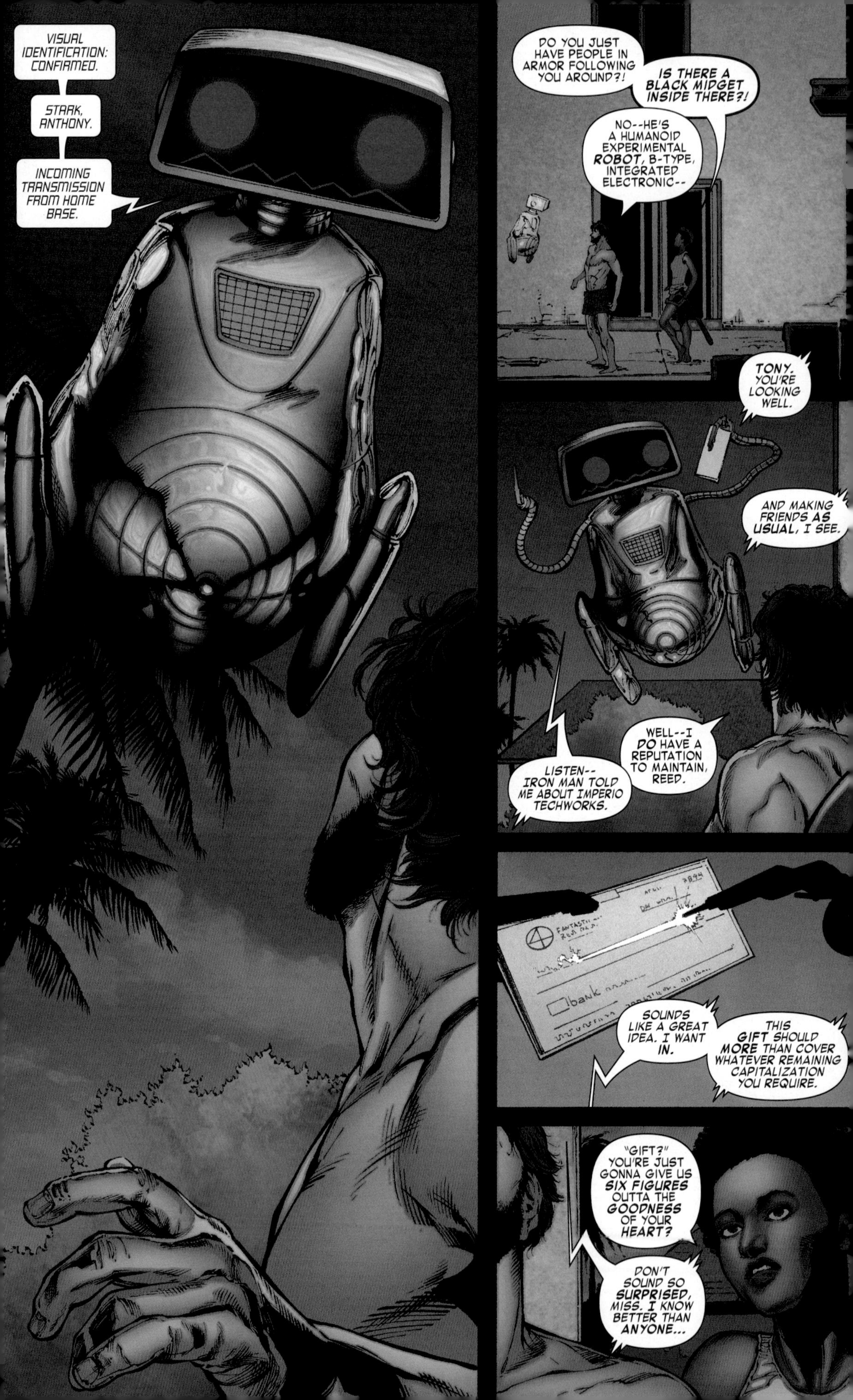

VISUAL IDENTIFICATION: CONFIRMED.
STARK, ANTHONY.
INCOMING TRANSMISSION FROM HOME BASE.
DO YOU JUST HAVE PEOPLE IN ARMOR FOLLOWING YOU AROUND?!
IS THERE A BLACK MIDGET INSIDE THERE?!
NO--HE'S A HUMANOID EXPERIMENTAL ROBOT, B-TYPE, INTEGRATED ELECTRONIC--
TONY. YOU'RE LOOKING WELL.
AND MAKING FRIENDS AS USUAL, I SEE.
WELL--I DO HAVE A REPUTATION TO MAINTAIN, REED.
LISTEN--IRON MAN TOLD ME ABOUT IMPERIO TECHWORKS.
SOUNDS LIKE A GREAT IDEA. I WANT IN.
THIS GIFT SHOULD MORE THAN COVER WHATEVER REMAINING CAPITALIZATION YOU REQUIRE.
"GIFT?" YOU'RE JUST GONNA GIVE US SIX FIGURES OUTTA THE GOODNESS OF YOUR HEART?
DON'T SOUND SO SURPRISED, MISS. I KNOW BETTER THAN ANYONE...

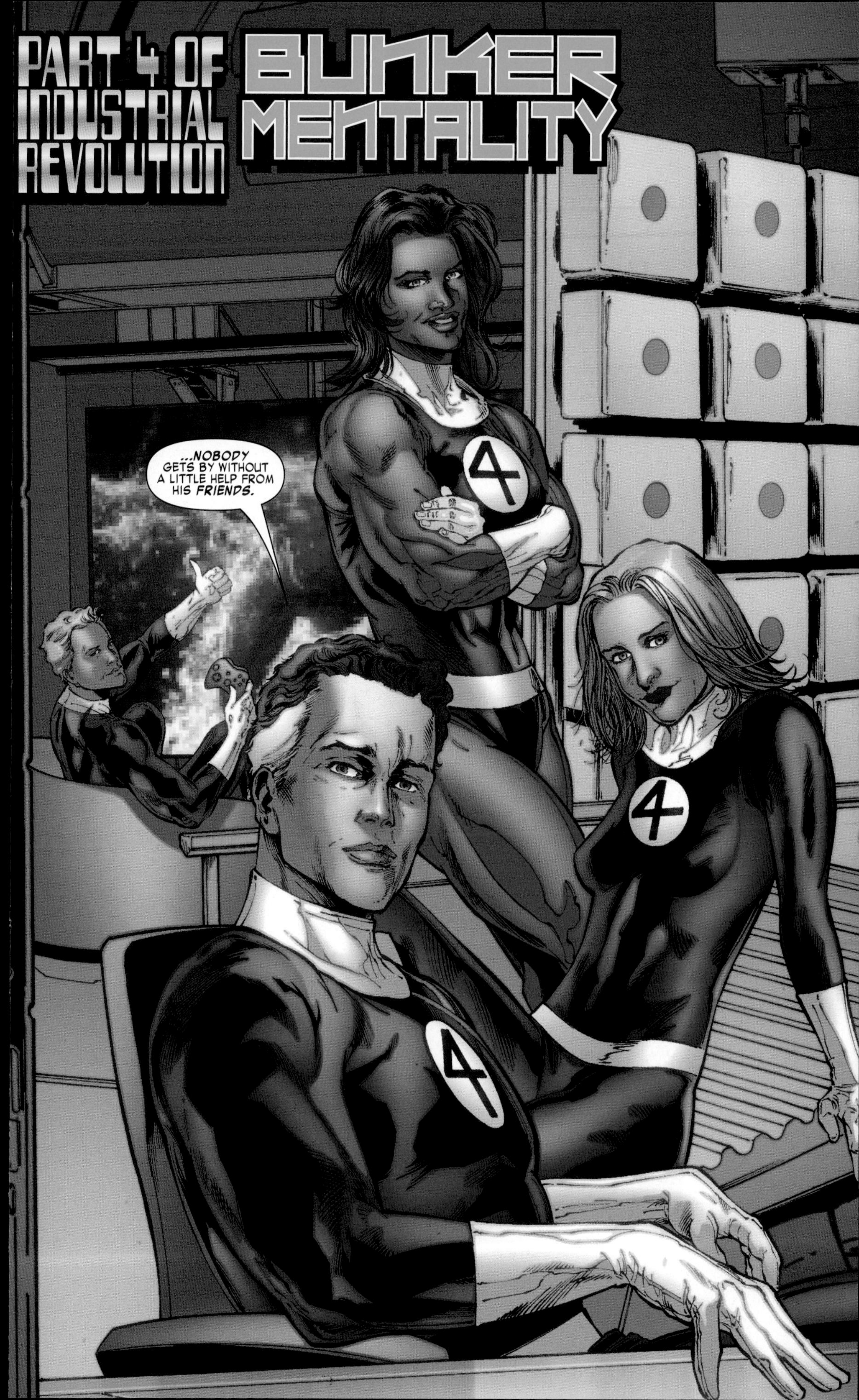
PART 4 OF INDUSTRIAL REVOLUTION
BUNKER MENTALITY
...NOBODY GETS BY WITHOUT A LITTLE HELP FROM HIS FRIENDS.

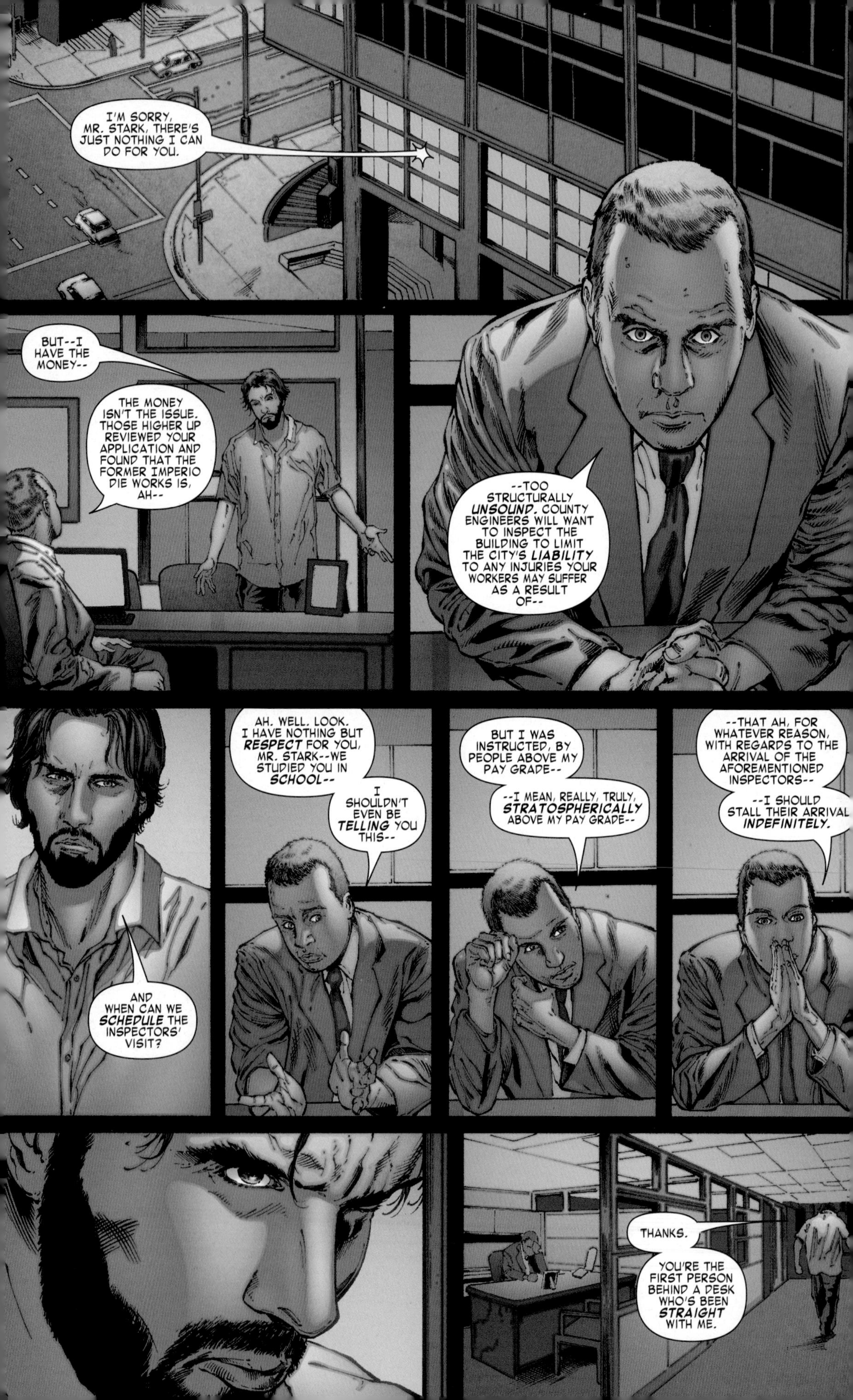
I'M SORRY, MR. STARK, THERE'S JUST NOTHING I CAN DO FOR YOU.
BUT--I HAVE THE MONEY--
THE MONEY ISN'T THE ISSUE. THOSE HIGHER UP REVIEWED YOUR APPLICATION AND FOUND THAT THE FORMER IMPERIO DIE WORKS IS, AH--
--TOO STRUCTURALLY UNSOUND. COUNTY ENGINEERS WILL WANT TO INSPECT THE BUILDING TO LIMIT THE CITY'S LIABILITY TO ANY INJURIES YOUR WORKERS MAY SUFFER AS A RESULT OF--
AND WHEN CAN WE SCHEDULE THE INSPECTORS' VISIT?
AH. WELL. LOOK. I HAVE NOTHING BUT RESPECT FOR YOU, MR. STARK--WE STUDIED YOU IN SCHOOL--
I SHOULDN'T EVEN BE TELLING YOU THIS--
BUT I WAS INSTRUCTED, BY PEOPLE ABOVE MY PAY GRADE--
--I MEAN, REALLY, TRULY, STRATOSPHERICALLY ABOVE MY PAY GRADE--
--THAT AH, FOR WHATEVER REASON, WITH REGARDS TO THE ARRIVAL OF THE AFOREMENTIONED INSPECTORS--
--I SHOULD STALL THEIR ARRIVAL INDEFINITELY.
THANKS.
YOU'RE THE FIRST PERSON BEHIND A DESK WHO'S BEEN STRAIGHT WITH ME.

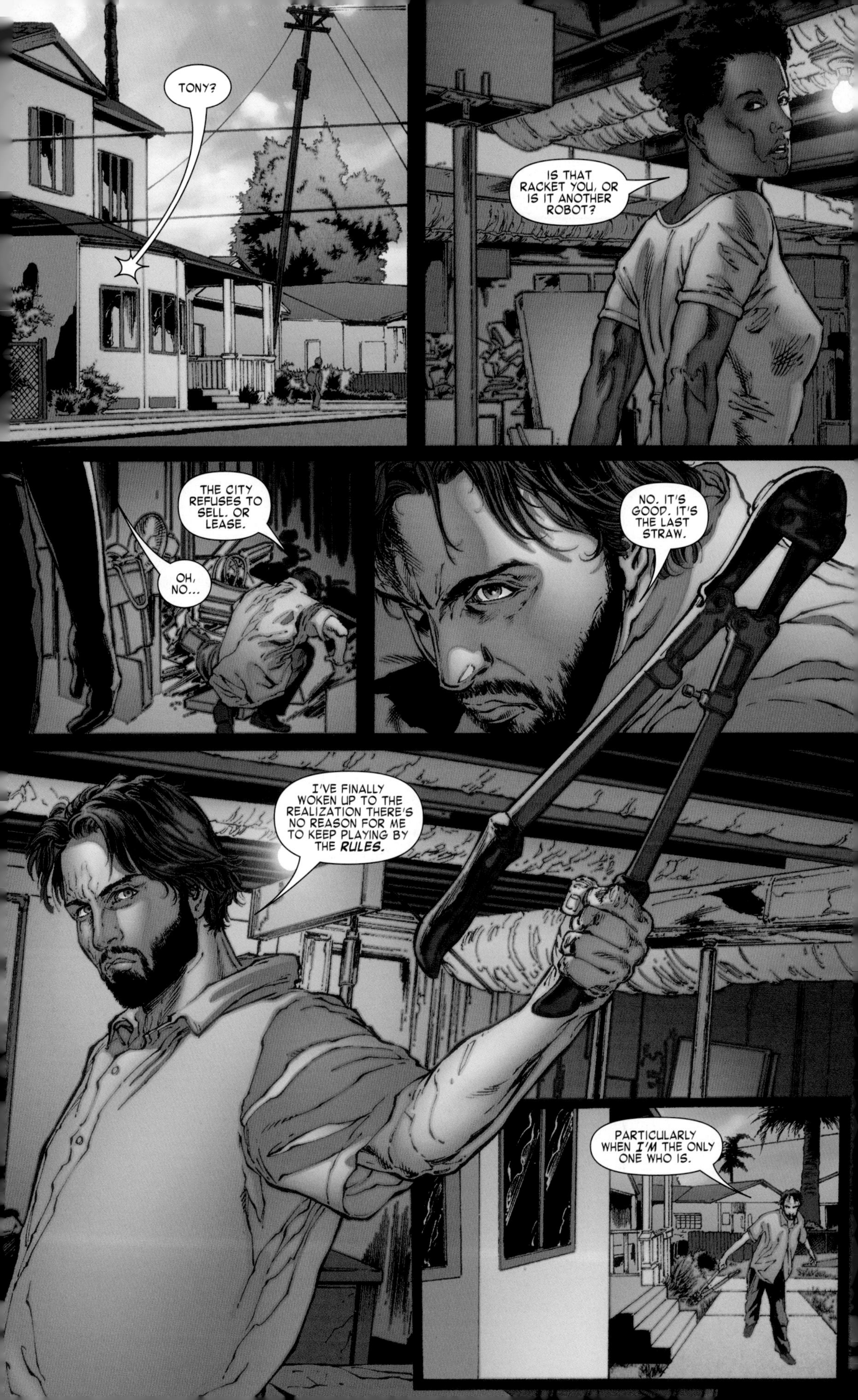
TONY?
IS THAT RACKET YOU, OR IS IT ANOTHER ROBOT?
THE CITY REFUSES TO SELL. OR LEASE.
OH, NO...
NO. IT'S GOOD. IT'S THE LAST STRAW.
I'VE FINALLY WOKEN UP TO THE REALIZATION THERE'S NO REASON FOR ME TO KEEP PLAYING BY THE *RULES.*
PARTICULARLY WHEN *I'M* THE ONLY ONE WHO IS.

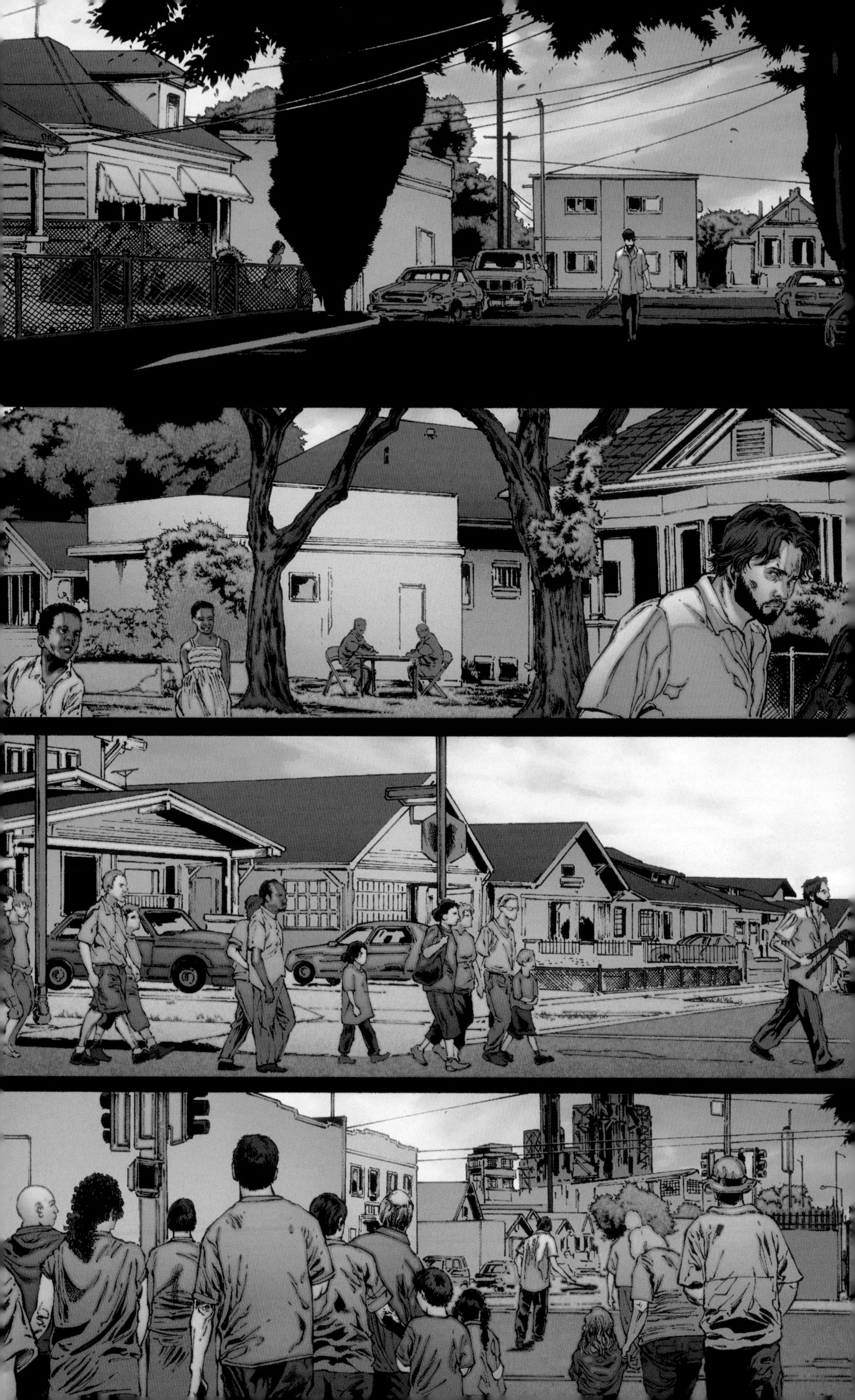

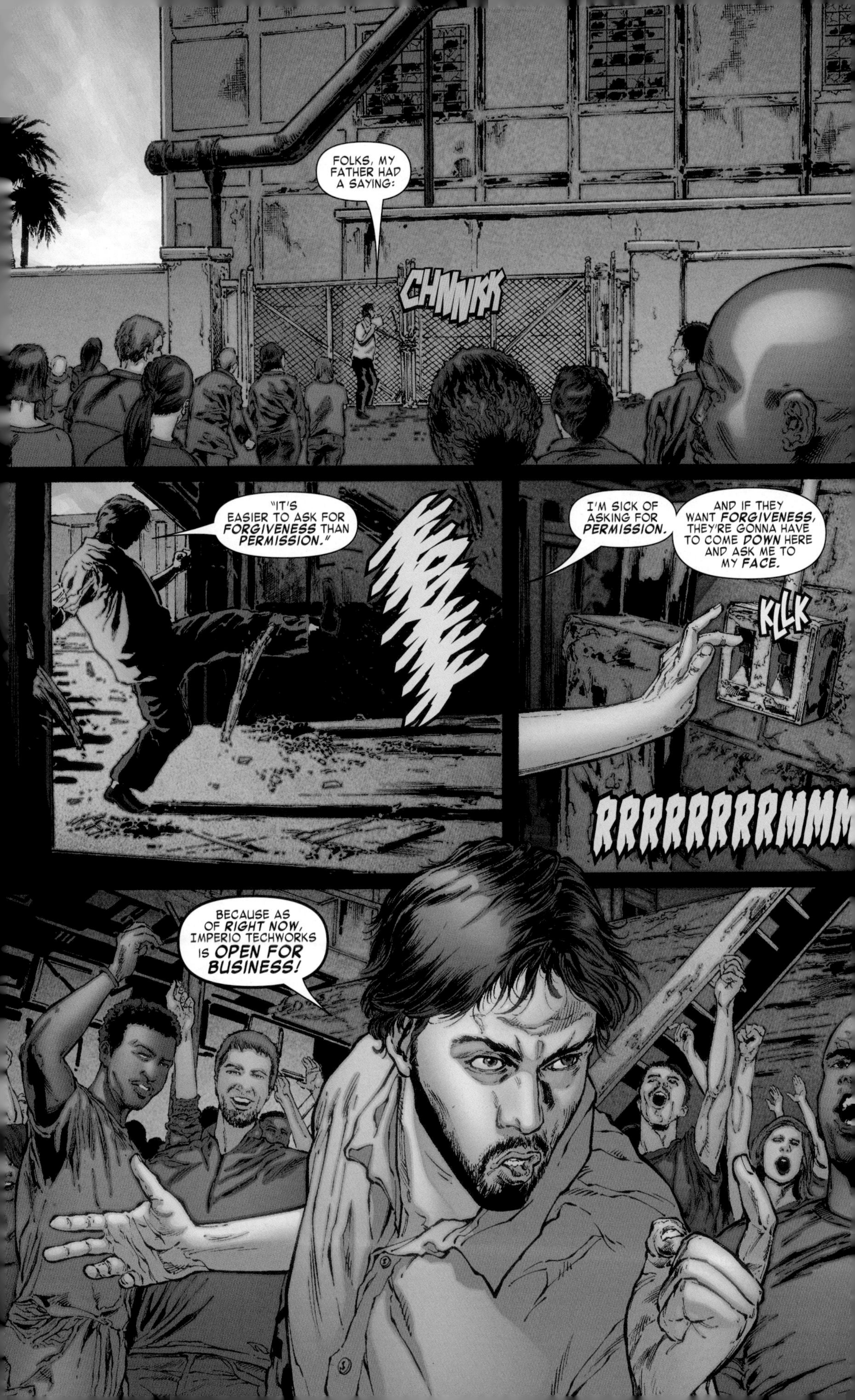
FOLKS, MY FATHER HAD A SAYING:
CHNNKK
"IT'S EASIER TO ASK FOR FORGIVENESS THAN PERMISSION."
I'M SICK OF ASKING FOR PERMISSION.
AND IF THEY WANT FORGIVENESS, THEY'RE GONNA HAVE TO COME DOWN HERE AND ASK ME TO MY FACE.
KLLK
RRRRRRRRMMM
BECAUSE AS OF RIGHT NOW, IMPERIO TECHWORKS IS OPEN FOR BUSINESS!

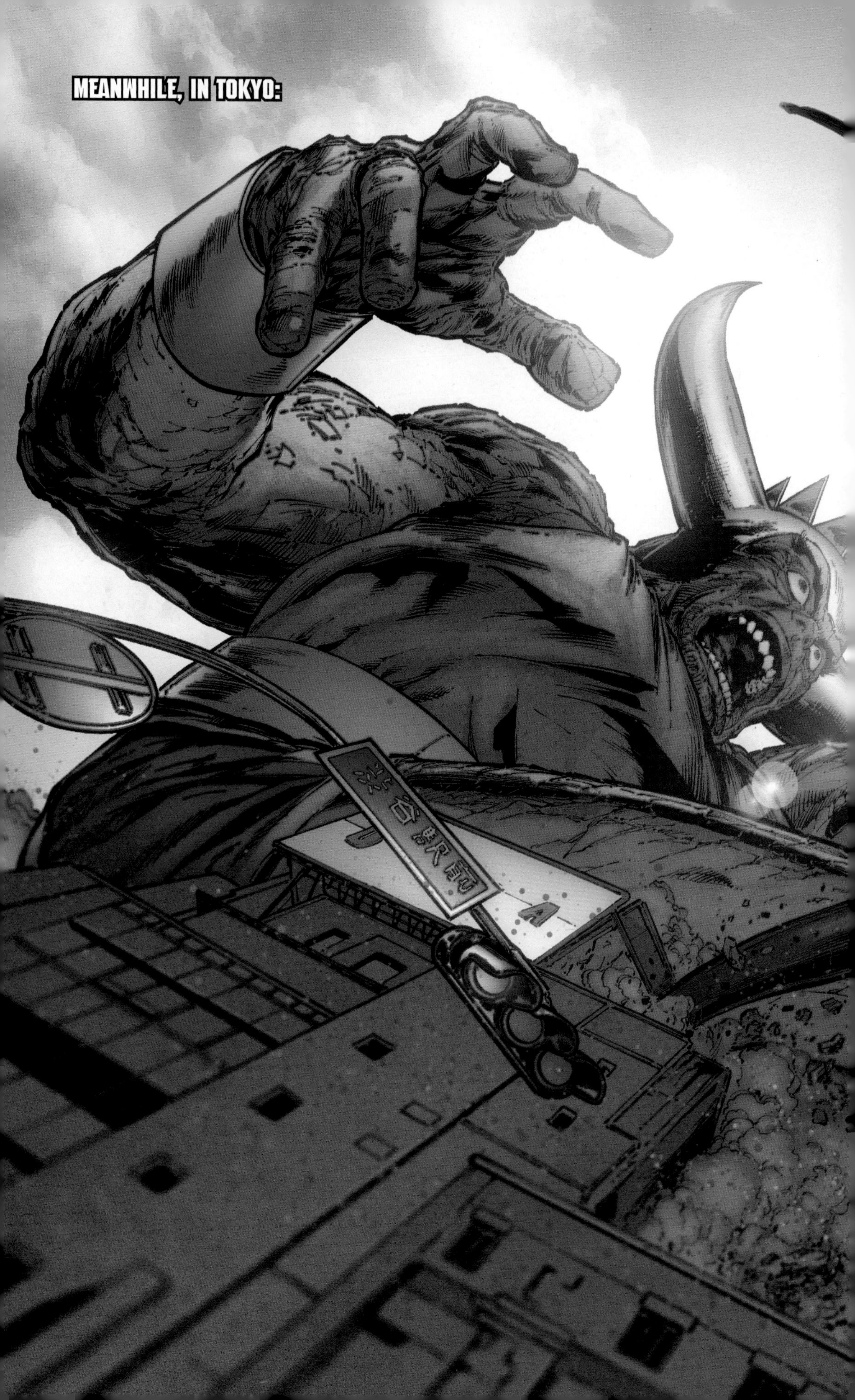
MEANWHILE, IN TOKYO:

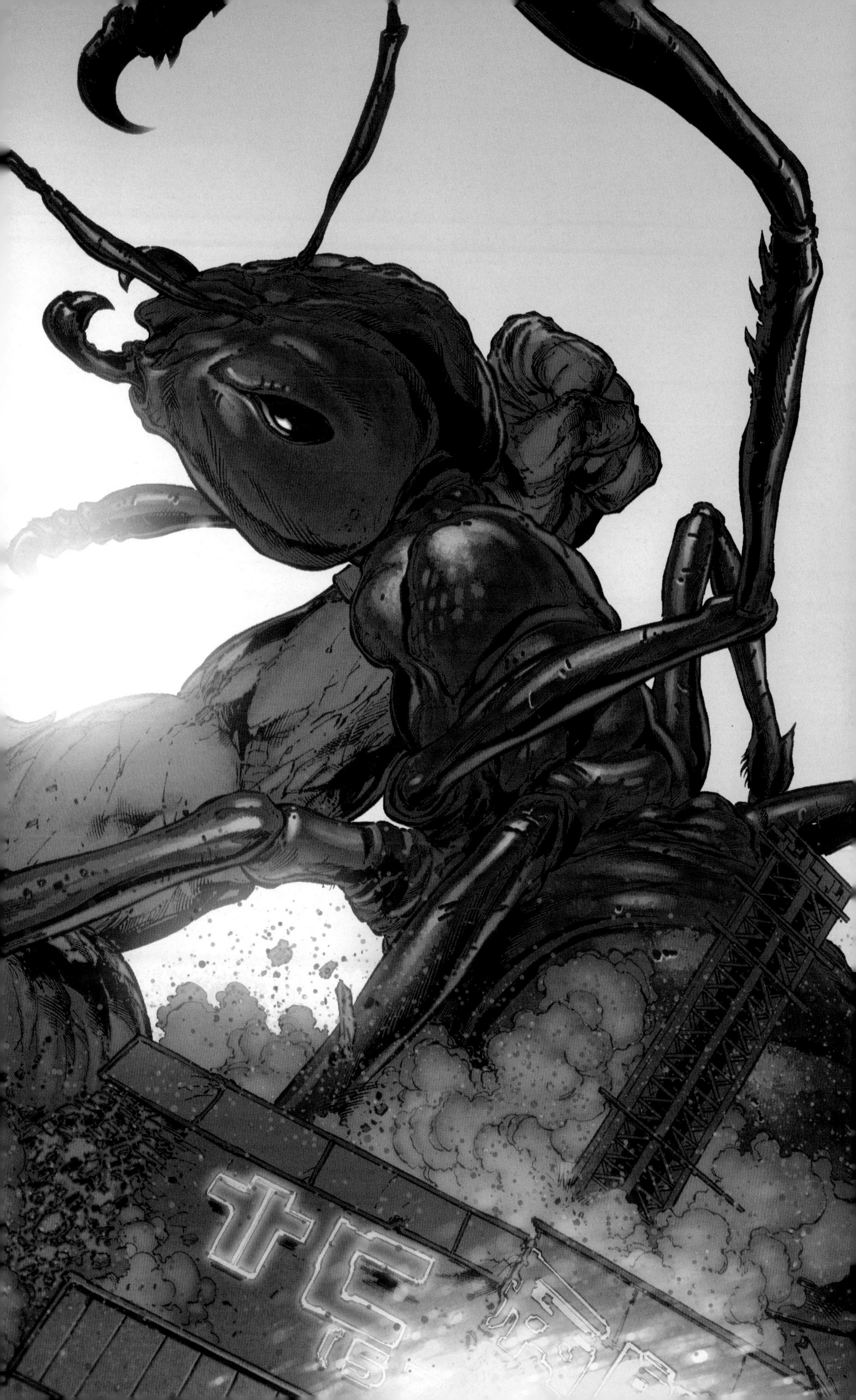

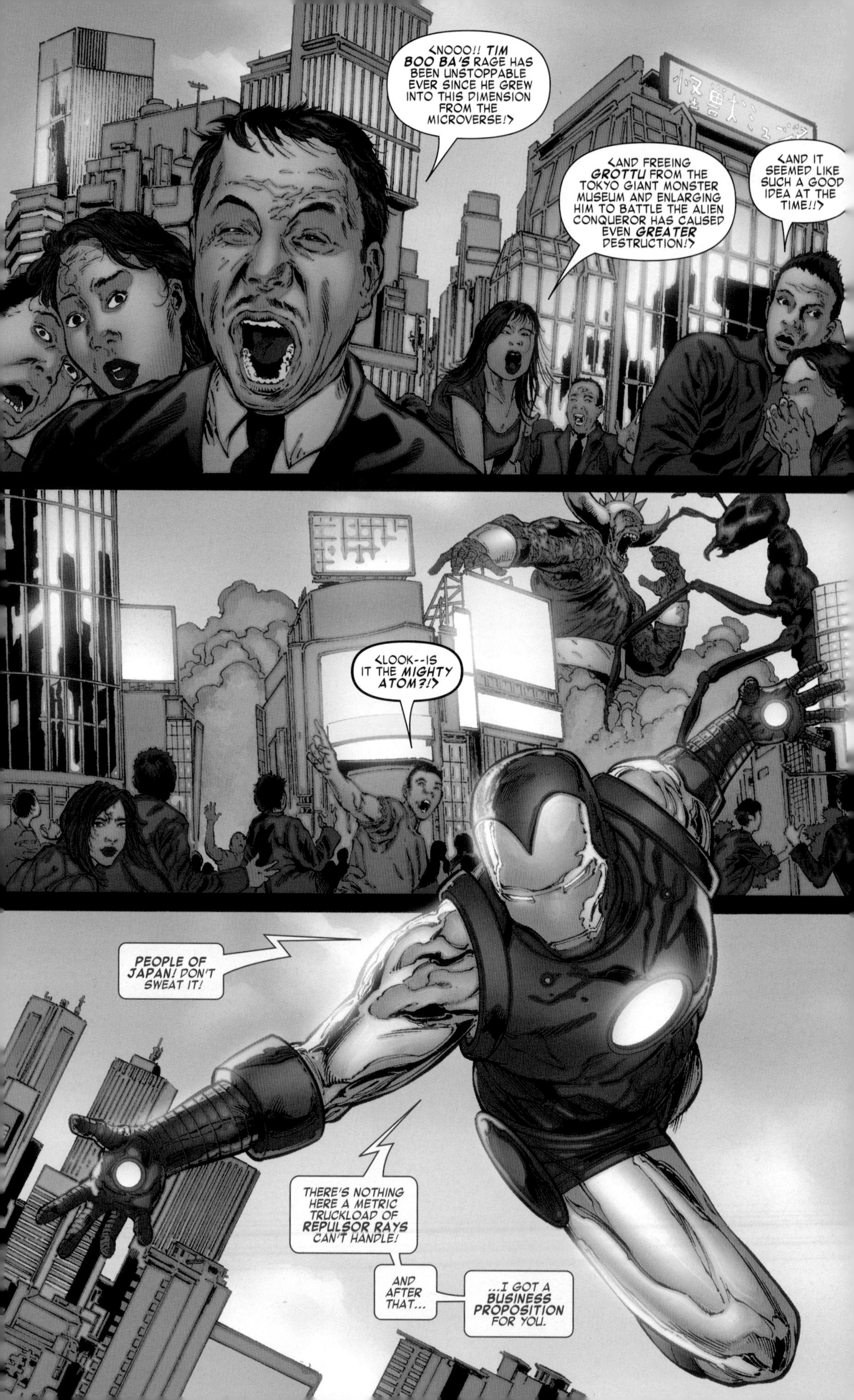

<NOOO!! TIM BOO BA'S RAGE HAS BEEN UNSTOPPABLE EVER SINCE HE GREW INTO THIS DIMENSION FROM THE MICROVERSE!>
<AND FREEING GROTTU FROM THE TOKYO GIANT MONSTER MUSEUM AND ENLARGING HIM TO BATTLE THE ALIEN CONQUEROR HAS CAUSED EVEN GREATER DESTRUCTION!>
<AND IT SEEMED LIKE SUCH A GOOD IDEA AT THE TIME!!>
<LOOK--IS IT THE MIGHTY ATOM?!>
PEOPLE OF JAPAN! DON'T SWEAT IT!
THERE'S NOTHING HERE A METRIC TRUCKLOAD OF REPULSOR RAYS CAN'T HANDLE!
AND AFTER THAT...
...I GOT A BUSINESS PROPOSITION FOR YOU.

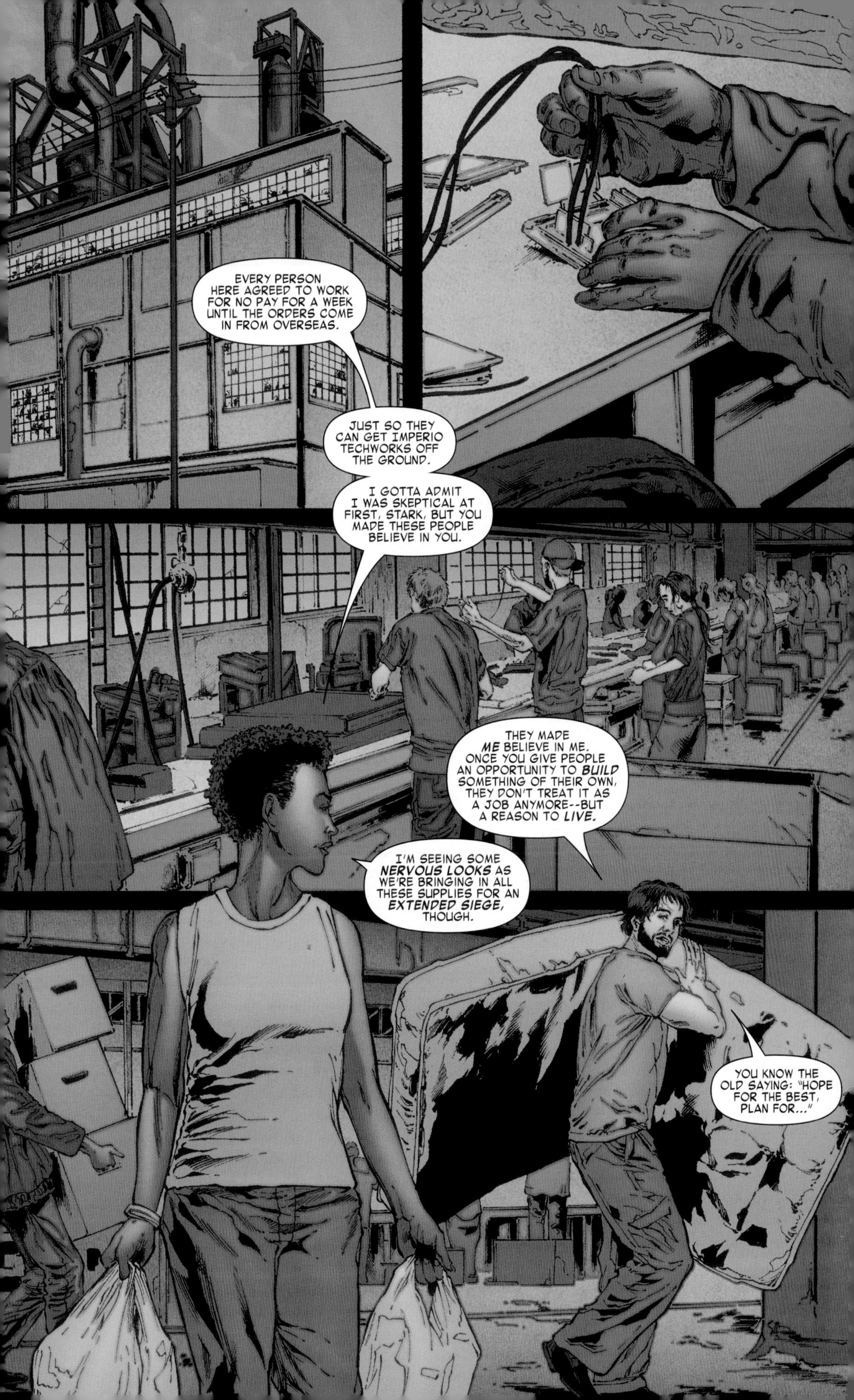
EVERY PERSON HERE AGREED TO WORK FOR NO PAY FOR A WEEK UNTIL THE ORDERS COME IN FROM OVERSEAS.
JUST SO THEY CAN GET IMPERIO TECHWORKS OFF THE GROUND.
I GOTTA ADMIT I WAS SKEPTICAL AT FIRST, STARK, BUT YOU MADE THESE PEOPLE BELIEVE IN YOU.
THEY MADE *ME* BELIEVE IN ME. ONCE YOU GIVE PEOPLE AN OPPORTUNITY TO *BUILD* SOMETHING OF THEIR OWN, THEY DON'T TREAT IT AS A JOB ANYMORE--BUT A REASON TO *LIVE.*
I'M SEEING SOME *NERVOUS LOOKS* AS WE'RE BRINGING IN ALL THESE SUPPLIES FOR AN *EXTENDED SIEGE,* THOUGH.
YOU KNOW THE OLD SAYING: "HOPE FOR THE BEST, PLAN FOR..."

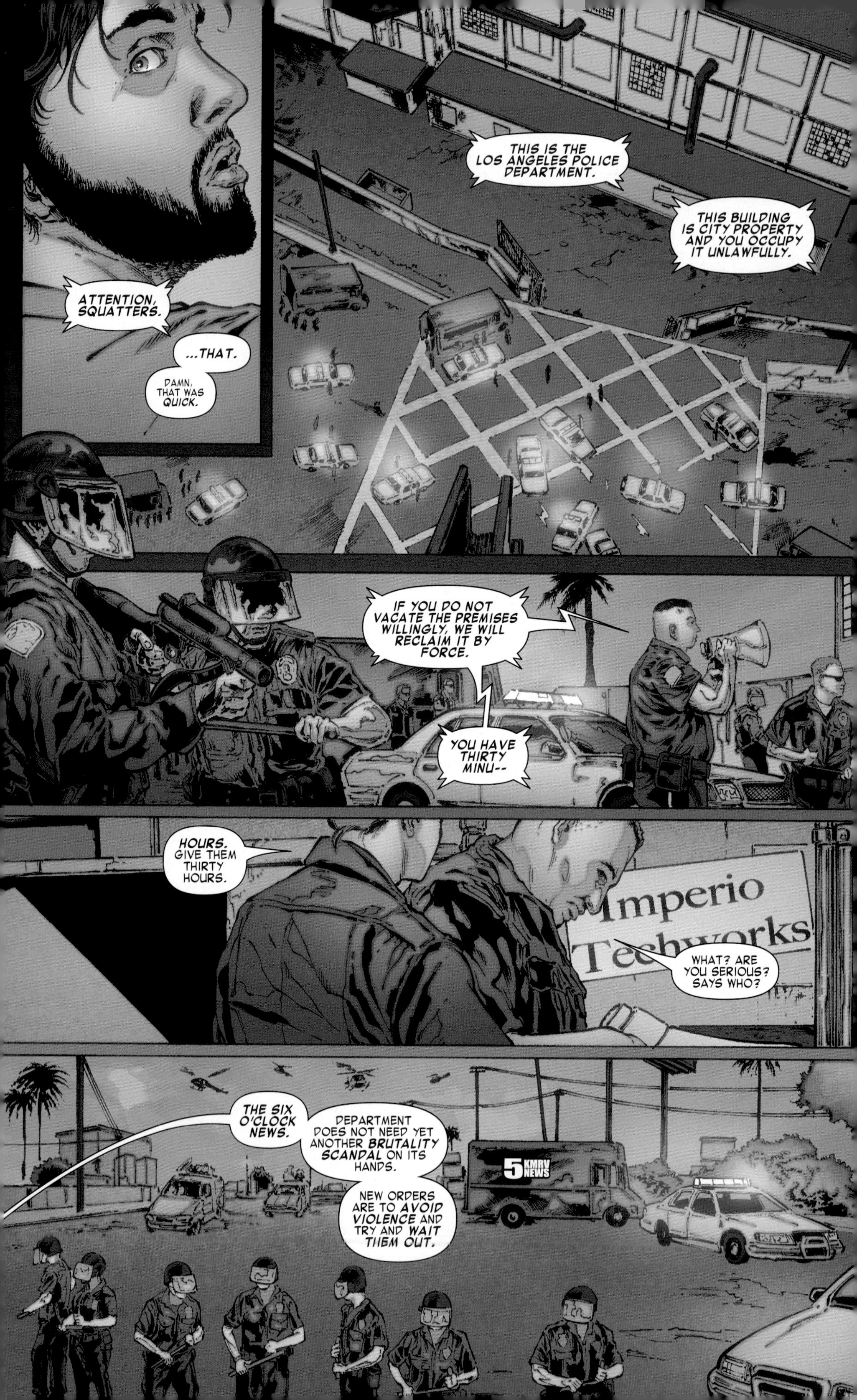
THIS IS THE LOS ANGELES POLICE DEPARTMENT.
THIS BUILDING IS CITY PROPERTY AND YOU OCCUPY IT UNLAWFULLY.
ATTENTION, SQUATTERS.
...THAT.
DAMN, THAT WAS QUICK.
IF YOU DO NOT VACATE THE PREMISES WILLINGLY, WE WILL RECLAIM IT BY FORCE.
YOU HAVE THIRTY MINU--
HOURS. GIVE THEM THIRTY HOURS.
Imperio Techworks
WHAT? ARE YOU SERIOUS? SAYS WHO?
THE SIX O'CLOCK NEWS.
DEPARTMENT DOES NOT NEED YET ANOTHER BRUTALITY SCANDAL ON ITS HANDS.
NEW ORDERS ARE TO AVOID VIOLENCE AND TRY AND WAIT THEM OUT.
5 KMRV NEWS

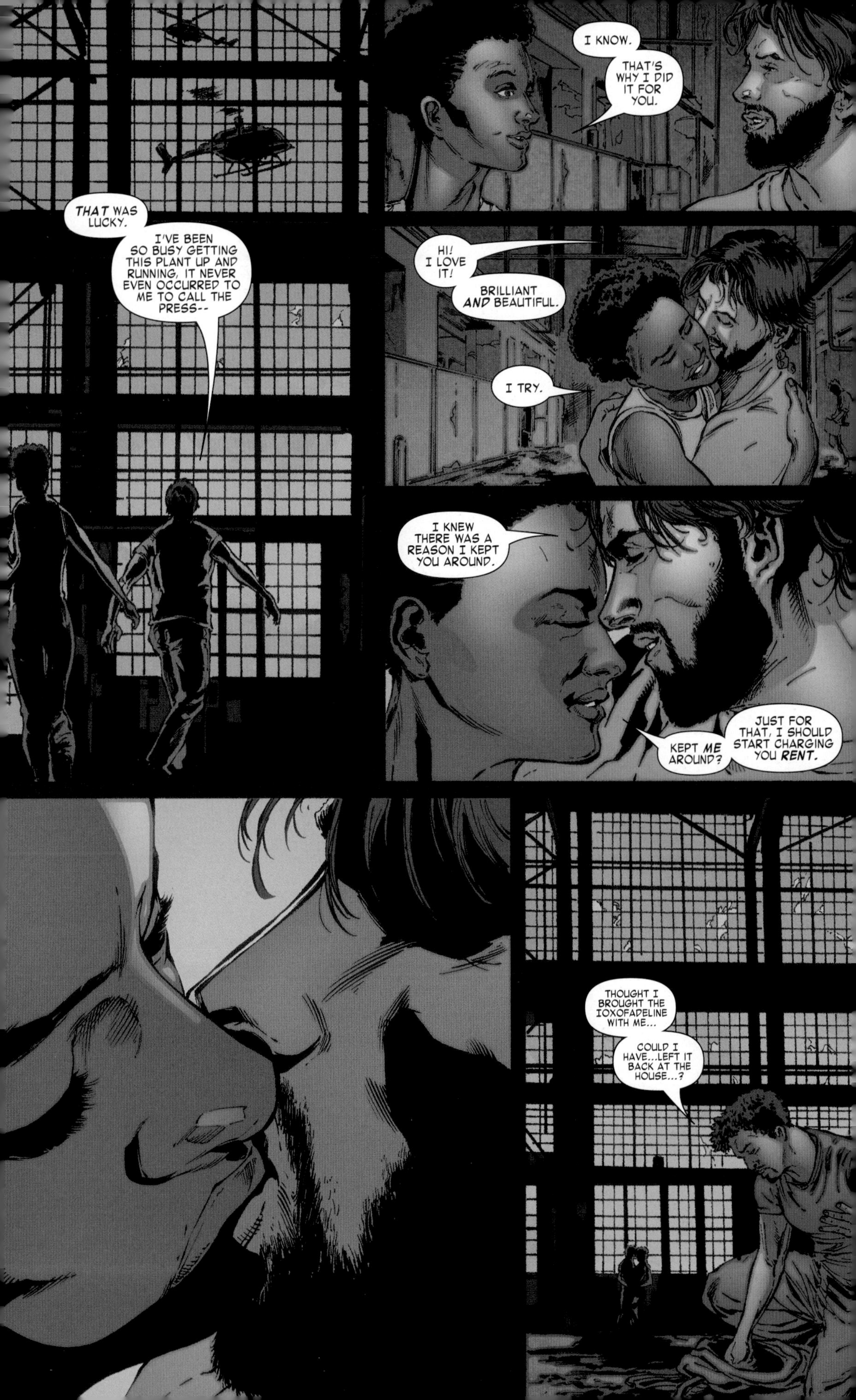
THAT WAS LUCKY.
I'VE BEEN SO BUSY GETTING THIS PLANT UP AND RUNNING, IT NEVER EVEN OCCURRED TO ME TO CALL THE PRESS--
I KNOW.
THAT'S WHY I DID IT FOR YOU.
HI! I LOVE IT!
BRILLIANT AND BEAUTIFUL.
I TRY.
I KNEW THERE WAS A REASON I KEPT YOU AROUND.
KEPT ME AROUND?
JUST FOR THAT, I SHOULD START CHARGING YOU RENT.
THOUGHT I BROUGHT THE IOXOFADELINE WITH ME...
COULD I HAVE...LEFT IT BACK AT THE HOUSE...?

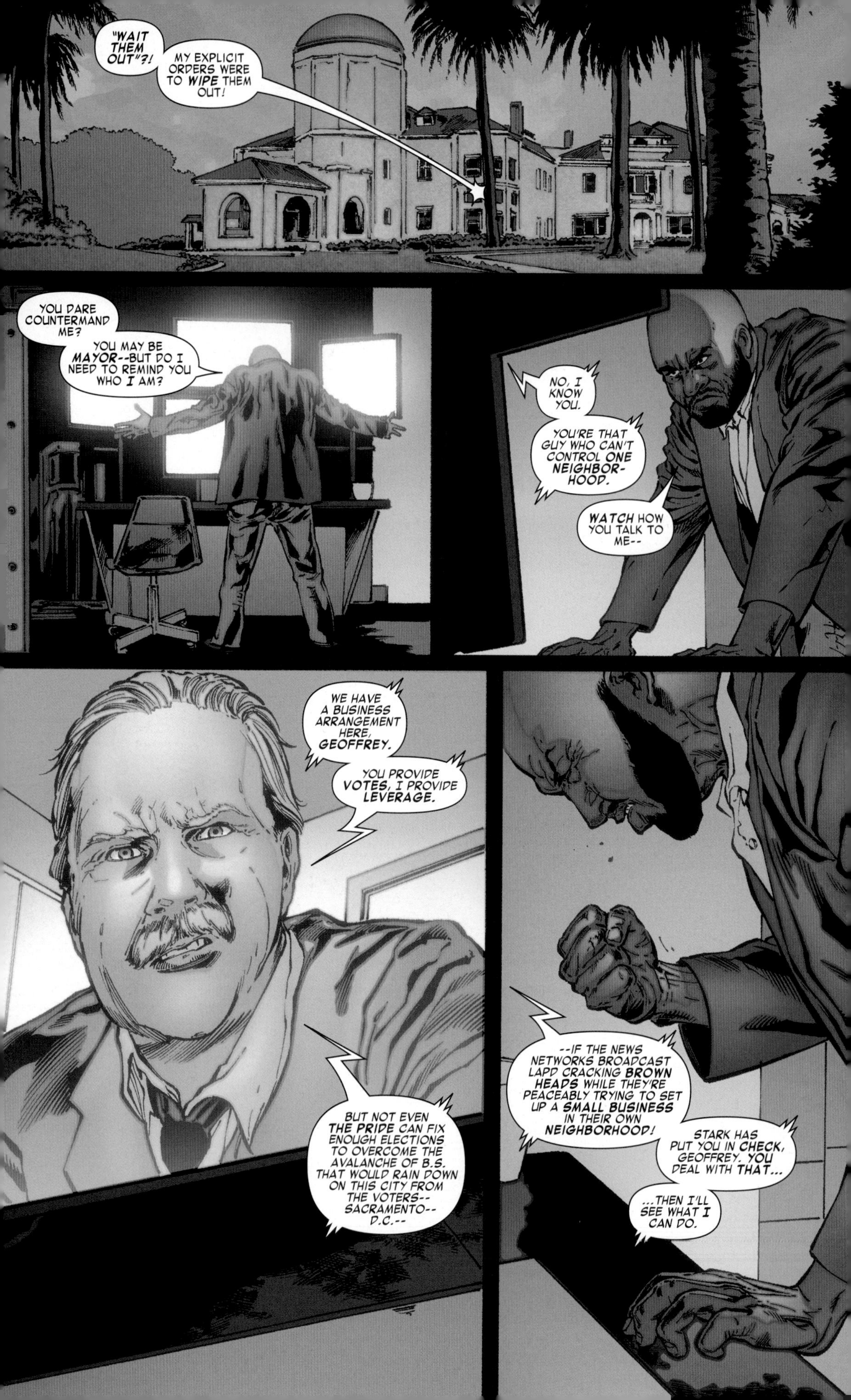
"WAIT THEM OUT"?!
MY EXPLICIT ORDERS WERE TO WIPE THEM OUT!
YOU DARE COUNTERMAND ME?
YOU MAY BE MAYOR--BUT DO I NEED TO REMIND YOU WHO I AM?
NO, I KNOW YOU.
YOU'RE THAT GUY WHO CAN'T CONTROL ONE NEIGHBOR-HOOD.
WATCH HOW YOU TALK TO ME--
WE HAVE A BUSINESS ARRANGEMENT HERE, GEOFFREY.
YOU PROVIDE VOTES, I PROVIDE LEVERAGE.
BUT NOT EVEN THE PRIDE CAN FIX ENOUGH ELECTIONS TO OVERCOME THE AVALANCHE OF B.S. THAT WOULD RAIN DOWN ON THIS CITY FROM THE VOTERS-- SACRAMENTO-- D.C.--
--IF THE NEWS NETWORKS BROADCAST LAPD CRACKING BROWN HEADS WHILE THEY'RE PEACEABLY TRYING TO SET UP A SMALL BUSINESS IN THEIR OWN NEIGHBORHOOD!
STARK HAS PUT YOU IN CHECK, GEOFFREY. YOU DEAL WITH THAT...
...THEN I'LL SEE WHAT I CAN DO.

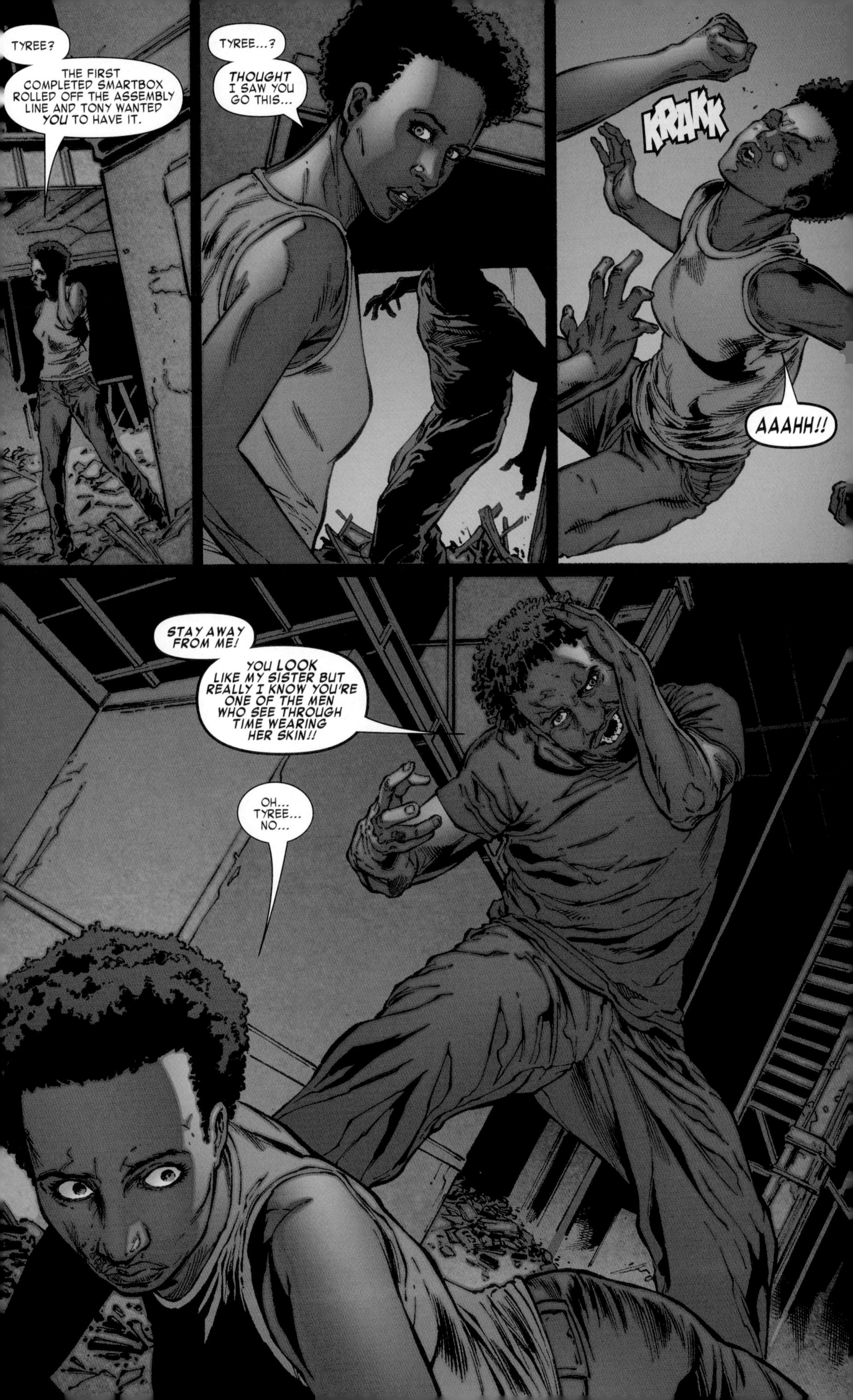
TYREE?
THE FIRST COMPLETED SMARTBOX ROLLED OFF THE ASSEMBLY LINE AND TONY WANTED YOU TO HAVE IT.
TYREE...?
THOUGHT I SAW YOU GO THIS...
KRAKK
AAAHH!!
STAY AWAY FROM ME!
YOU LOOK LIKE MY SISTER BUT REALLY I KNOW YOU'RE ONE OF THE MEN WHO SEE THROUGH TIME WEARING HER SKIN!!
OH... TYREE... NO...

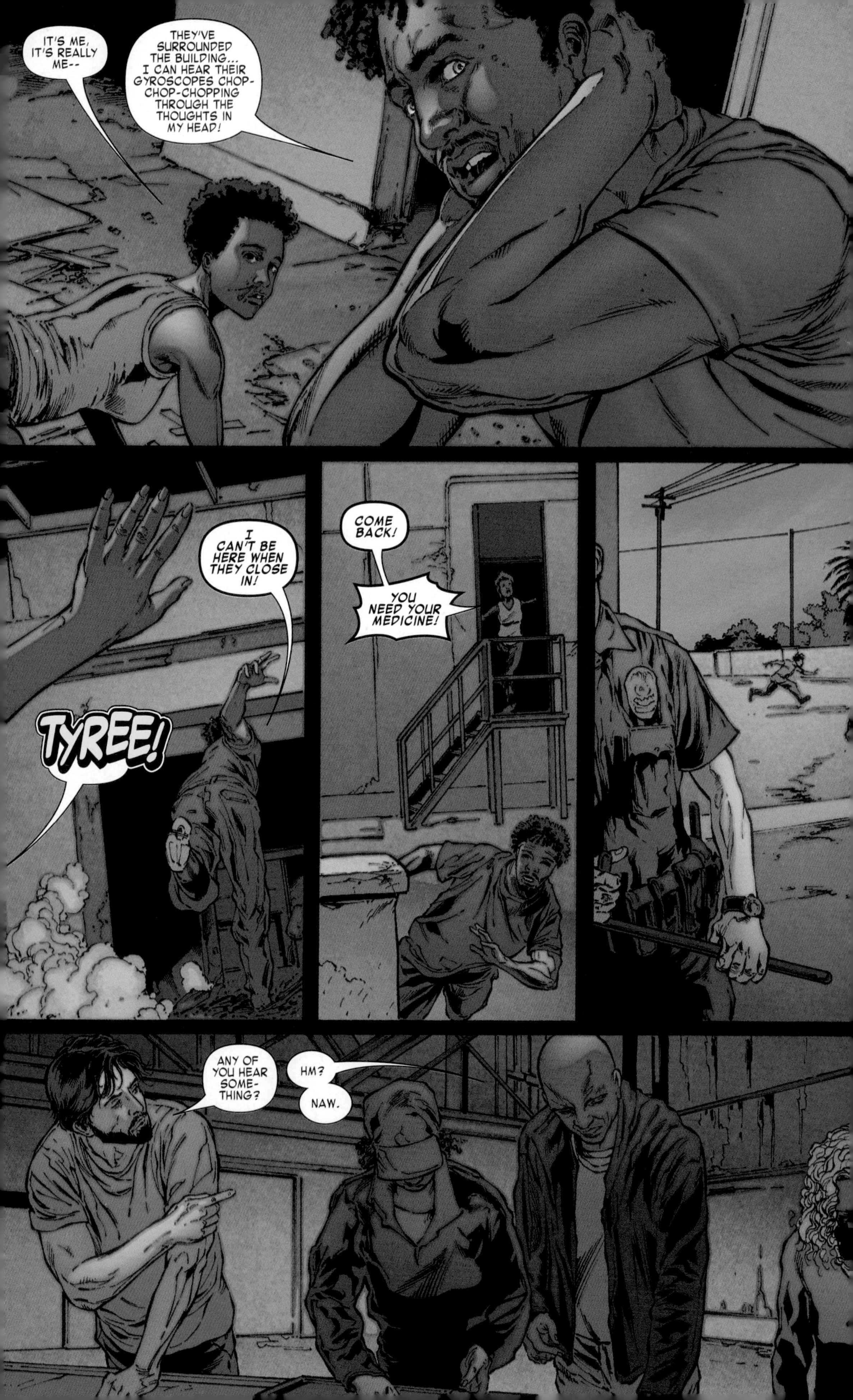
IT'S ME, IT'S REALLY ME--
THEY'VE SURROUNDED THE BUILDING... I CAN HEAR THEIR GYROSCOPES CHOP-CHOP-CHOPPING THROUGH THE THOUGHTS IN MY HEAD!
I CAN'T BE HERE WHEN THEY CLOSE IN!
TYREE!
COME BACK!
YOU NEED YOUR MEDICINE!
ANY OF YOU HEAR SOME-THING?
HM?
NAW.

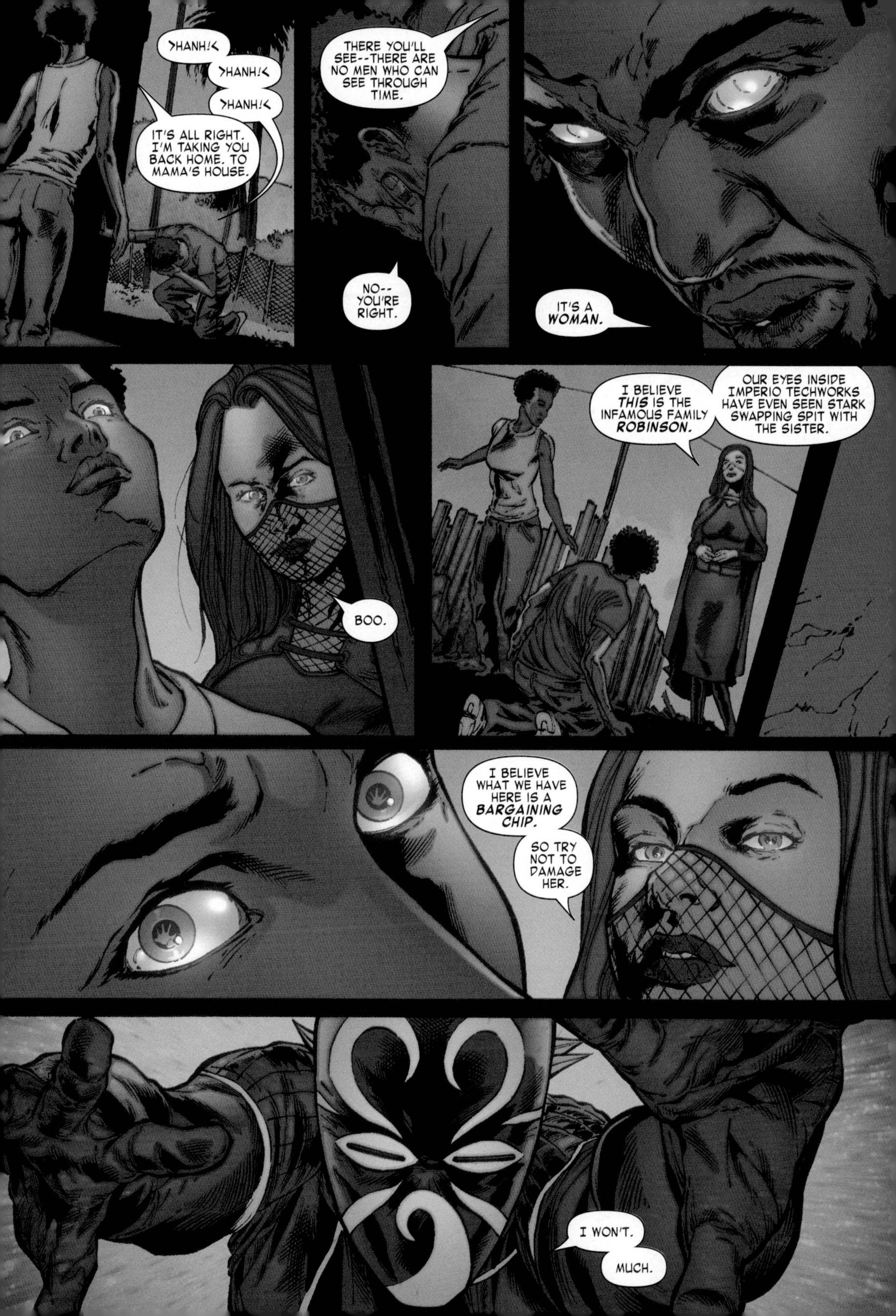

>HANH!<
>HANH!<
>HANH!<
IT'S ALL RIGHT. I'M TAKING YOU BACK HOME. TO MAMA'S HOUSE.
THERE YOU'LL SEE--THERE ARE NO MEN WHO CAN SEE THROUGH TIME.
NO--YOU'RE RIGHT.
IT'S A WOMAN.
BOO.
I BELIEVE THIS IS THE INFAMOUS FAMILY ROBINSON.
OUR EYES INSIDE IMPERIO TECHWORKS HAVE EVEN SEEN STARK SWAPPING SPIT WITH THE SISTER.
I BELIEVE WHAT WE HAVE HERE IS A BARGAINING CHIP.
SO TRY NOT TO DAMAGE HER.
I WON'T.
MUCH.

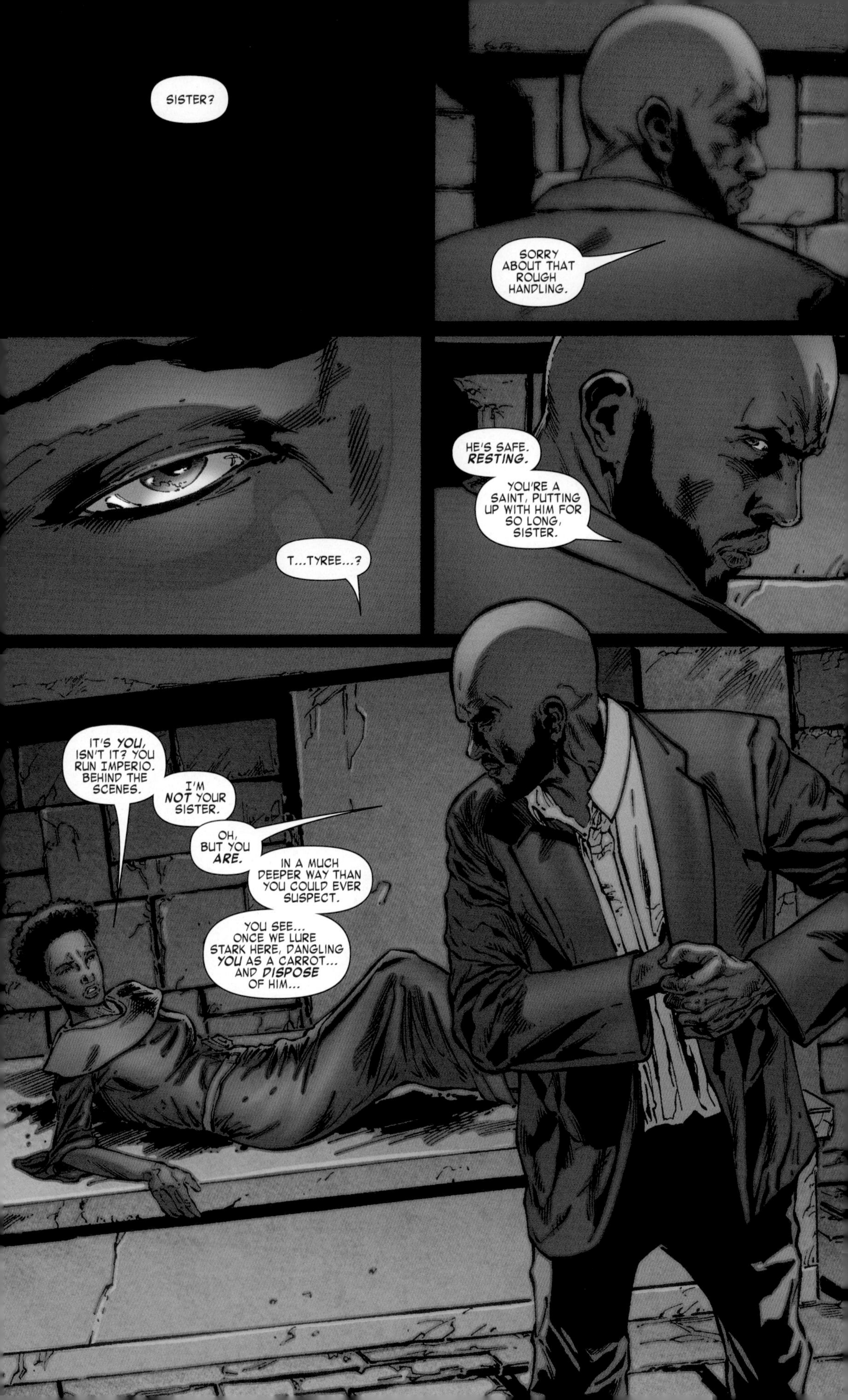
SISTER?
SORRY ABOUT THAT ROUGH HANDLING.
HE'S SAFE. RESTING.
YOU'RE A SAINT, PUTTING UP WITH HIM FOR SO LONG, SISTER.
T...TYREE...?
IT'S YOU, ISN'T IT? YOU RUN IMPERIO. BEHIND THE SCENES.
I'M NOT YOUR SISTER.
OH, BUT YOU ARE.
IN A MUCH DEEPER WAY THAN YOU COULD EVER SUSPECT.
YOU SEE... ONCE WE LURE STARK HERE, DANGLING YOU AS A CARROT... AND DISPOSE OF HIM...

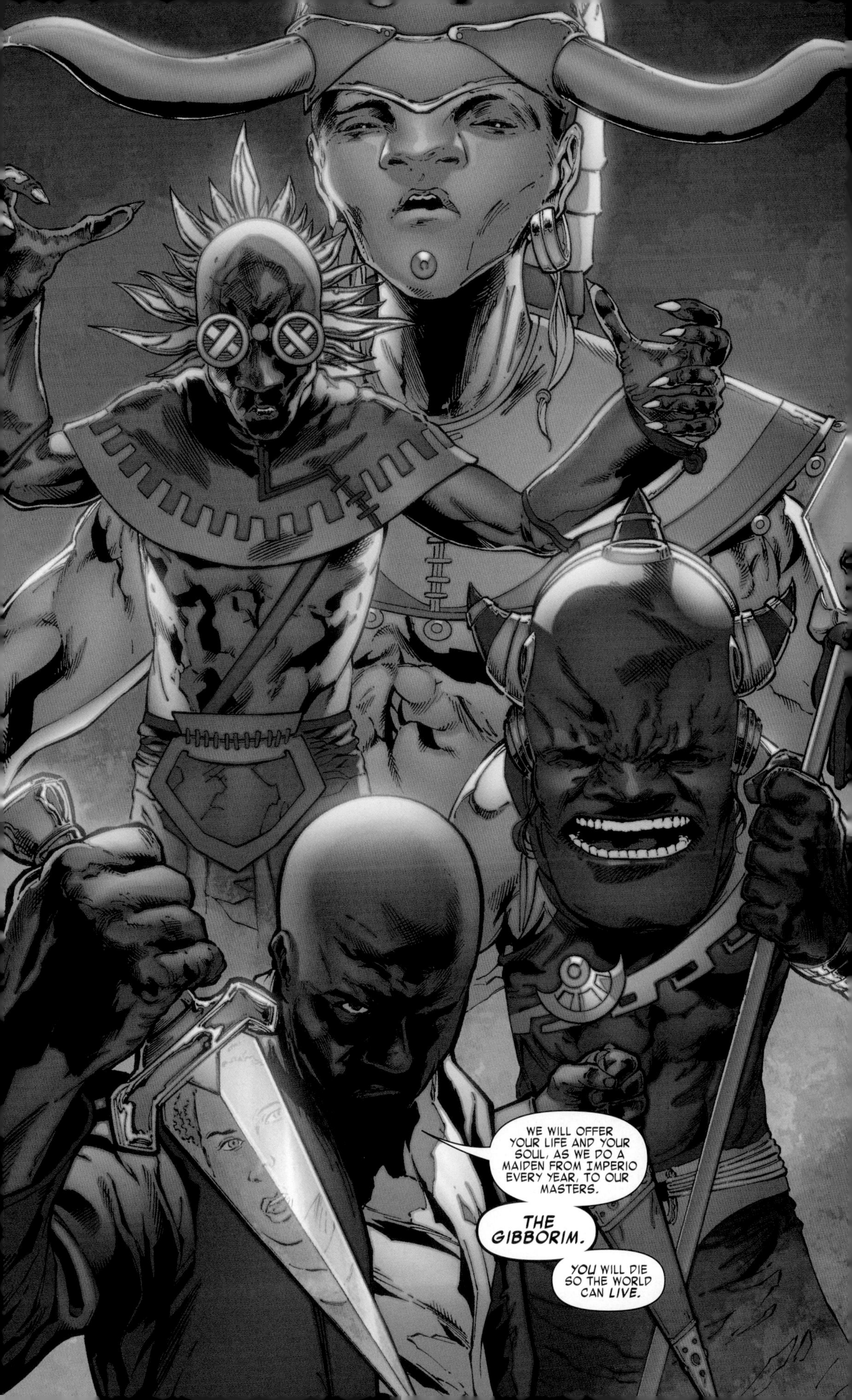
WE WILL OFFER YOUR LIFE AND YOUR SOUL, AS WE DO A MAIDEN FROM IMPERIO EVERY YEAR, TO OUR MASTERS.
THE GIBBORIM.
YOU WILL DIE SO THE WORLD CAN LIVE.

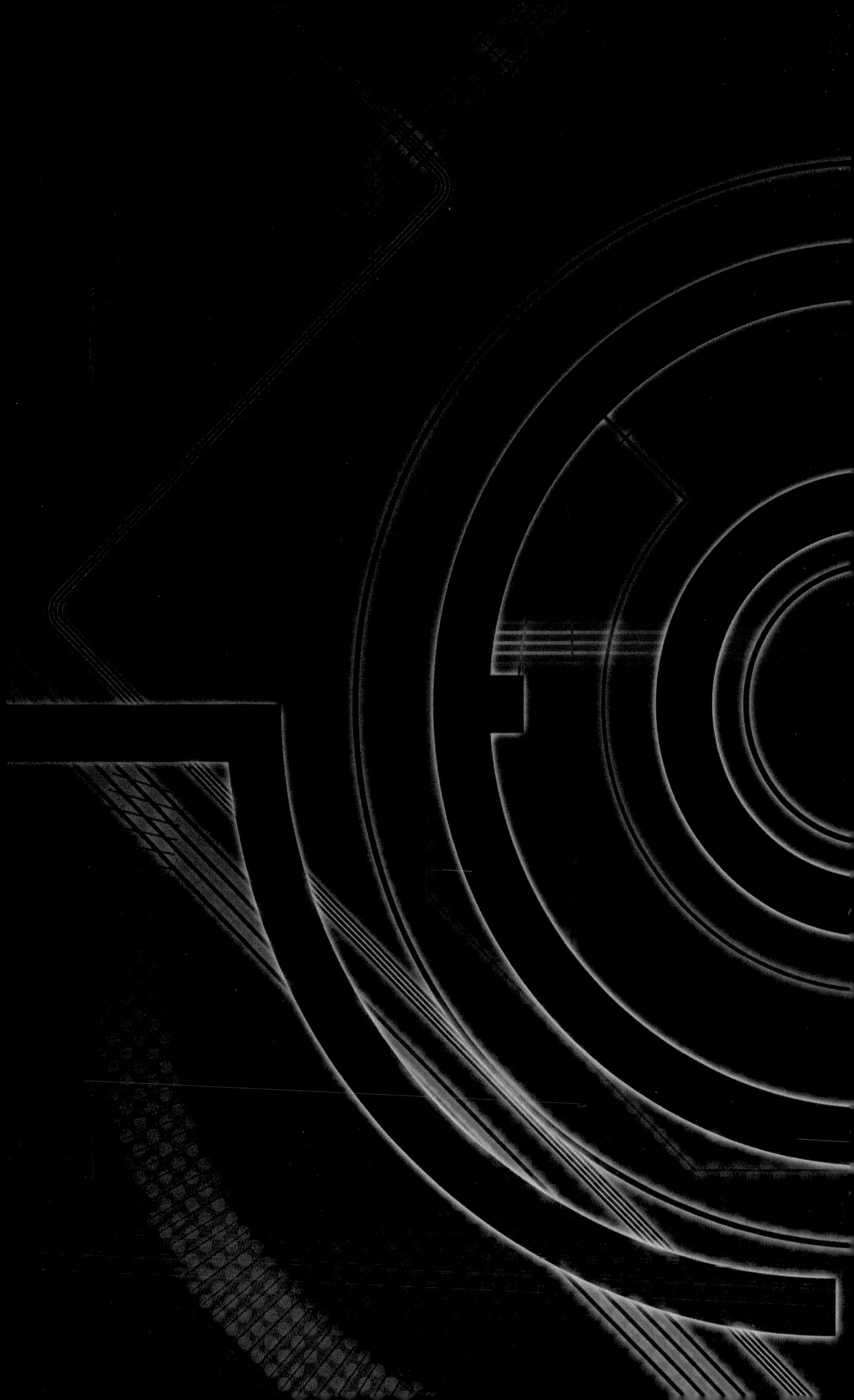

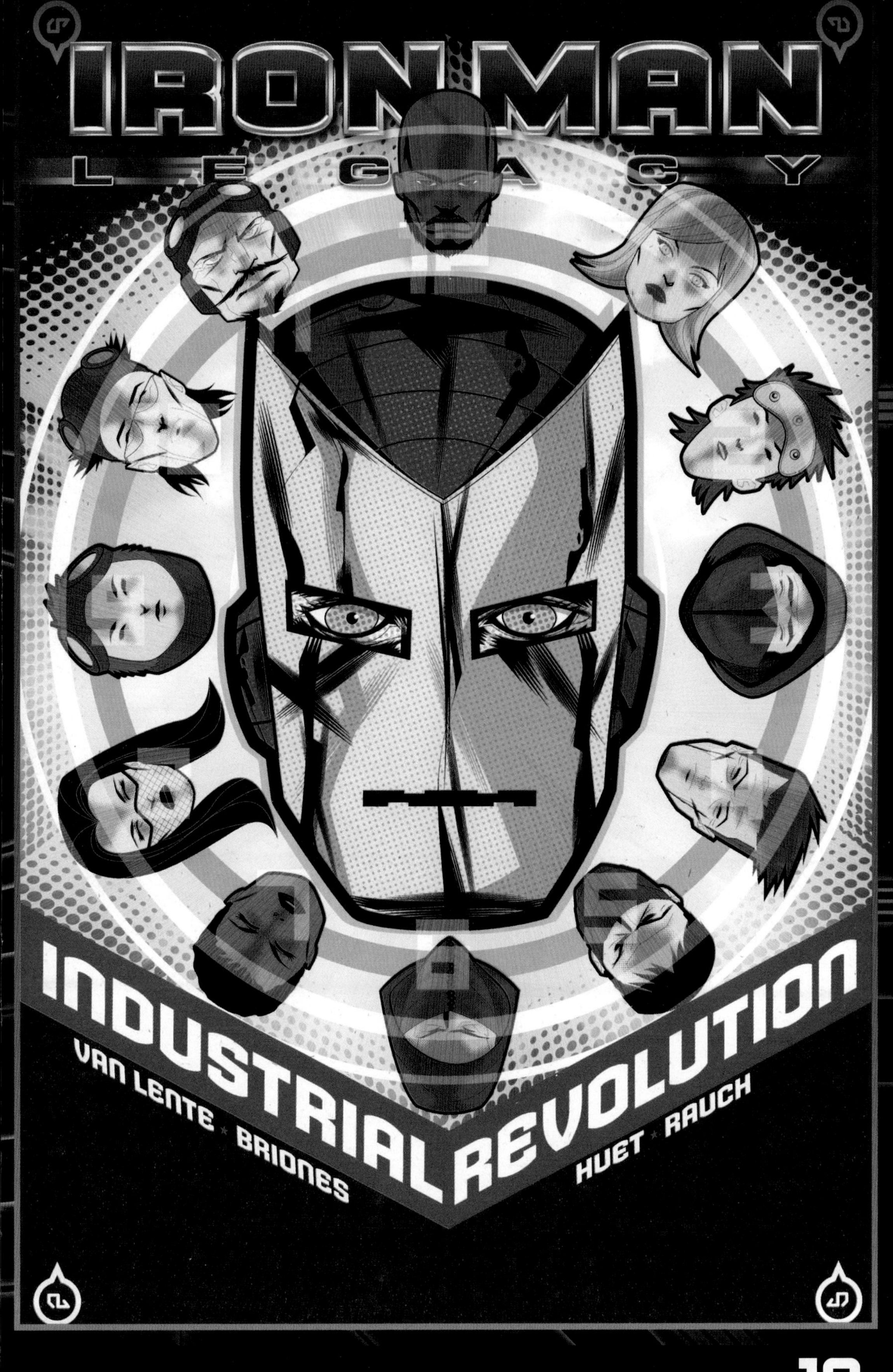
IRON MAN
LEGACY
INDUSTRIAL REVOLUTION
VAN LENTE • BRIONES
HUET • RAUCH

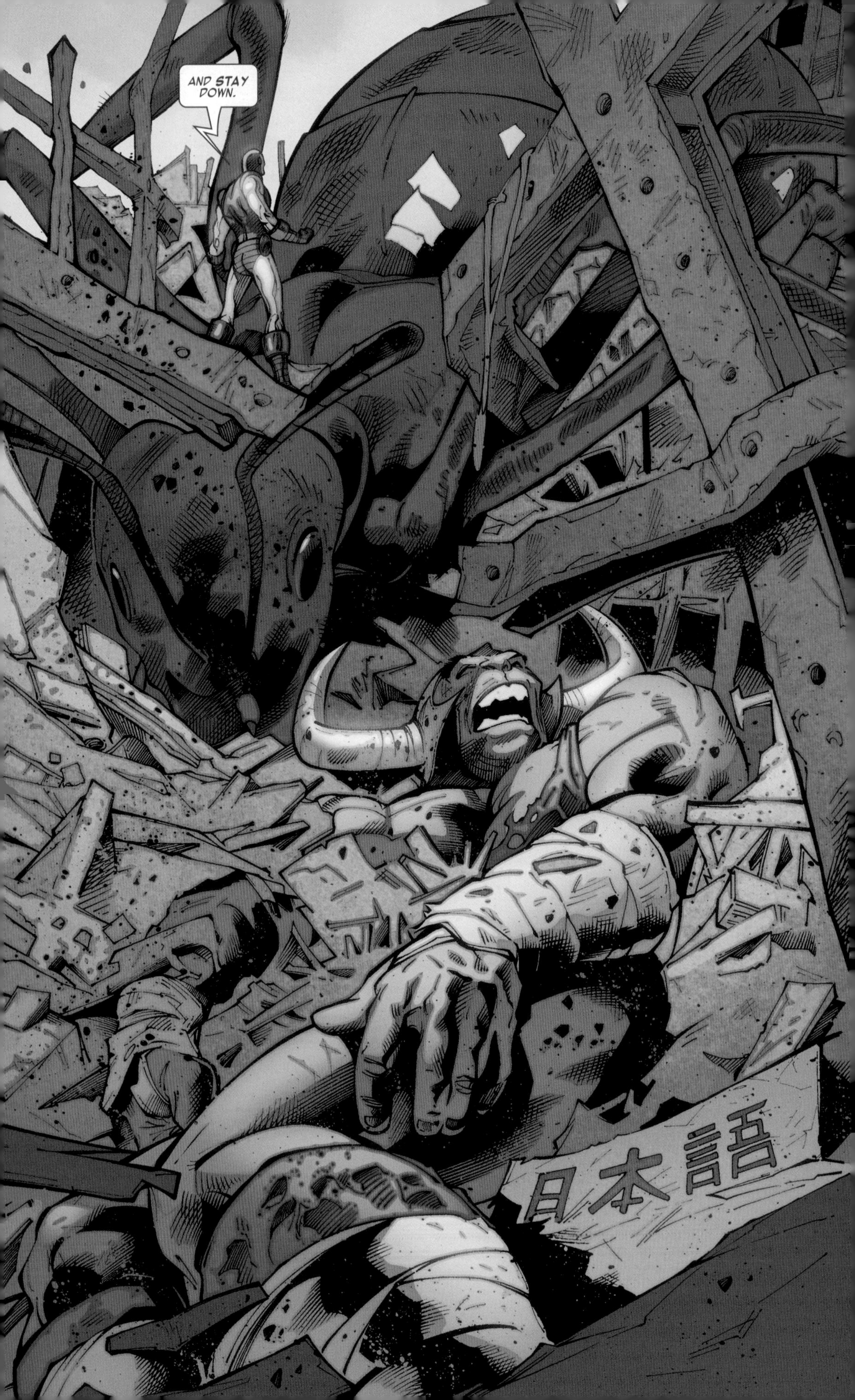
AND STAY DOWN.
日本語

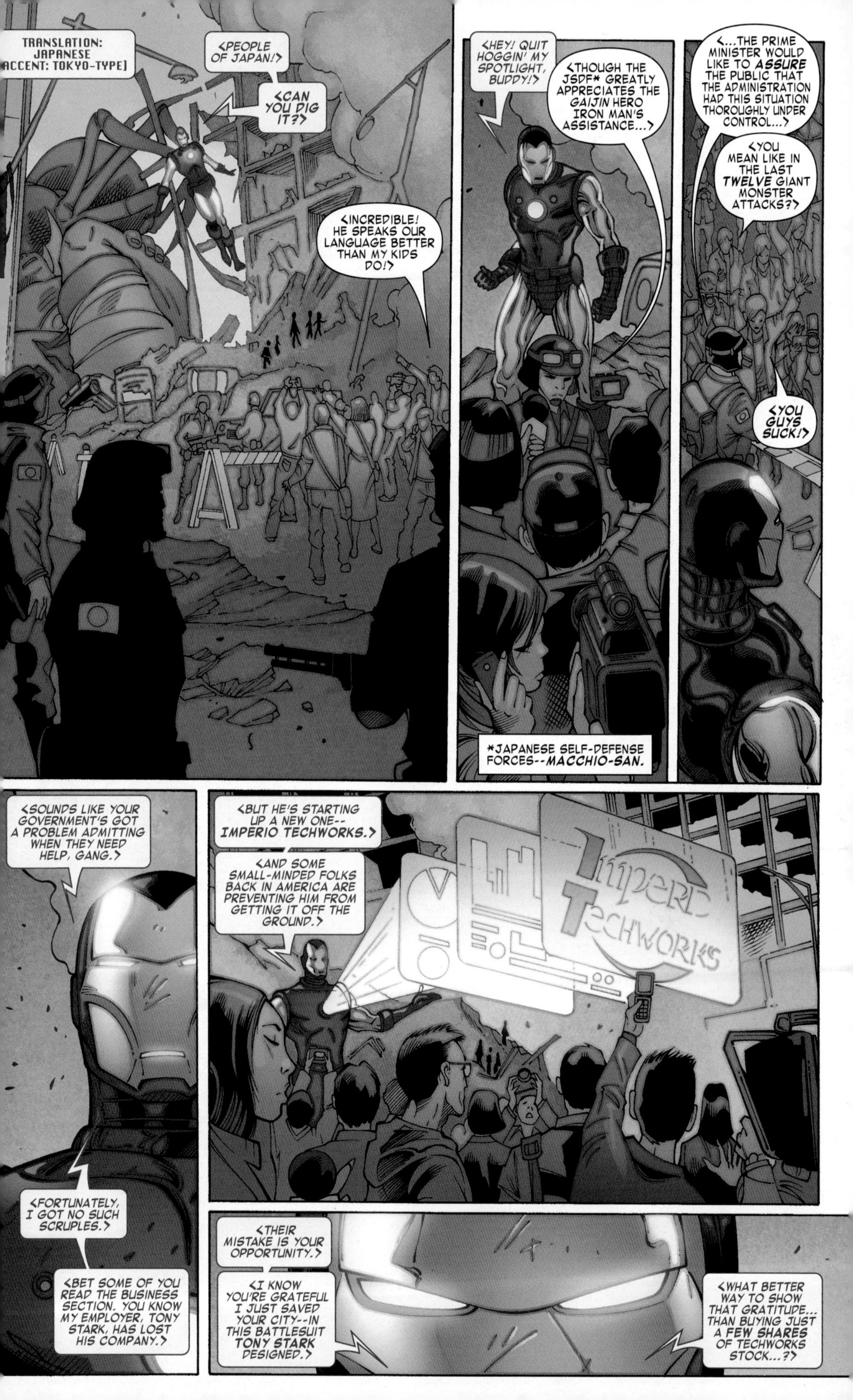

TRANSLATION: JAPANESE [ACCENT: TOKYO-TYPE]
<PEOPLE OF JAPAN!>
<CAN YOU DIG IT?>
<INCREDIBLE! HE SPEAKS OUR LANGUAGE BETTER THAN MY KIDS DO!>
<THOUGH THE JSDF* GREATLY APPRECIATES THE GAIJIN HERO IRON MAN'S ASSISTANCE...>
<HEY! QUIT HOGGIN' MY SPOTLIGHT, BUDDY!>
*JAPANESE SELF-DEFENSE FORCES--MACCHIO-SAN.
<...THE PRIME MINISTER WOULD LIKE TO ASSURE THE PUBLIC THAT THE ADMINISTRATION HAD THIS SITUATION THOROUGHLY UNDER CONTROL...>
<YOU MEAN LIKE IN THE LAST TWELVE GIANT MONSTER ATTACKS?>
<YOU GUYS SUCK!>
<SOUNDS LIKE YOUR GOVERNMENT'S GOT A PROBLEM ADMITTING WHEN THEY NEED HELP, GANG.>
<FORTUNATELY, I GOT NO SUCH SCRUPLES.>
<BET SOME OF YOU READ THE BUSINESS SECTION. YOU KNOW MY EMPLOYER, TONY STARK, HAS LOST HIS COMPANY.>
<BUT HE'S STARTING UP A NEW ONE-- IMPERIO TECHWORKS.>
<AND SOME SMALL-MINDED FOLKS BACK IN AMERICA ARE PREVENTING HIM FROM GETTING IT OFF THE GROUND.>
IMPERIO TECHWORKS
<THEIR MISTAKE IS YOUR OPPORTUNITY.>
<I KNOW YOU'RE GRATEFUL I JUST SAVED YOUR CITY--IN THIS BATTLESUIT TONY STARK DESIGNED.>
<WHAT BETTER WAY TO SHOW THAT GRATITUDE... THAN BUYING JUST A FEW SHARES OF TECHWORKS STOCK...?>

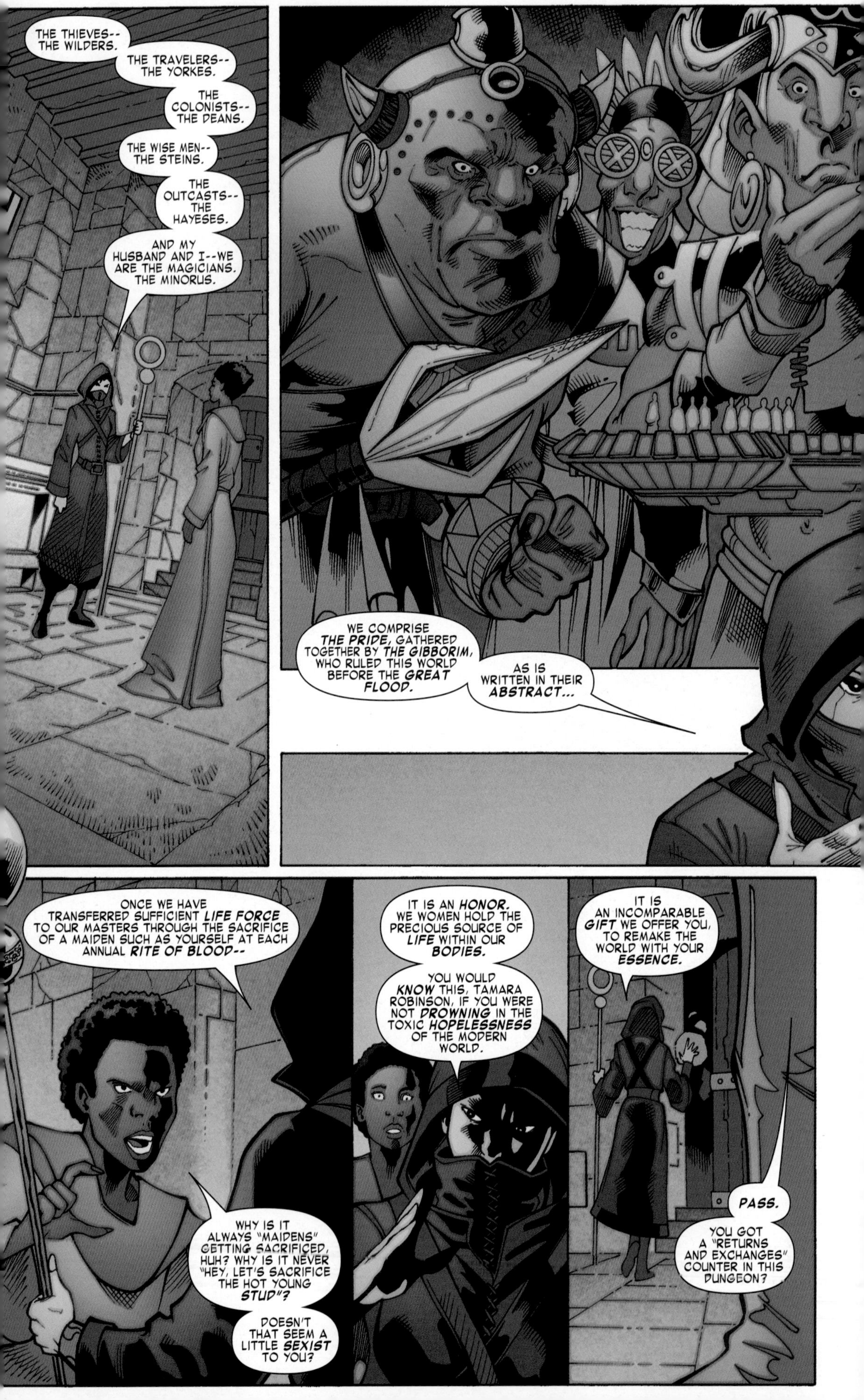
THE THIEVES-- THE WILDERS.
THE TRAVELERS-- THE YORKES.
THE COLONISTS-- THE DEANS.
THE WISE MEN-- THE STEINS.
THE OUTCASTS-- THE HAYESES.
AND MY HUSBAND AND I--WE ARE THE MAGICIANS. THE MINORUS.
WE COMPRISE THE PRIDE, GATHERED TOGETHER BY THE GIBBORIM, WHO RULED THIS WORLD BEFORE THE GREAT FLOOD.
AS IS WRITTEN IN THEIR ABSTRACT...
ONCE WE HAVE TRANSFERRED SUFFICIENT LIFE FORCE TO OUR MASTERS THROUGH THE SACRIFICE OF A MAIDEN SUCH AS YOURSELF AT EACH ANNUAL RITE OF BLOOD--
WHY IS IT ALWAYS "MAIDENS" GETTING SACRIFICED, HUH? WHY IS IT NEVER "HEY, LET'S SACRIFICE THE HOT YOUNG STUD"?
DOESN'T THAT SEEM A LITTLE SEXIST TO YOU?
IT IS AN HONOR. WE WOMEN HOLD THE PRECIOUS SOURCE OF LIFE WITHIN OUR BODIES.
YOU WOULD KNOW THIS, TAMARA ROBINSON, IF YOU WERE NOT DROWNING IN THE TOXIC HOPELESSNESS OF THE MODERN WORLD.
IT IS AN INCOMPARABLE GIFT WE OFFER YOU, TO REMAKE THE WORLD WITH YOUR ESSENCE.
PASS.
YOU GOT A "RETURNS AND EXCHANGES" COUNTER IN THIS DUNGEON?

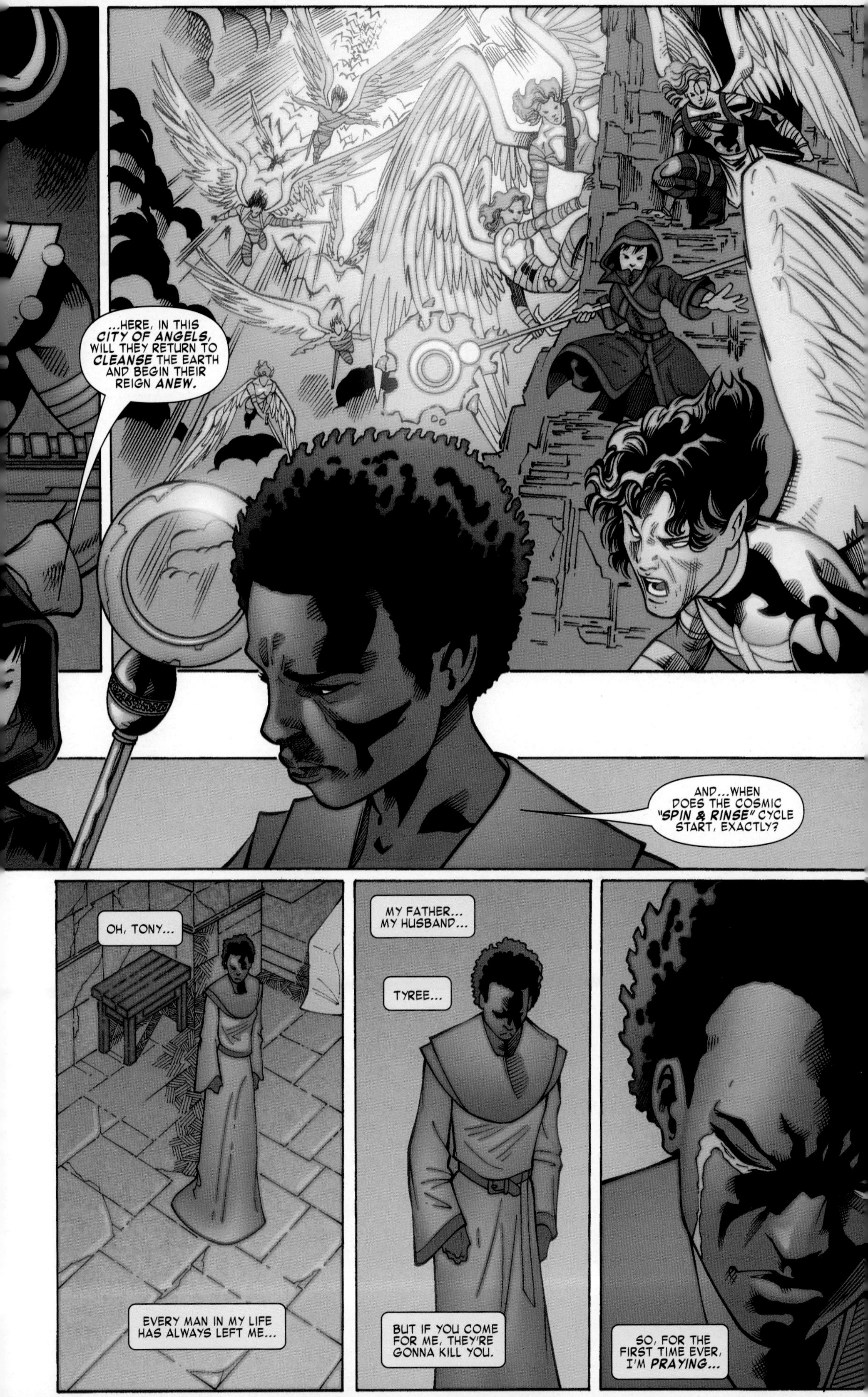
...HERE, IN THIS CITY OF ANGELS, WILL THEY RETURN TO CLEANSE THE EARTH AND BEGIN THEIR REIGN ANEW.
AND...WHEN DOES THE COSMIC "SPIN & RINSE" CYCLE START, EXACTLY?
OH, TONY...
EVERY MAN IN MY LIFE HAS ALWAYS LEFT ME...
MY FATHER... MY HUSBAND...
TYREE...
BUT IF YOU COME FOR ME, THEY'RE GONNA KILL YOU.
SO, FOR THE FIRST TIME EVER, I'M PRAYING...

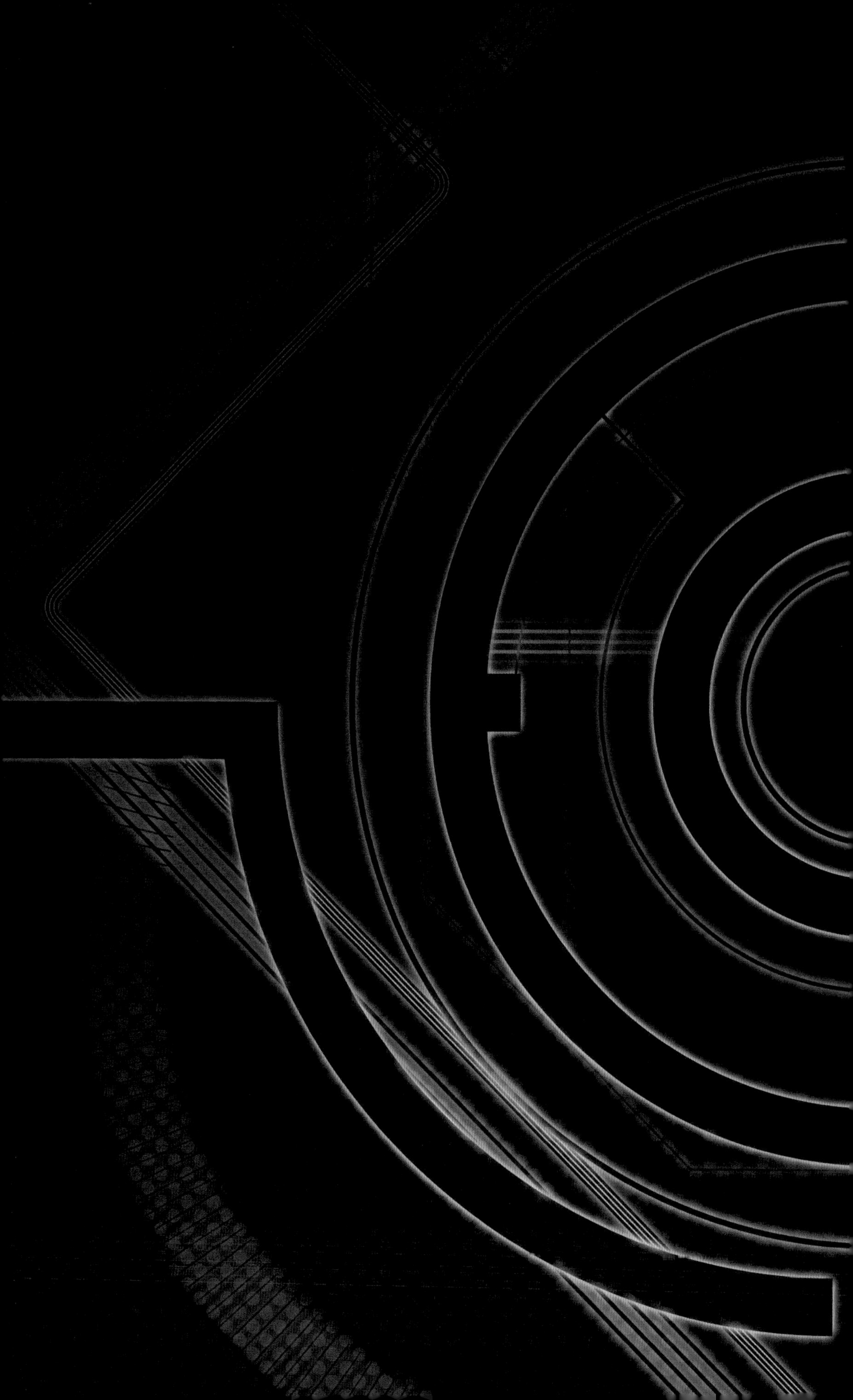

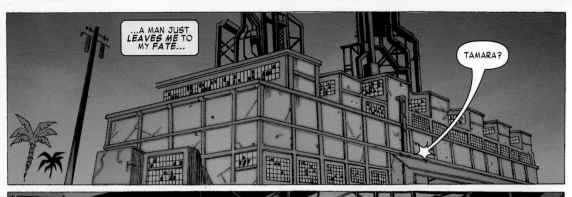

...A MAN JUST *LEAVES* ME TO MY *FATE*...

TAMARA?

TAMARA... WHERE *ARE* YOU?

HEY! TRYING TO CATCH SOME Z'S OVER HERE!

SORRY.

TYREE?

LIKE I TURNED AROUND, AND THEY WERE BOTH *GONE*.

COULD THEY HAVE BOTH GONE BACK HOME? BUT WITHOUT TELLING ME?

AND HOW COULD THEY HAVE GOTTEN PAST THE RING OF L.A.P.D. STILL OUTSIDE...?

STARK. AT LAST.

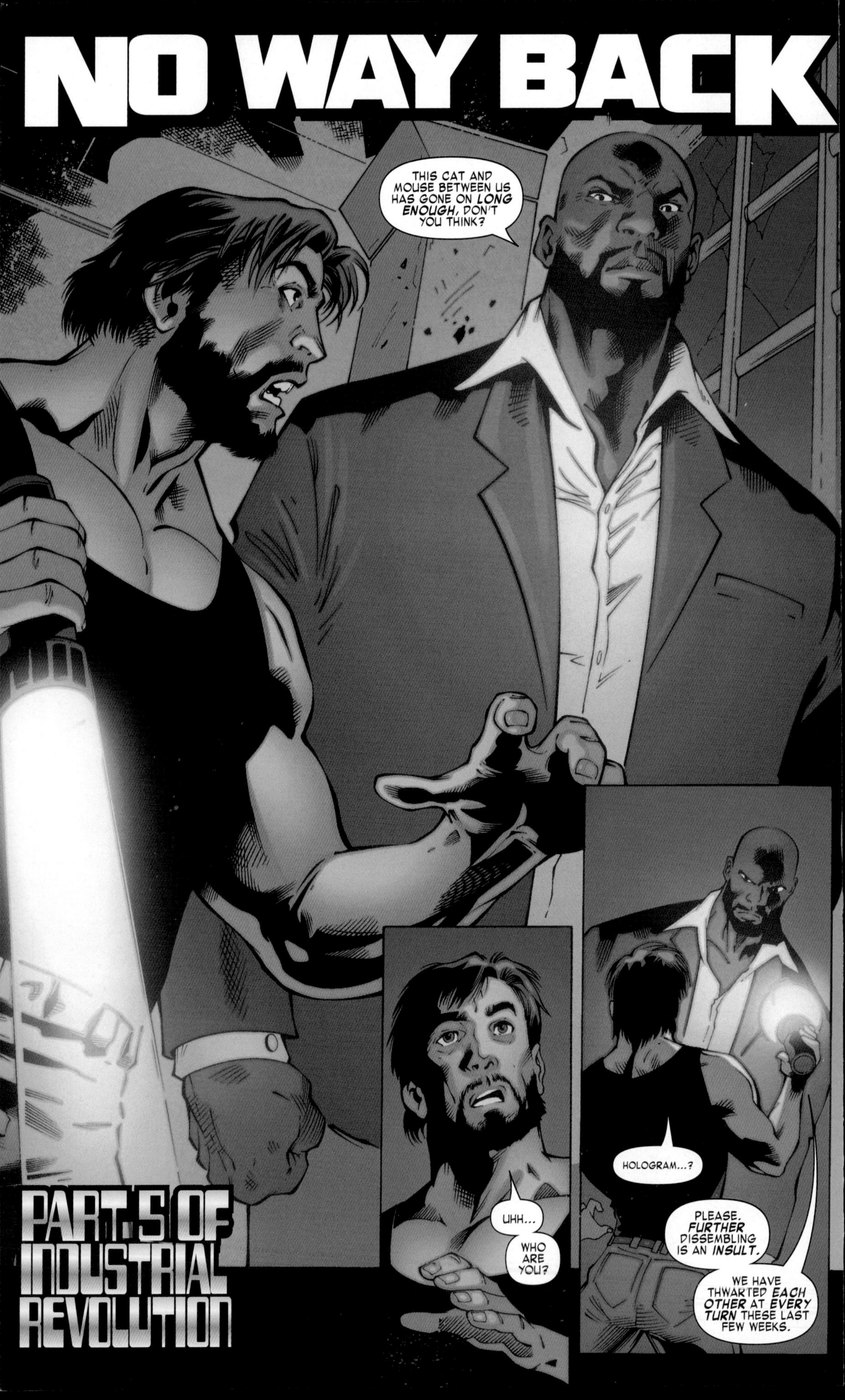
NO WAY BACK
THIS CAT AND MOUSE BETWEEN US HAS GONE ON LONG ENOUGH, DON'T YOU THINK?
UHH...
WHO ARE YOU?
HOLOGRAM...?
PLEASE. FURTHER DISSEMBLING IS AN INSULT.
WE HAVE THWARTED EACH OTHER AT EVERY TURN THESE LAST FEW WEEKS.
PART 5 OF INDUSTRIAL REVOLUTION

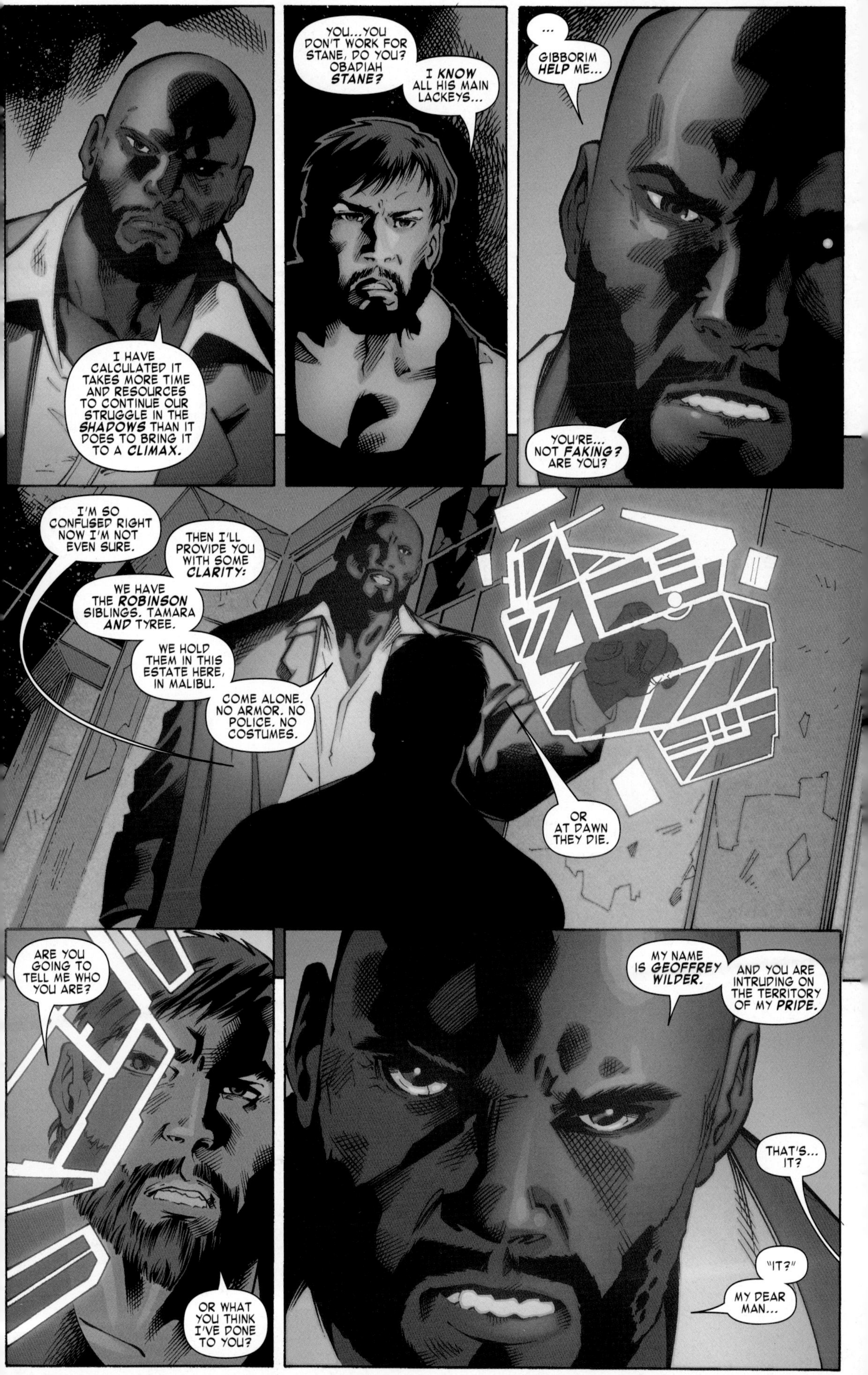
I HAVE CALCULATED IT TAKES MORE TIME AND RESOURCES TO CONTINUE OUR STRUGGLE IN THE SHADOWS THAN IT DOES TO BRING IT TO A CLIMAX.
YOU...YOU DON'T WORK FOR STANE, DO YOU? OBADIAH STANE?
I KNOW ALL HIS MAIN LACKEYS...
...
GIBBORIM HELP ME...
YOU'RE... NOT FAKING? ARE YOU?
I'M SO CONFUSED RIGHT NOW I'M NOT EVEN SURE.
THEN I'LL PROVIDE YOU WITH SOME CLARITY:
WE HAVE THE ROBINSON SIBLINGS. TAMARA AND TYREE.
WE HOLD THEM IN THIS ESTATE HERE, IN MALIBU.
COME ALONE. NO ARMOR. NO POLICE. NO COSTUMES.
OR AT DAWN THEY DIE.
ARE YOU GOING TO TELL ME WHO YOU ARE?
OR WHAT YOU THINK I'VE DONE TO YOU?
MY NAME IS GEOFFREY WILDER.
AND YOU ARE INTRUDING ON THE TERRITORY OF MY PRIDE.
THAT'S... IT?
"IT?"
MY DEAR MAN...

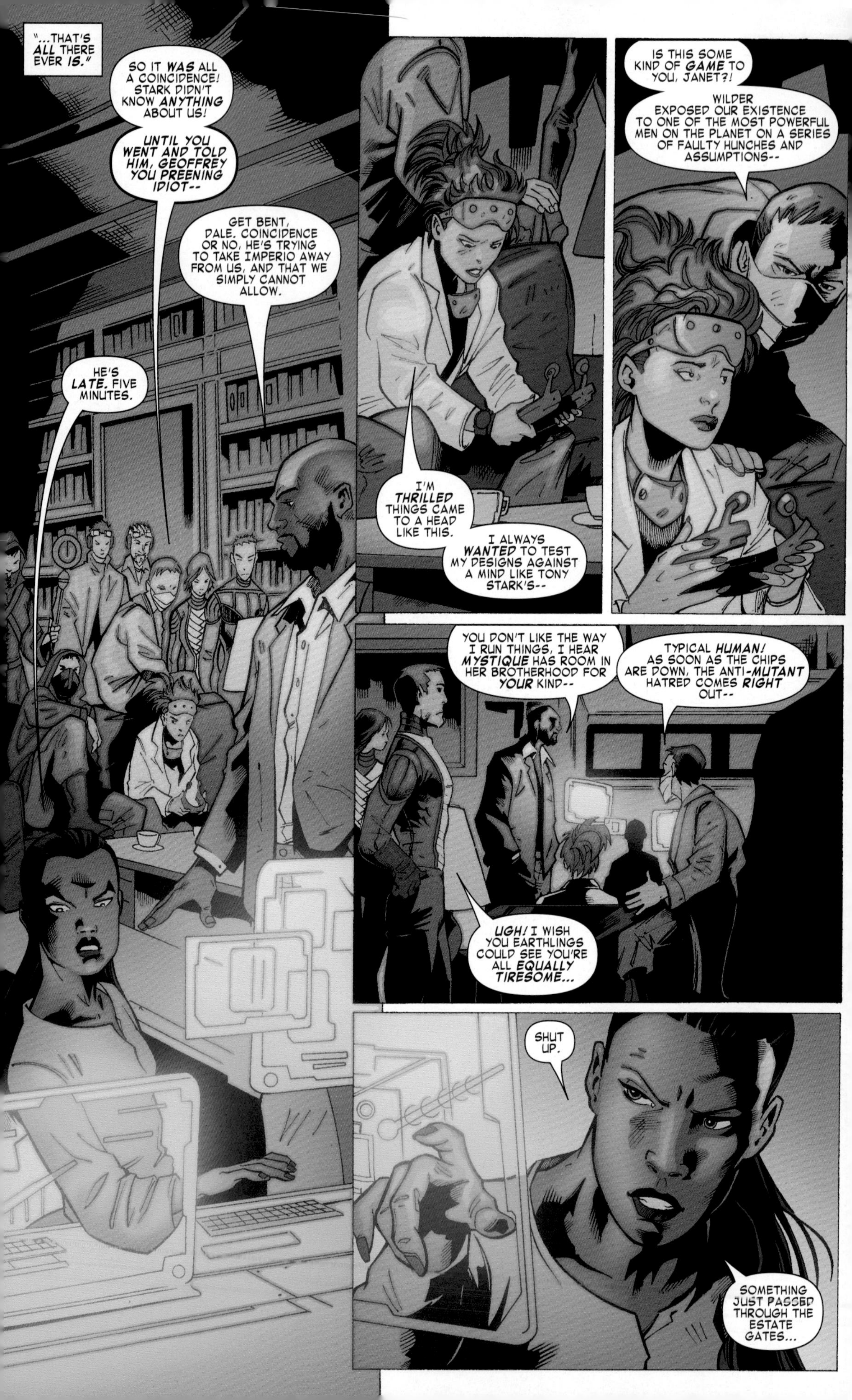
"...THAT'S ALL THERE EVER IS."
SO IT WAS ALL A COINCIDENCE! STARK DIDN'T KNOW ANYTHING ABOUT US!
UNTIL YOU WENT AND TOLD HIM, GEOFFREY YOU PREENING IDIOT--
GET BENT, DALE. COINCIDENCE OR NO, HE'S TRYING TO TAKE IMPERIO AWAY FROM US, AND THAT WE SIMPLY CANNOT ALLOW.
HE'S LATE. FIVE MINUTES.
I'M THRILLED THINGS CAME TO A HEAD LIKE THIS.
I ALWAYS WANTED TO TEST MY DESIGNS AGAINST A MIND LIKE TONY STARK'S--
IS THIS SOME KIND OF GAME TO YOU, JANET?!
WILDER EXPOSED OUR EXISTENCE TO ONE OF THE MOST POWERFUL MEN ON THE PLANET ON A SERIES OF FAULTY HUNCHES AND ASSUMPTIONS--
YOU DON'T LIKE THE WAY I RUN THINGS, I HEAR MYSTIQUE HAS ROOM IN HER BROTHERHOOD FOR YOUR KIND--
TYPICAL HUMAN! AS SOON AS THE CHIPS ARE DOWN, THE ANTI-MUTANT HATRED COMES RIGHT OUT--
UGH! I WISH YOU EARTHLINGS COULD SEE YOU'RE ALL EQUALLY TIRESOME...
SHUT UP.
SOMETHING JUST PASSED THROUGH THE ESTATE GATES...

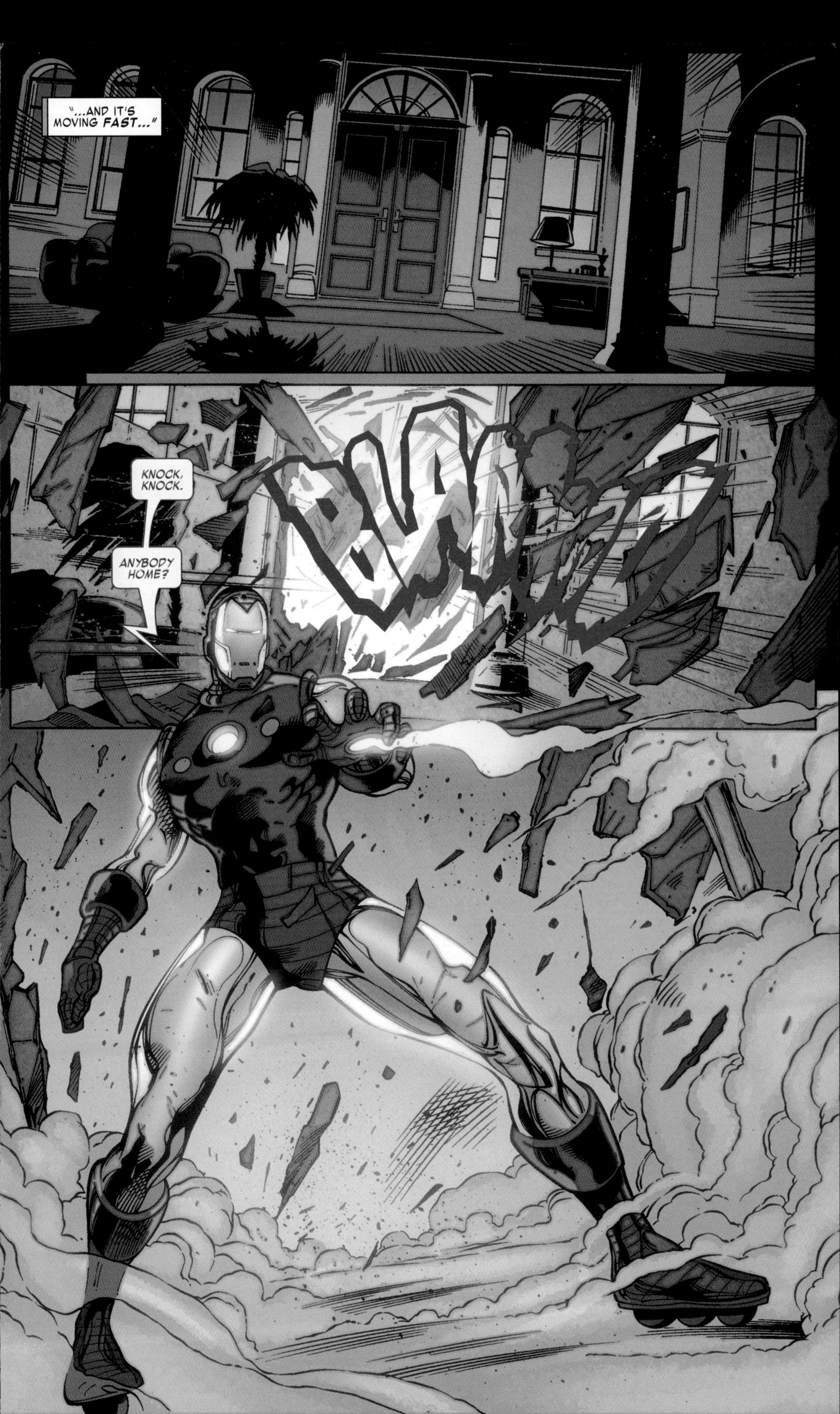
"...AND IT'S MOVING FAST..."
KNOCK, KNOCK.
ANYBODY HOME?

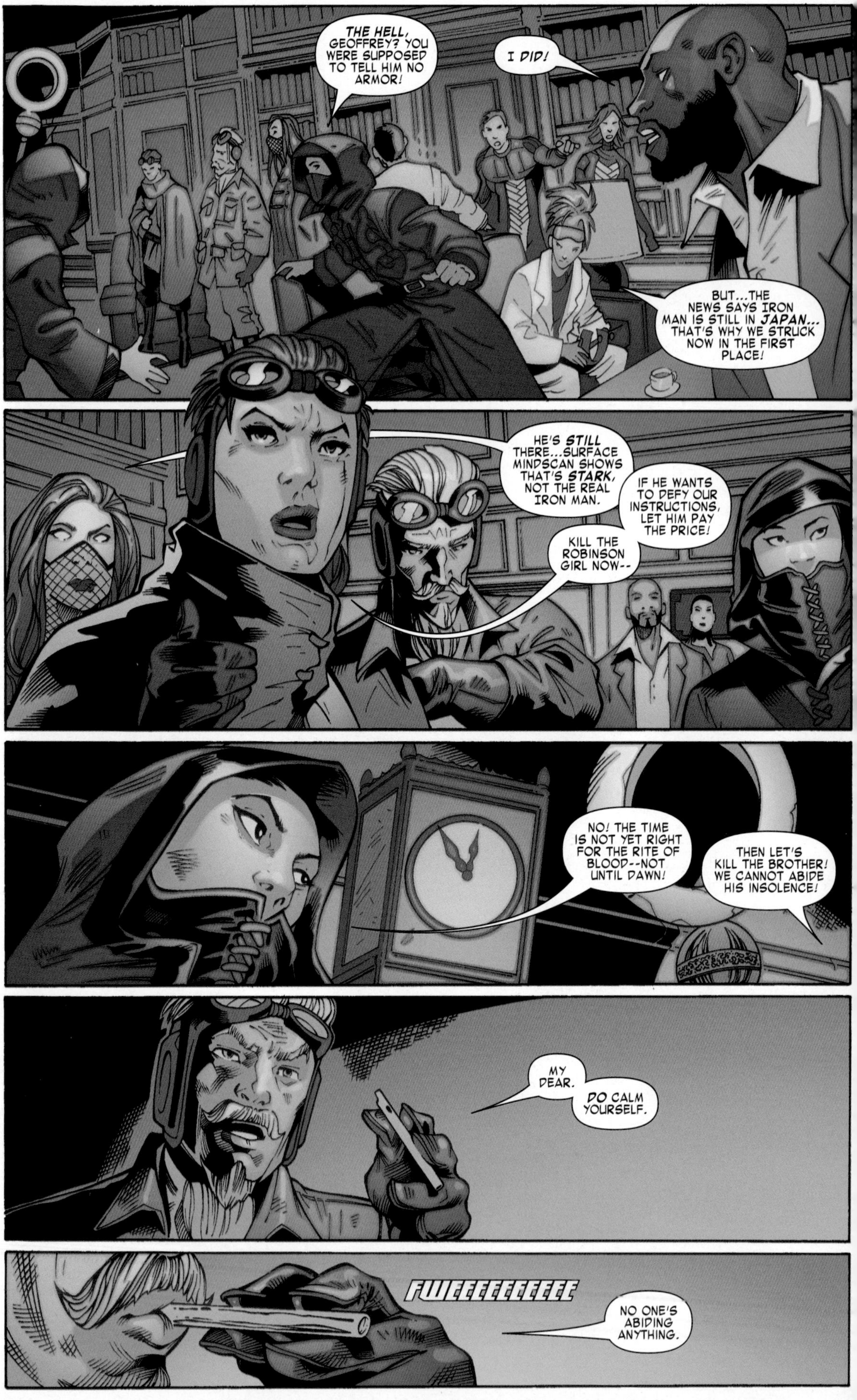
THE HELL, GEOFFREY? YOU WERE SUPPOSED TO TELL HIM NO ARMOR!
I DID!
BUT...THE NEWS SAYS IRON MAN IS STILL IN JAPAN... THAT'S WHY WE STRUCK NOW IN THE FIRST PLACE!
HE'S STILL THERE...SURFACE MINDSCAN SHOWS THAT'S STARK, NOT THE REAL IRON MAN.
IF HE WANTS TO DEFY OUR INSTRUCTIONS, LET HIM PAY THE PRICE!
KILL THE ROBINSON GIRL NOW--
NO! THE TIME IS NOT YET RIGHT FOR THE RITE OF BLOOD--NOT UNTIL DAWN!
THEN LET'S KILL THE BROTHER! WE CANNOT ABIDE HIS INSOLENCE!
MY DEAR.
DO CALM YOURSELF.
FWEEEEEEEEEE
NO ONE'S ABIDING ANYTHING.

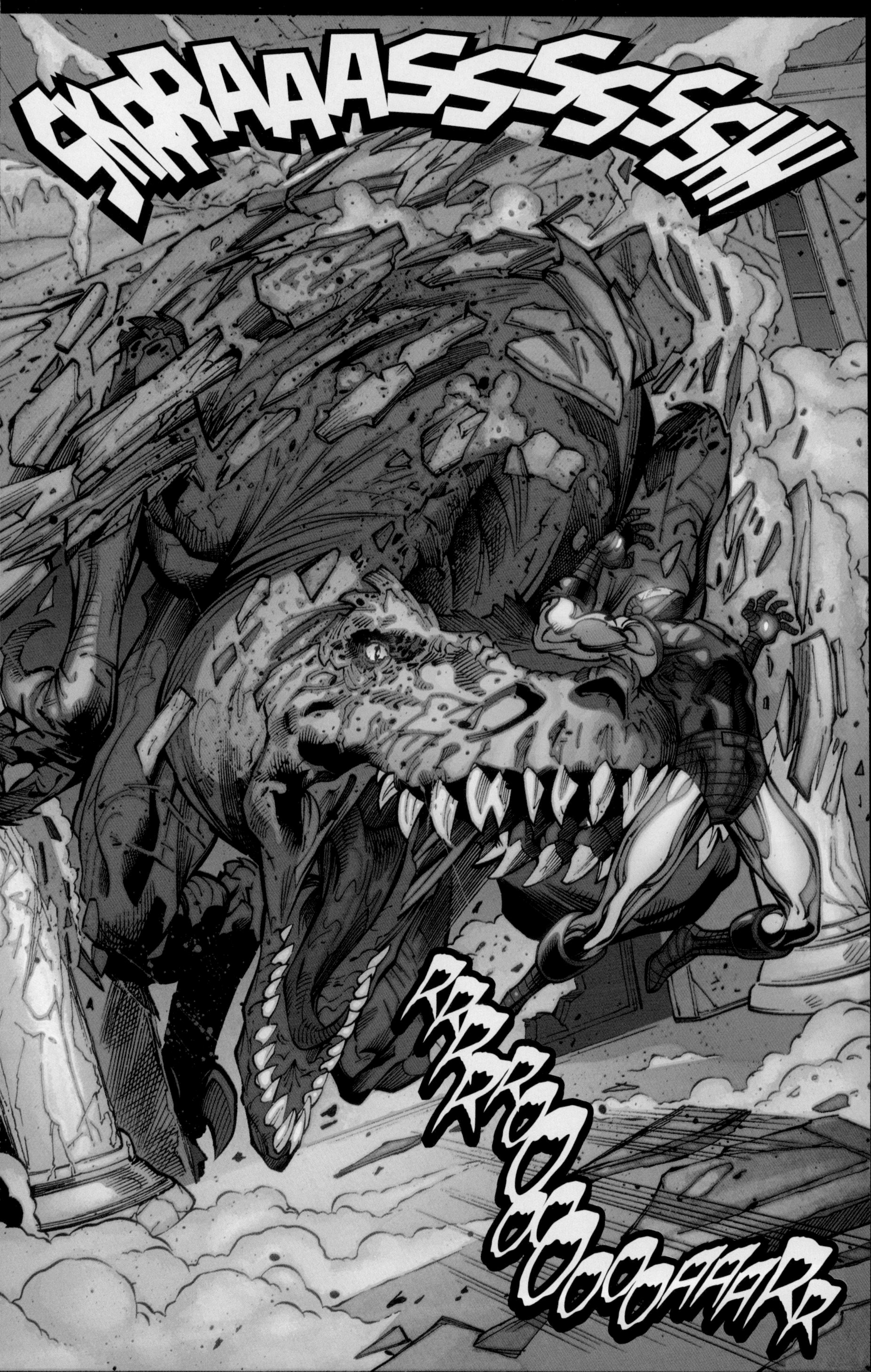
KRRAAASSSSSH
RRRROOOOOOOOAAARR

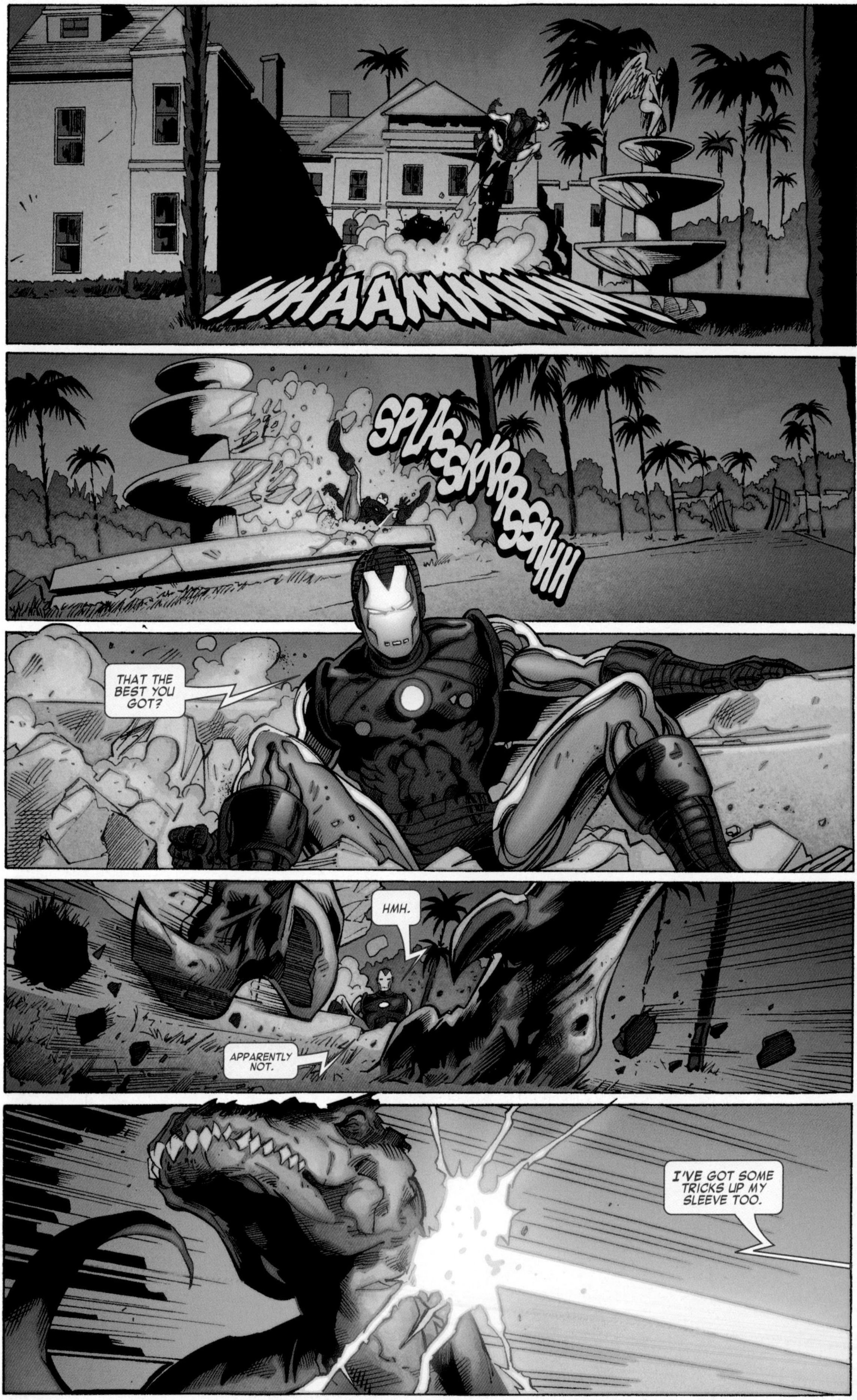
WHAAMMMM
SPLASSKKRRSSHHH
THAT THE BEST YOU GOT?
HMH.
APPARENTLY NOT.
I'VE GOT SOME TRICKS UP MY SLEEVE TOO.

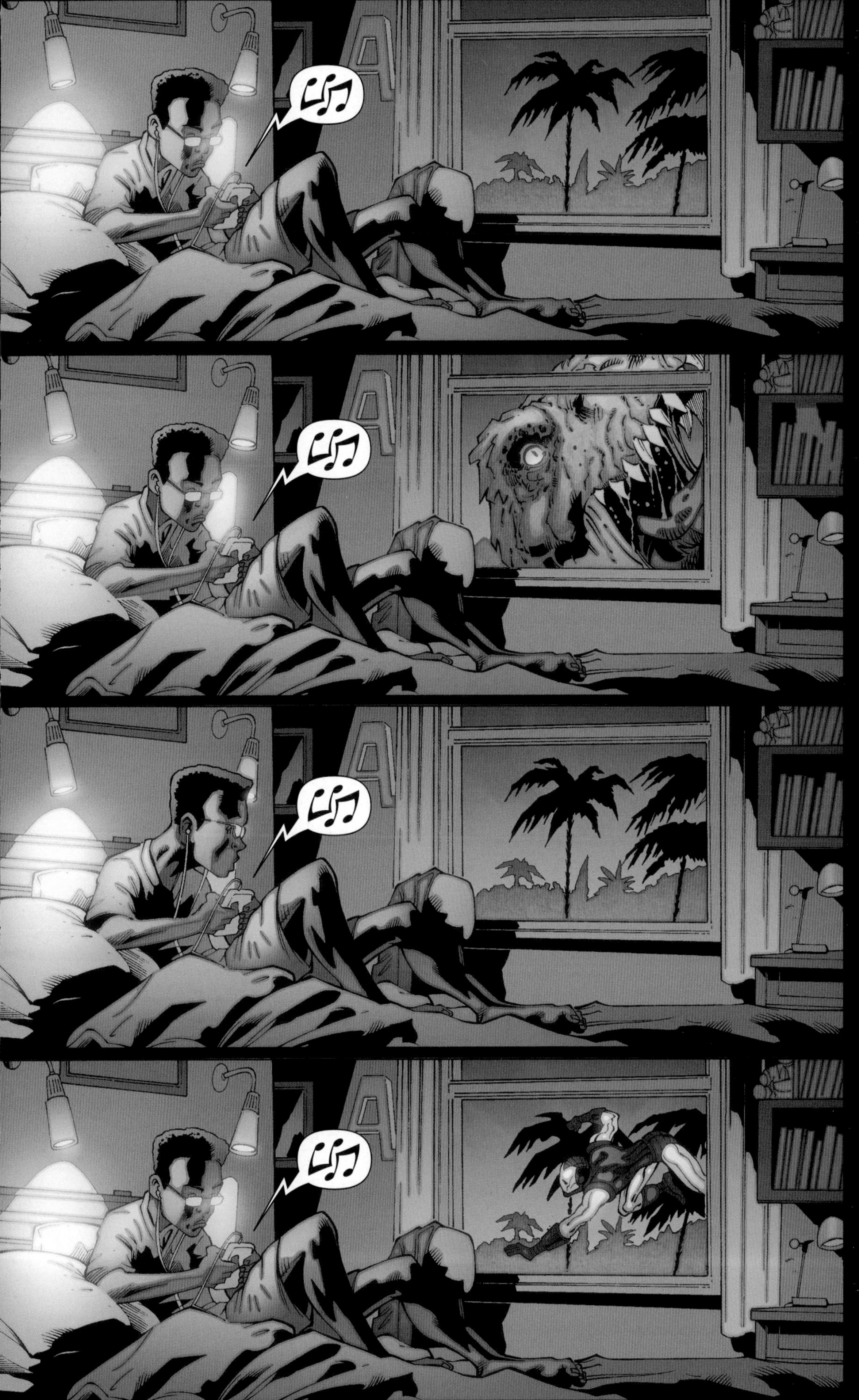

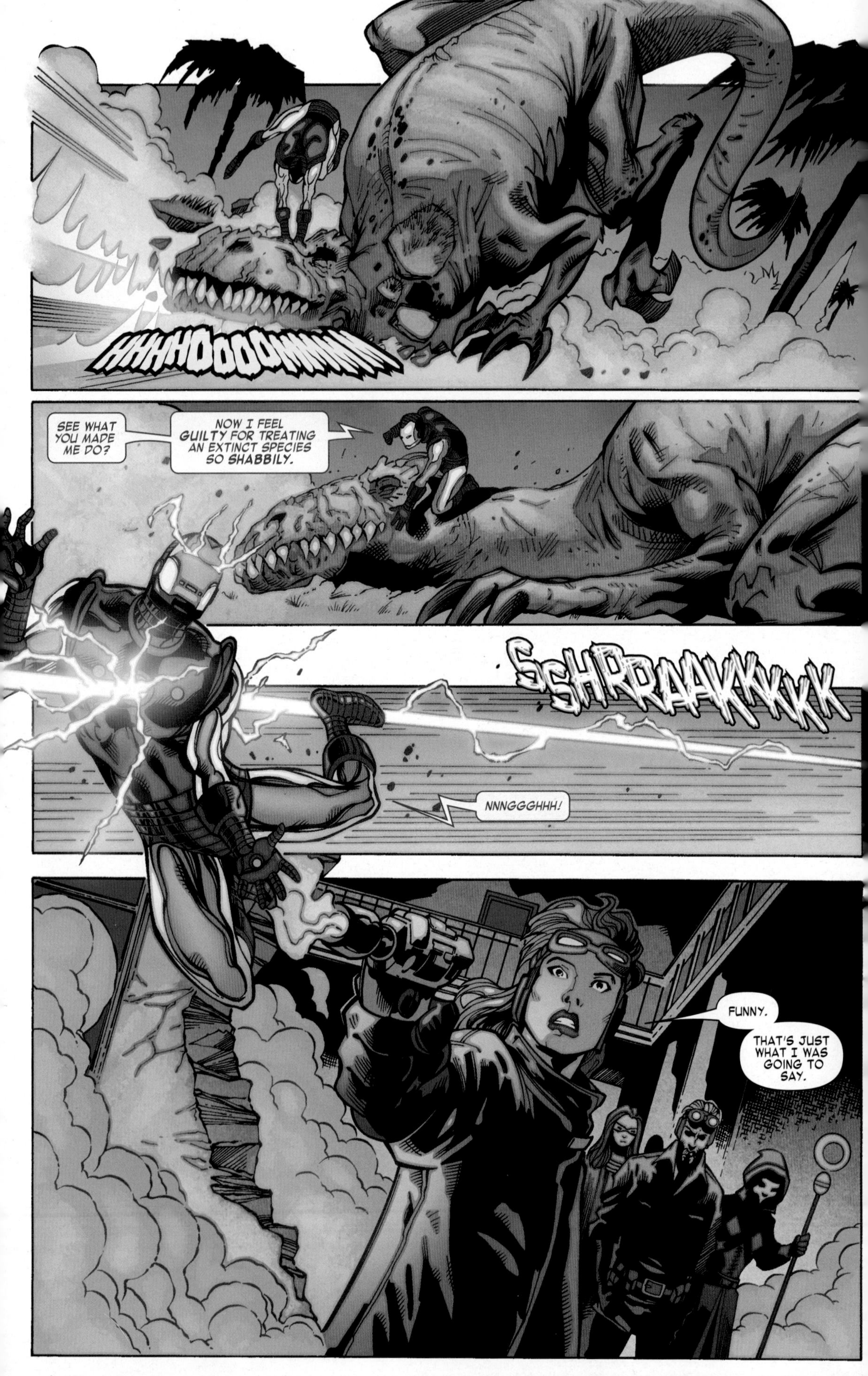
HHHHOOOOMMMM!
SEE WHAT YOU MADE ME DO?
NOW I FEEL GUILTY FOR TREATING AN EXTINCT SPECIES SO SHABBILY.
SSHRRAAKKKKK
NNNGGGHHH!
FUNNY.
THAT'S JUST WHAT I WAS GOING TO SAY.

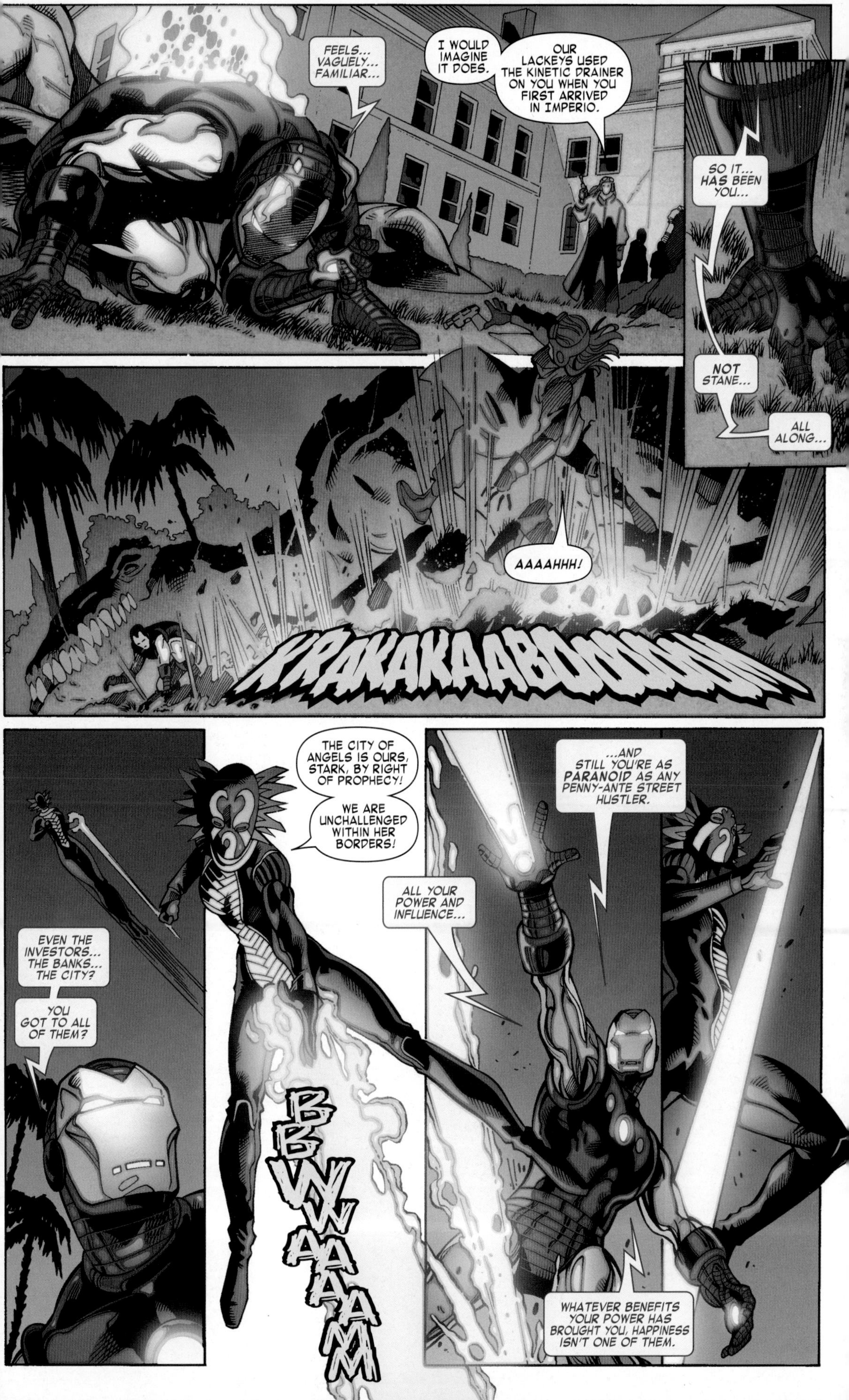
FEELS... VAGUELY... FAMILIAR...
I WOULD IMAGINE IT DOES.
OUR LACKEYS USED THE KINETIC DRAINER ON YOU WHEN YOU FIRST ARRIVED IN IMPERIO.
SO IT... HAS BEEN YOU...
NOT STANE...
ALL ALONG...
AAAAHHH!
KRAKAKAABOOOOOM
EVEN THE INVESTORS... THE BANKS... THE CITY?
YOU GOT TO ALL OF THEM?
THE CITY OF ANGELS IS OURS, STARK, BY RIGHT OF PROPHECY!
WE ARE UNCHALLENGED WITHIN HER BORDERS!
BBWAAAAM
ALL YOUR POWER AND INFLUENCE...
...AND STILL YOU'RE AS PARANOID AS ANY PENNY-ANTE STREET HUSTLER.
WHATEVER BENEFITS YOUR POWER HAS BROUGHT YOU, HAPPINESS ISN'T ONE OF THEM.

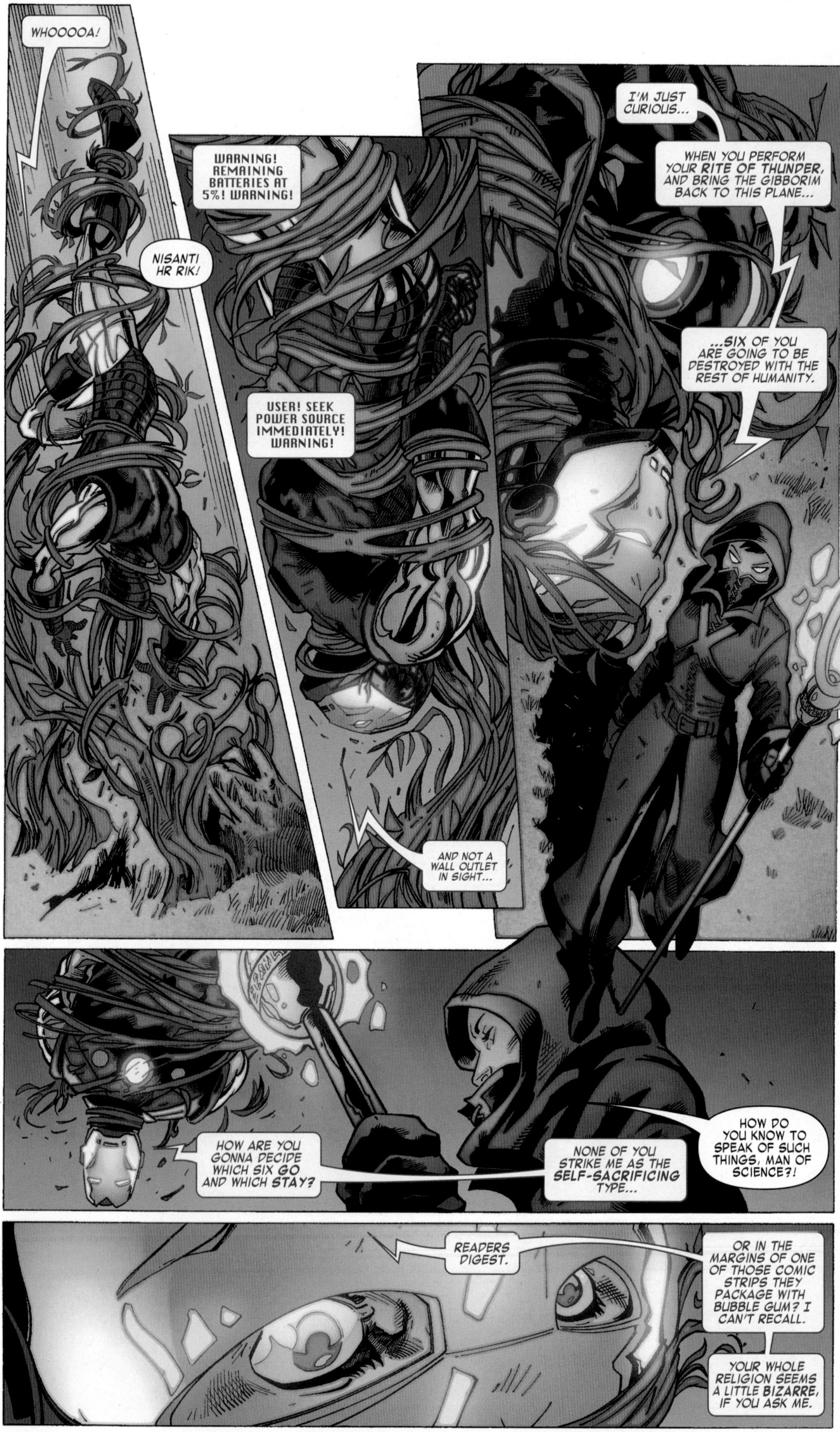
WHOOOOA!
NISANTI HR RIK!
WARNING! REMAINING BATTERIES AT 5%! WARNING!
USER! SEEK POWER SOURCE IMMEDIATELY! WARNING!
AND NOT A WALL OUTLET IN SIGHT...
I'M JUST CURIOUS...
WHEN YOU PERFORM YOUR RITE OF THUNDER, AND BRING THE GIBBORIM BACK TO THIS PLANE...
...SIX OF YOU ARE GOING TO BE DESTROYED WITH THE REST OF HUMANITY.
HOW ARE YOU GONNA DECIDE WHICH SIX GO AND WHICH STAY?
NONE OF YOU STRIKE ME AS THE SELF-SACRIFICING TYPE...
HOW DO YOU KNOW TO SPEAK OF SUCH THINGS, MAN OF SCIENCE?!
READERS DIGEST.
OR IN THE MARGINS OF ONE OF THOSE COMIC STRIPS THEY PACKAGE WITH BUBBLE GUM? I CAN'T RECALL.
YOUR WHOLE RELIGION SEEMS A LITTLE BIZARRE, IF YOU ASK ME.

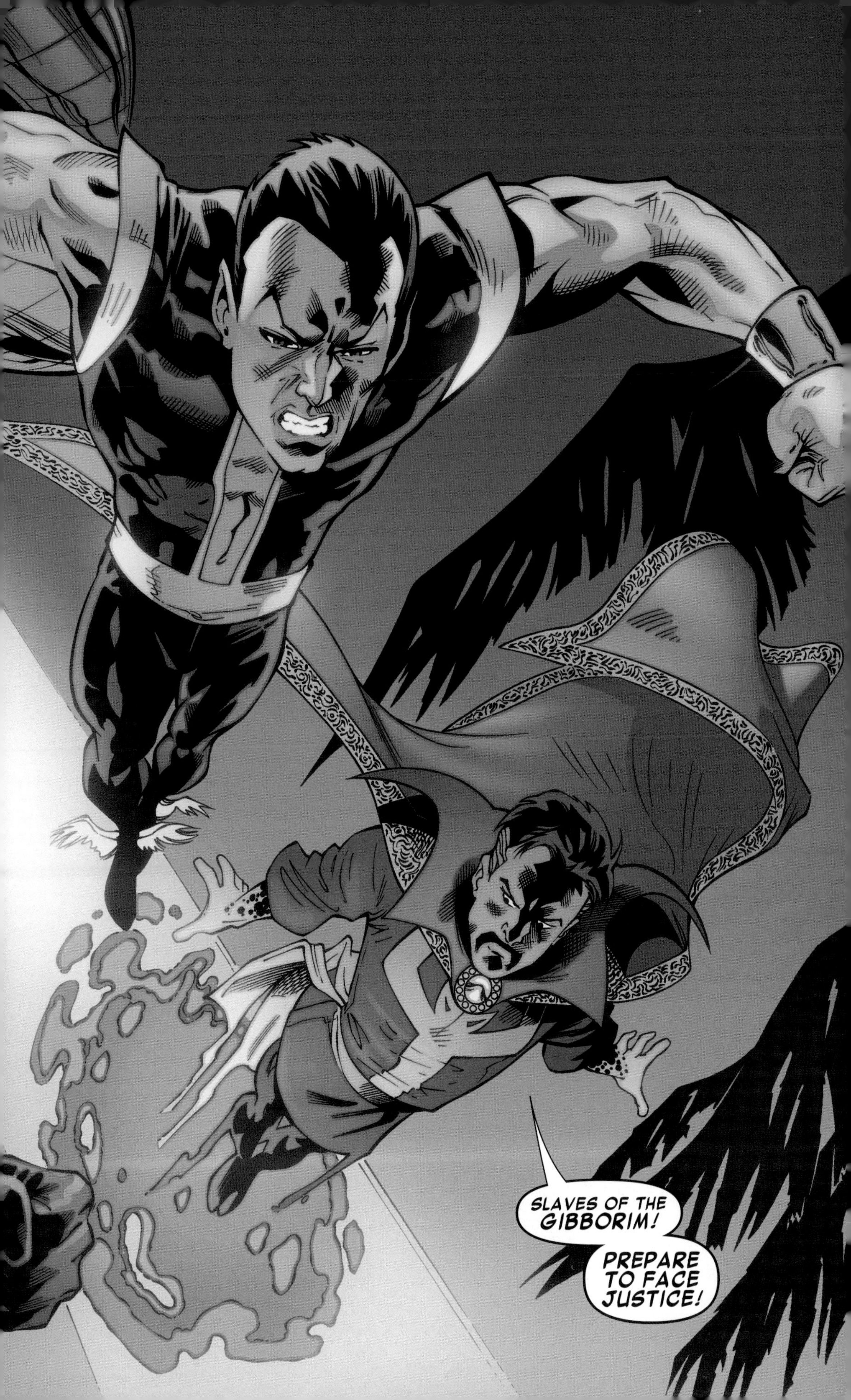
SLAVES OF THE GIBBORIM!
PREPARE TO FACE JUSTICE!

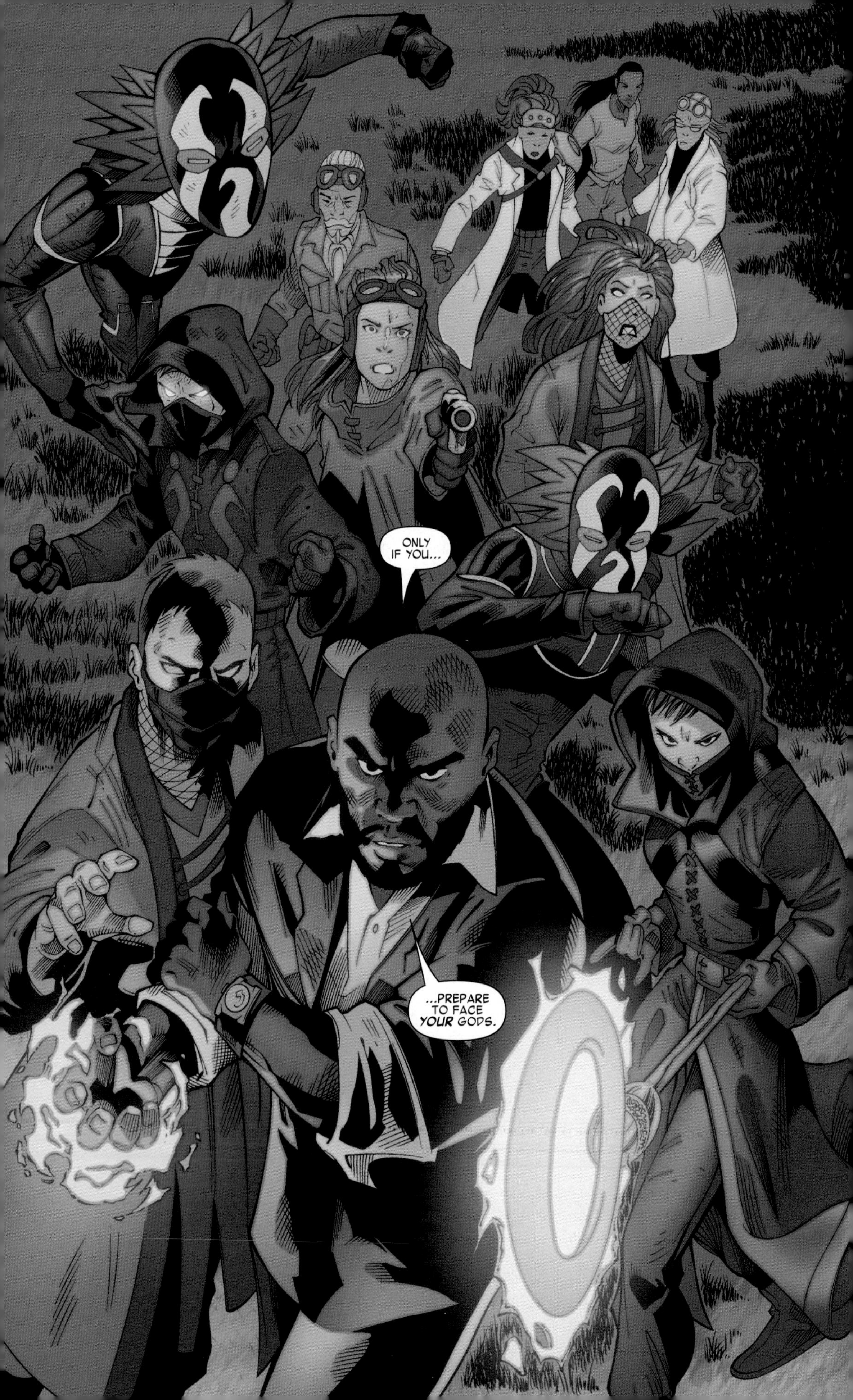
ONLY IF YOU...
...PREPARE TO FACE YOUR GODS.

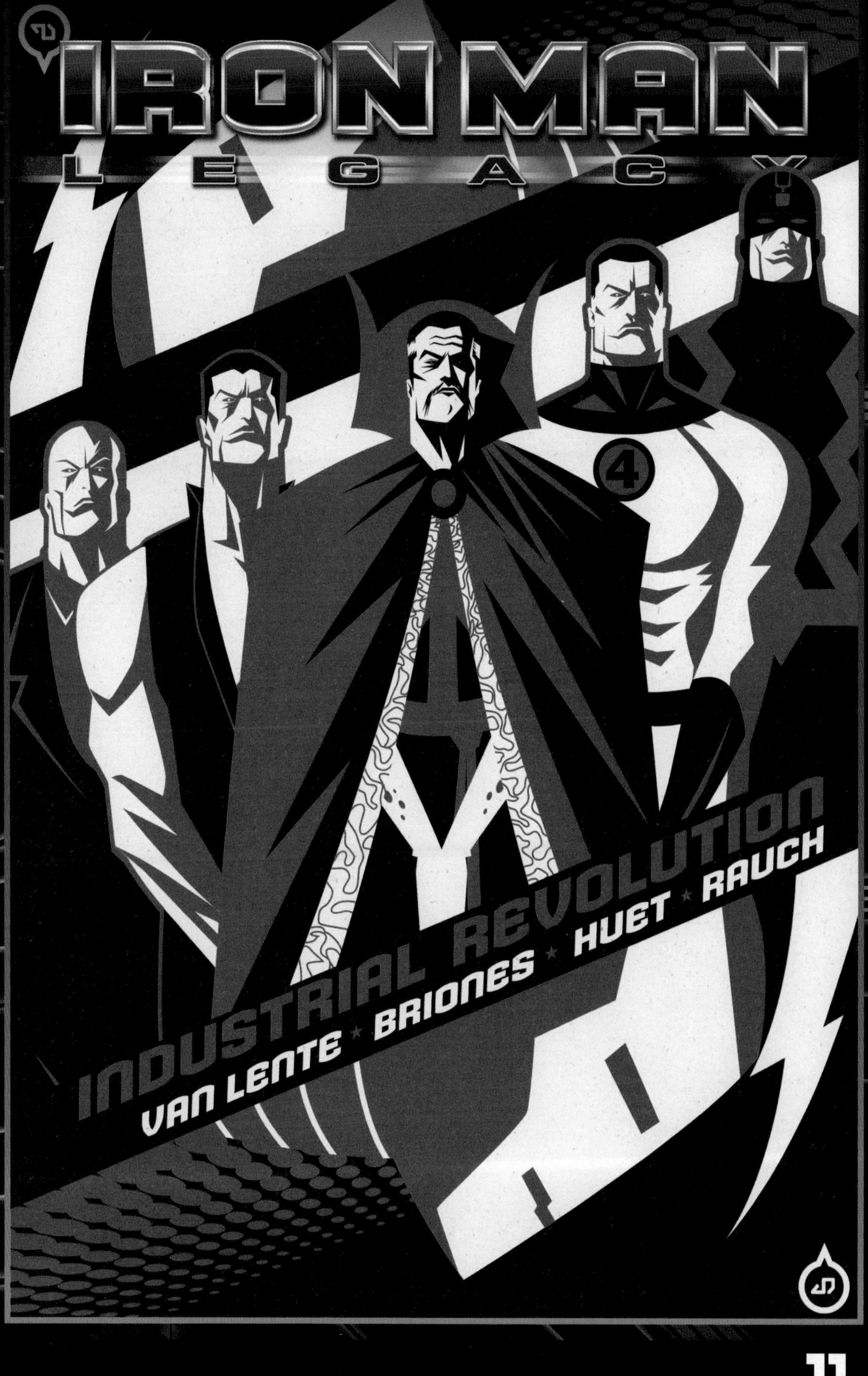
IRON MAN
LEGACY
INDUSTRIAL REVOLUTION
VAN LENTE • BRIONES • HUET • RAUCH

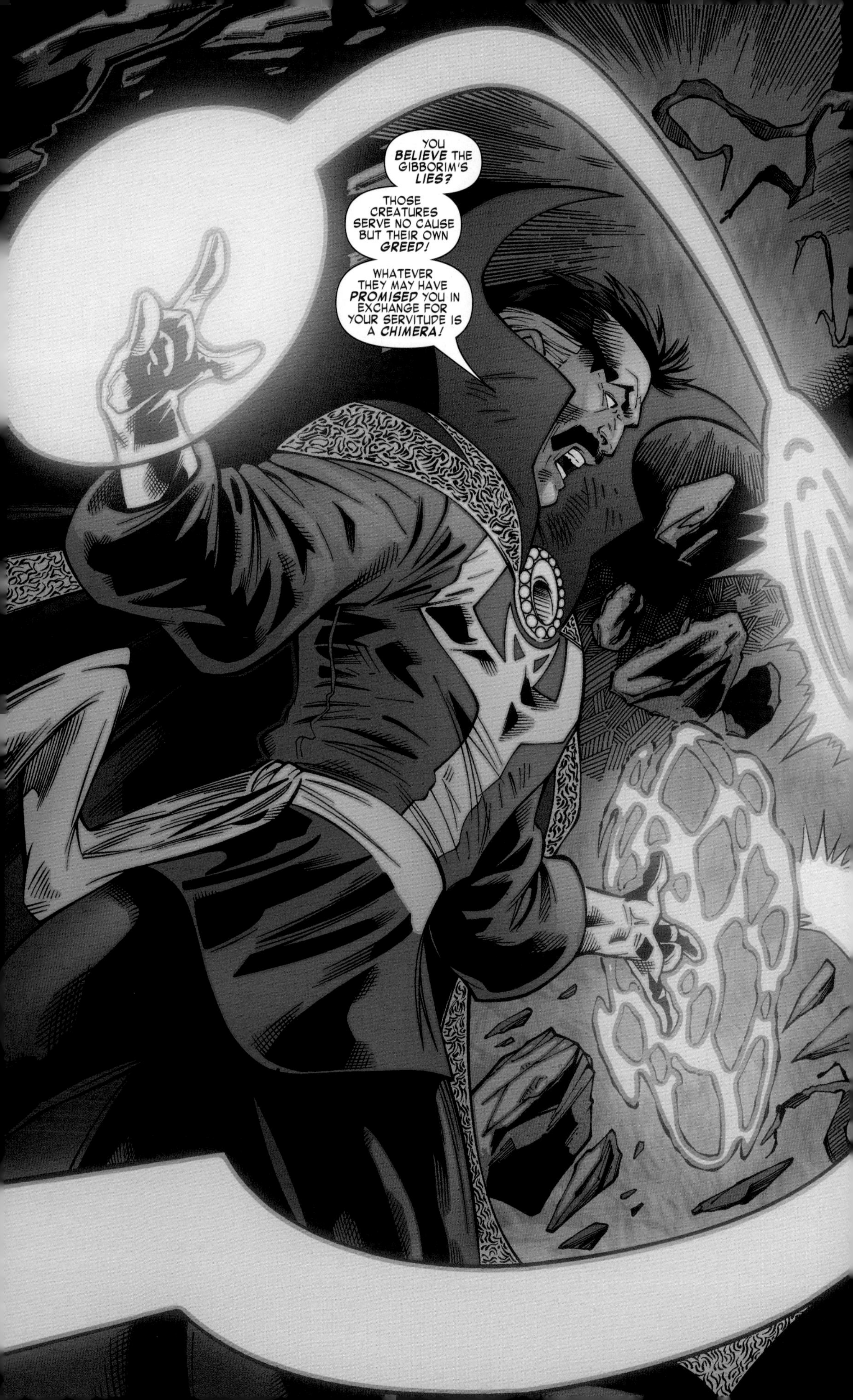
YOU BELIEVE THE GIBBORIM'S LIES?
THOSE CREATURES SERVE NO CAUSE BUT THEIR OWN GREED!
WHATEVER THEY MAY HAVE PROMISED YOU IN EXCHANGE FOR YOUR SERVITUDE IS A CHIMERA!

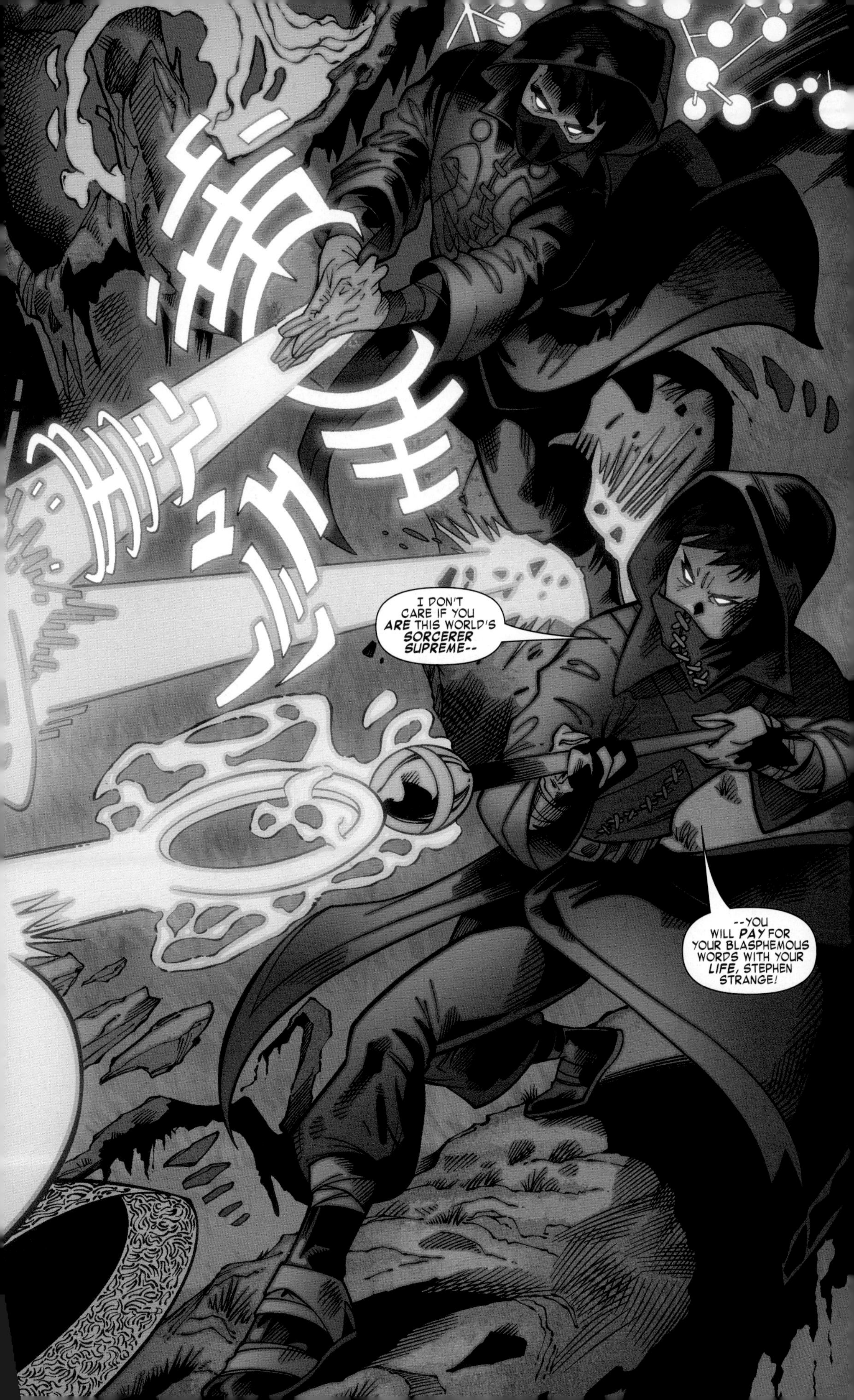
I DON'T CARE IF YOU ARE THIS WORLD'S SORCERER SUPREME--
--YOU WILL PAY FOR YOUR BLASPHEMOUS WORDS WITH YOUR LIFE, STEPHEN STRANGE!

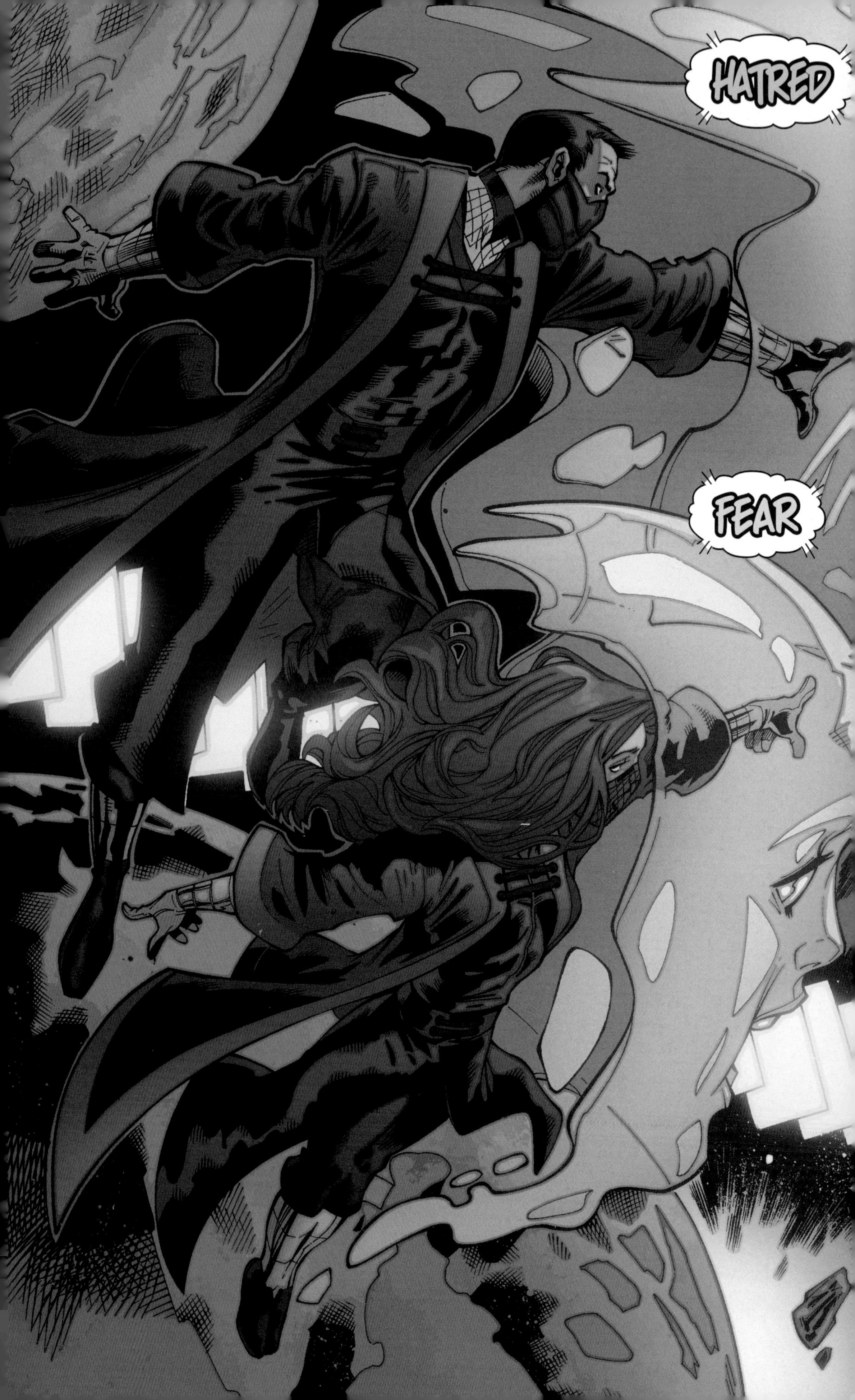
HATRED
FEAR

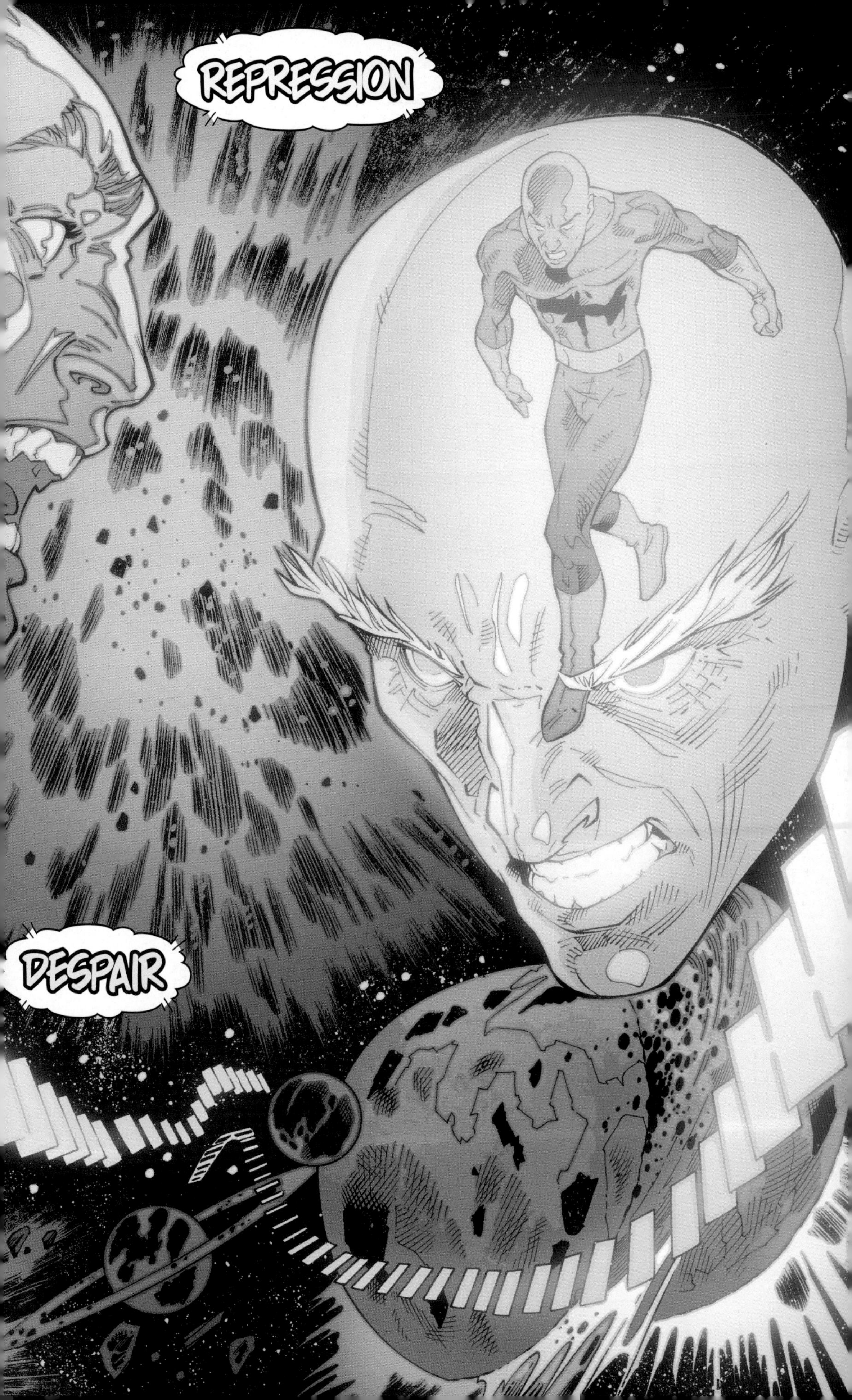
REPRESSION
DESPAIR

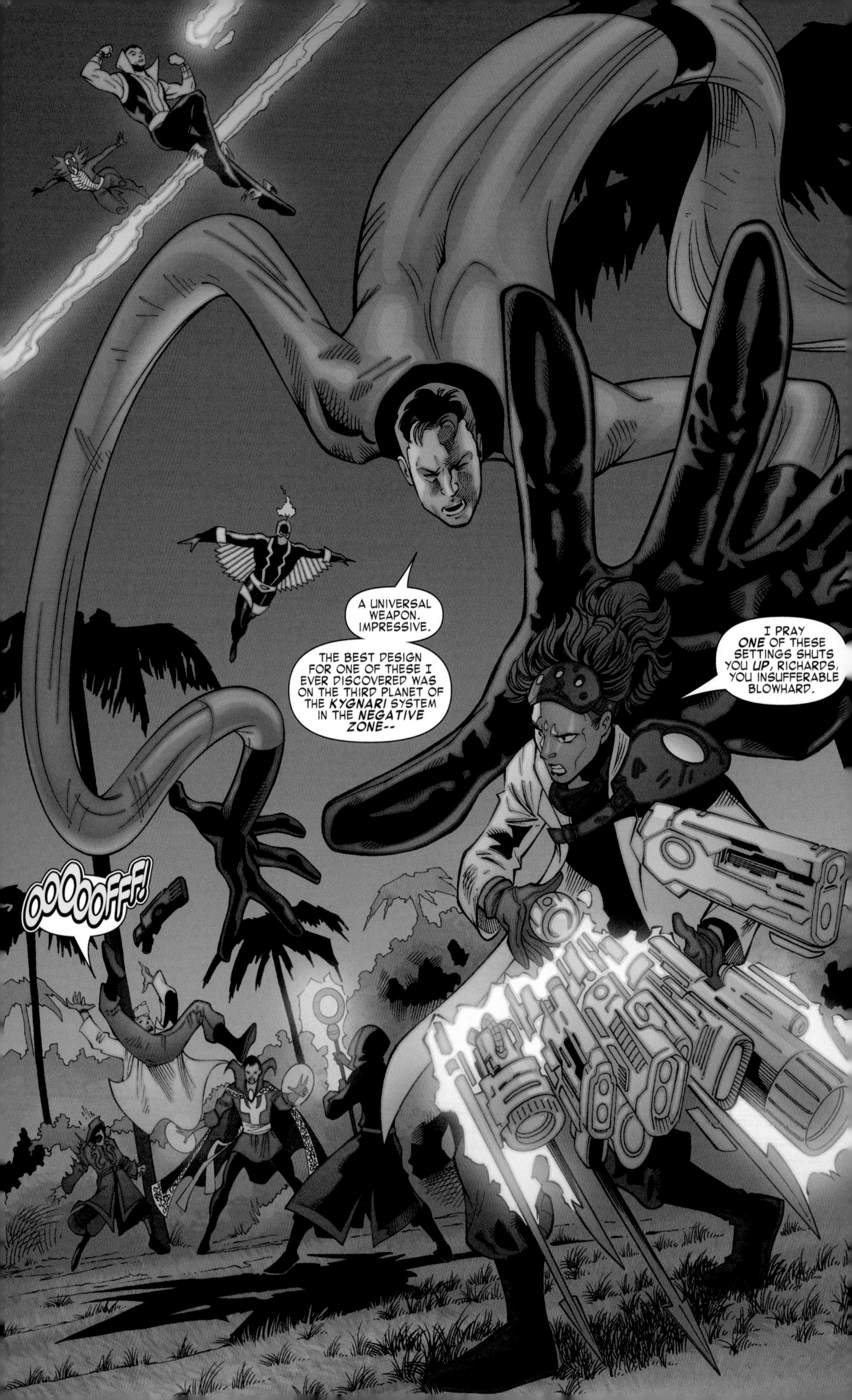
A UNIVERSAL WEAPON. IMPRESSIVE.
THE BEST DESIGN FOR ONE OF THESE I EVER DISCOVERED WAS ON THE THIRD PLANET OF THE KYGNARI SYSTEM IN THE NEGATIVE ZONE--
I PRAY ONE OF THESE SETTINGS SHUTS YOU UP, RICHARDS, YOU INSUFFERABLE BLOWHARD.
OOOOOFFF!

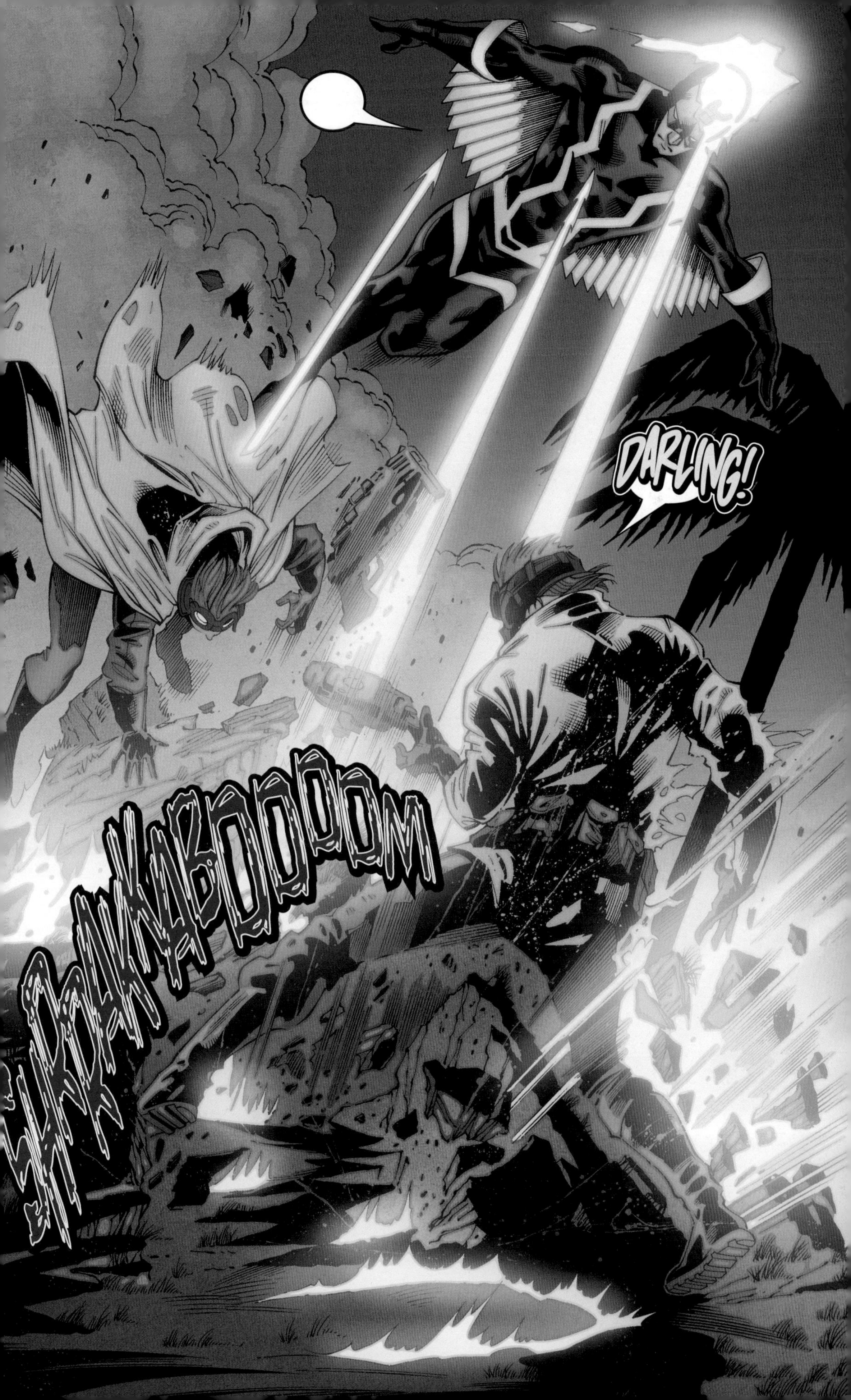
DARLING!
SHRAKABOOOOM

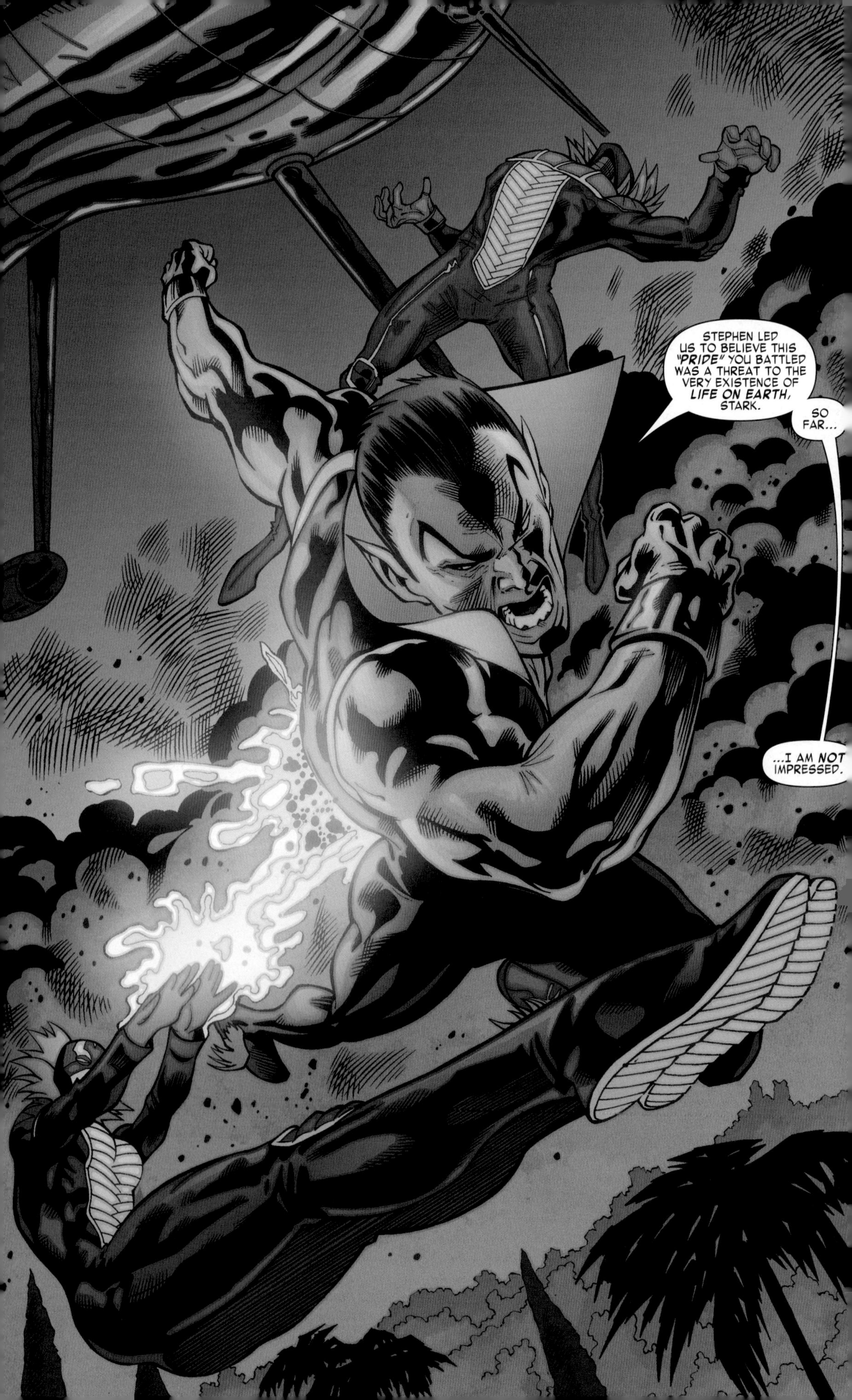
STEPHEN LED US TO BELIEVE THIS "PRIDE" YOU BATTLED WAS A THREAT TO THE VERY EXISTENCE OF LIFE ON EARTH, STARK.
SO FAR...
...I AM NOT IMPRESSED.

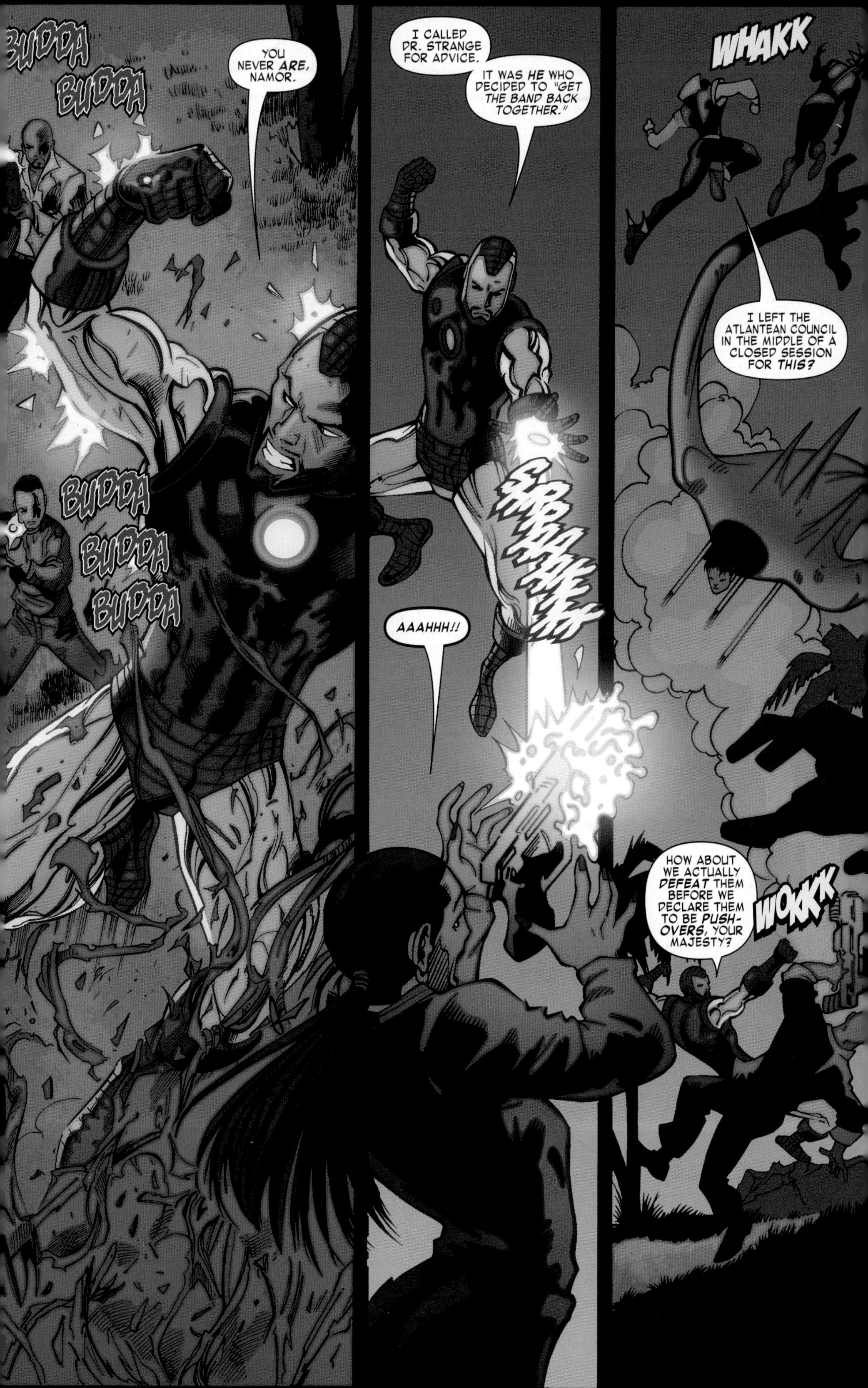
BUDDA
BUDDA
YOU NEVER ARE, NAMOR.
BUDDA
BUDDA
BUDDA
I CALLED DR. STRANGE FOR ADVICE.
IT WAS HE WHO DECIDED TO "GET THE BAND BACK TOGETHER."
AAAHHH!!
WHAKK
I LEFT THE ATLANTEAN COUNCIL IN THE MIDDLE OF A CLOSED SESSION FOR THIS?
HOW ABOUT WE ACTUALLY DEFEAT THEM BEFORE WE DECLARE THEM TO BE PUSH-OVERS, YOUR MAJESTY?
WOKKK

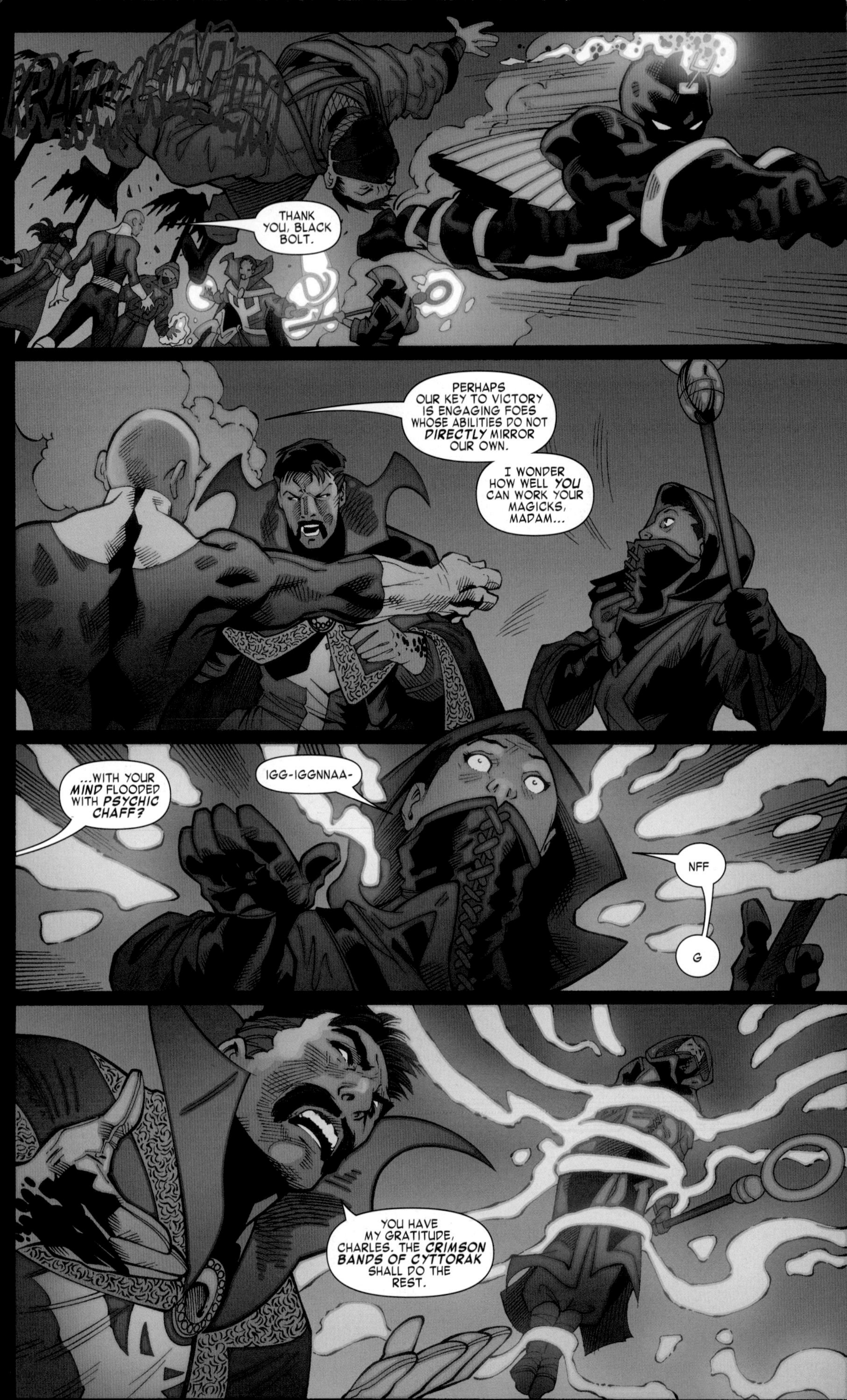
KRAKKAKOOOM
THANK YOU, BLACK BOLT.
PERHAPS OUR KEY TO VICTORY IS ENGAGING FOES WHOSE ABILITIES DO NOT DIRECTLY MIRROR OUR OWN.
I WONDER HOW WELL YOU CAN WORK YOUR MAGICKS, MADAM...
...WITH YOUR MIND FLOODED WITH PSYCHIC CHAFF?
IGG-IGGNNAA-
NFF
G
YOU HAVE MY GRATITUDE, CHARLES. THE CRIMSON BANDS OF CYTTORAK SHALL DO THE REST.

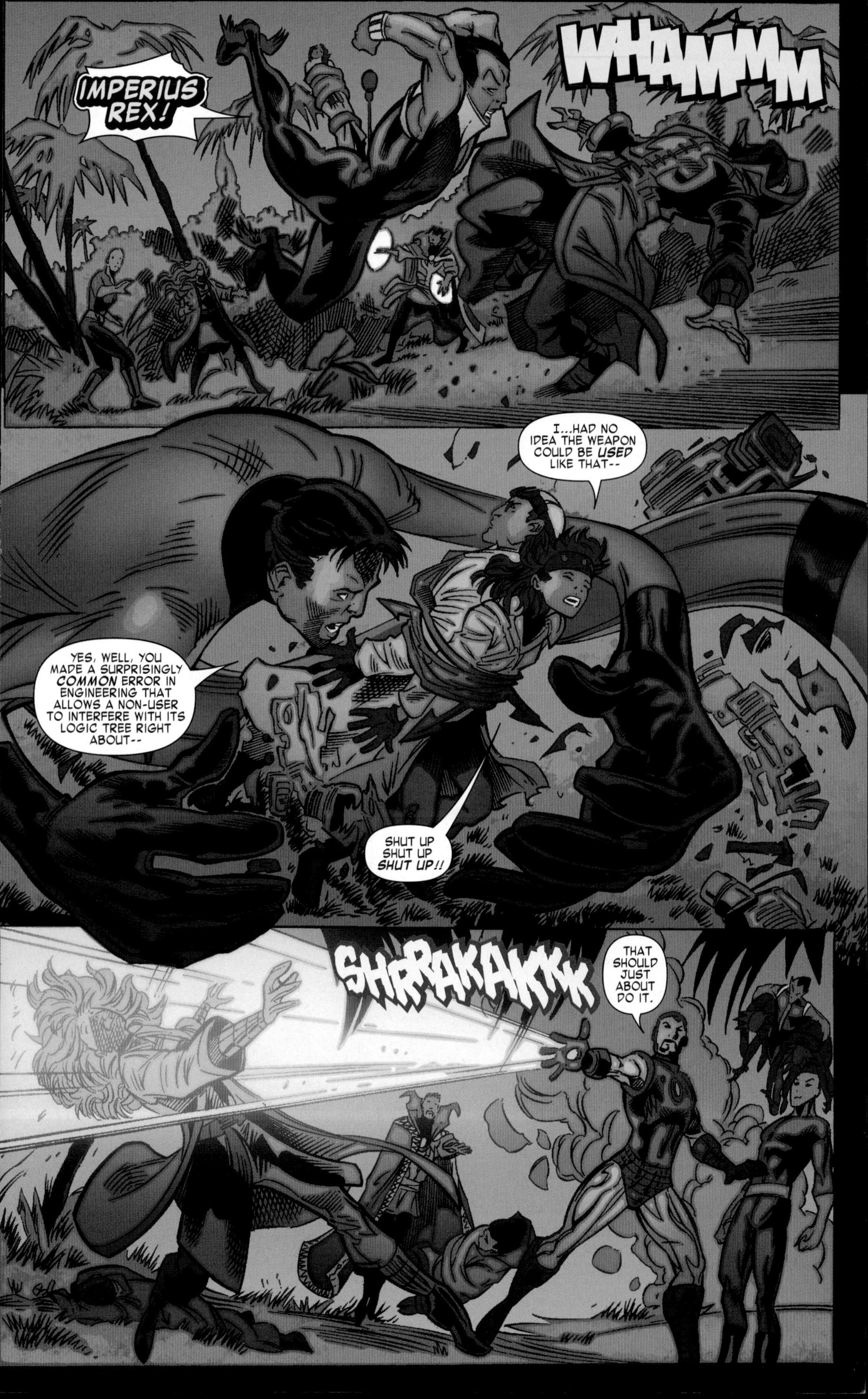
IMPERIUS REX!
WHAMMMM
I...HAD NO IDEA THE WEAPON COULD BE USED LIKE THAT--
YES, WELL, YOU MADE A SURPRISINGLY COMMON ERROR IN ENGINEERING THAT ALLOWS A NON-USER TO INTERFERE WITH ITS LOGIC TREE RIGHT ABOUT--
SHUT UP SHUT UP SHUT UP!!
SHRRAKAKKK
THAT SHOULD JUST ABOUT DO IT.

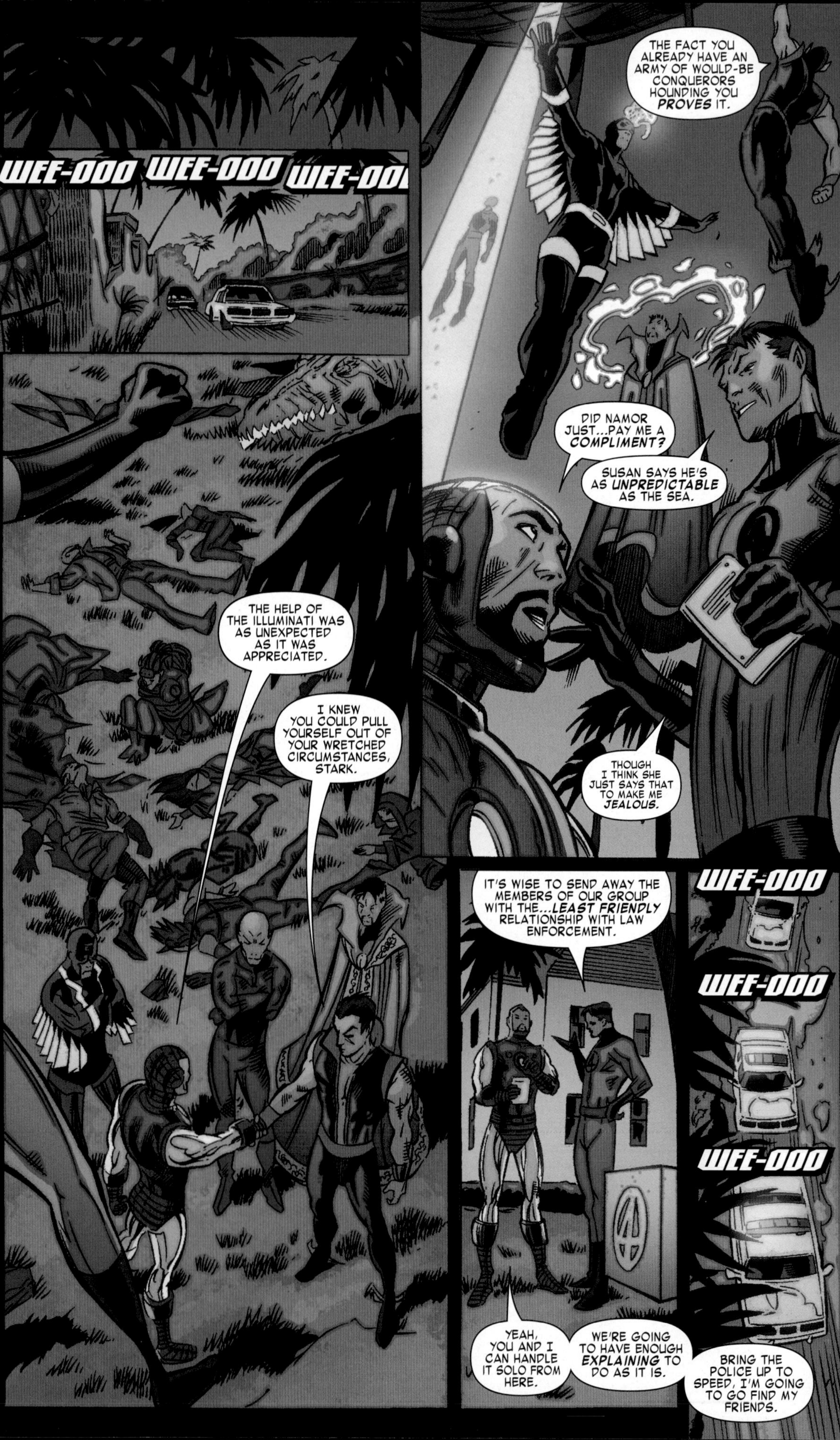
WEE-OOO WEE-OOO WEE-OO
THE FACT YOU ALREADY HAVE AN ARMY OF WOULD-BE CONQUERORS HOUNDING YOU PROVES IT.
DID NAMOR JUST...PAY ME A COMPLIMENT?
SUSAN SAYS HE'S AS UNPREDICTABLE AS THE SEA.
THOUGH I THINK SHE JUST SAYS THAT TO MAKE ME JEALOUS.
THE HELP OF THE ILLUMINATI WAS AS UNEXPECTED AS IT WAS APPRECIATED.
I KNEW YOU COULD PULL YOURSELF OUT OF YOUR WRETCHED CIRCUMSTANCES, STARK.
IT'S WISE TO SEND AWAY THE MEMBERS OF OUR GROUP WITH THE...LEAST FRIENDLY RELATIONSHIP WITH LAW ENFORCEMENT.
YEAH, YOU AND I CAN HANDLE IT SOLO FROM HERE.
WE'RE GOING TO HAVE ENOUGH EXPLAINING TO DO AS IT IS.
WEE-OOO
WEE-OOO
WEE-OOO
BRING THE POLICE UP TO SPEED, I'M GOING TO GO FIND MY FRIENDS.

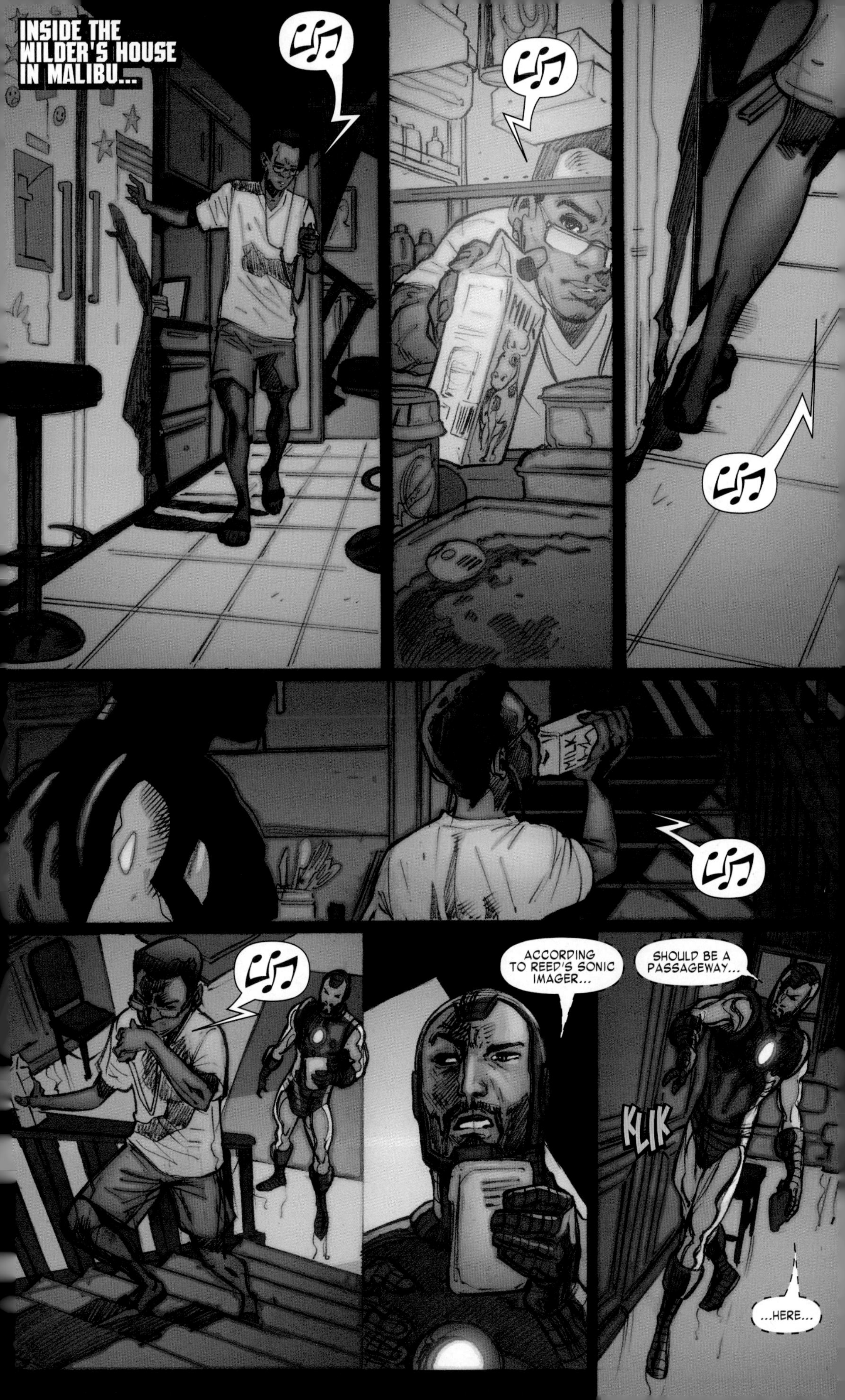

INSIDE THE WILDER'S HOUSE IN MALIBU...
ACCORDING TO REED'S SONIC IMAGER...
SHOULD BE A PASSAGEWAY...
KLIK
...HERE...

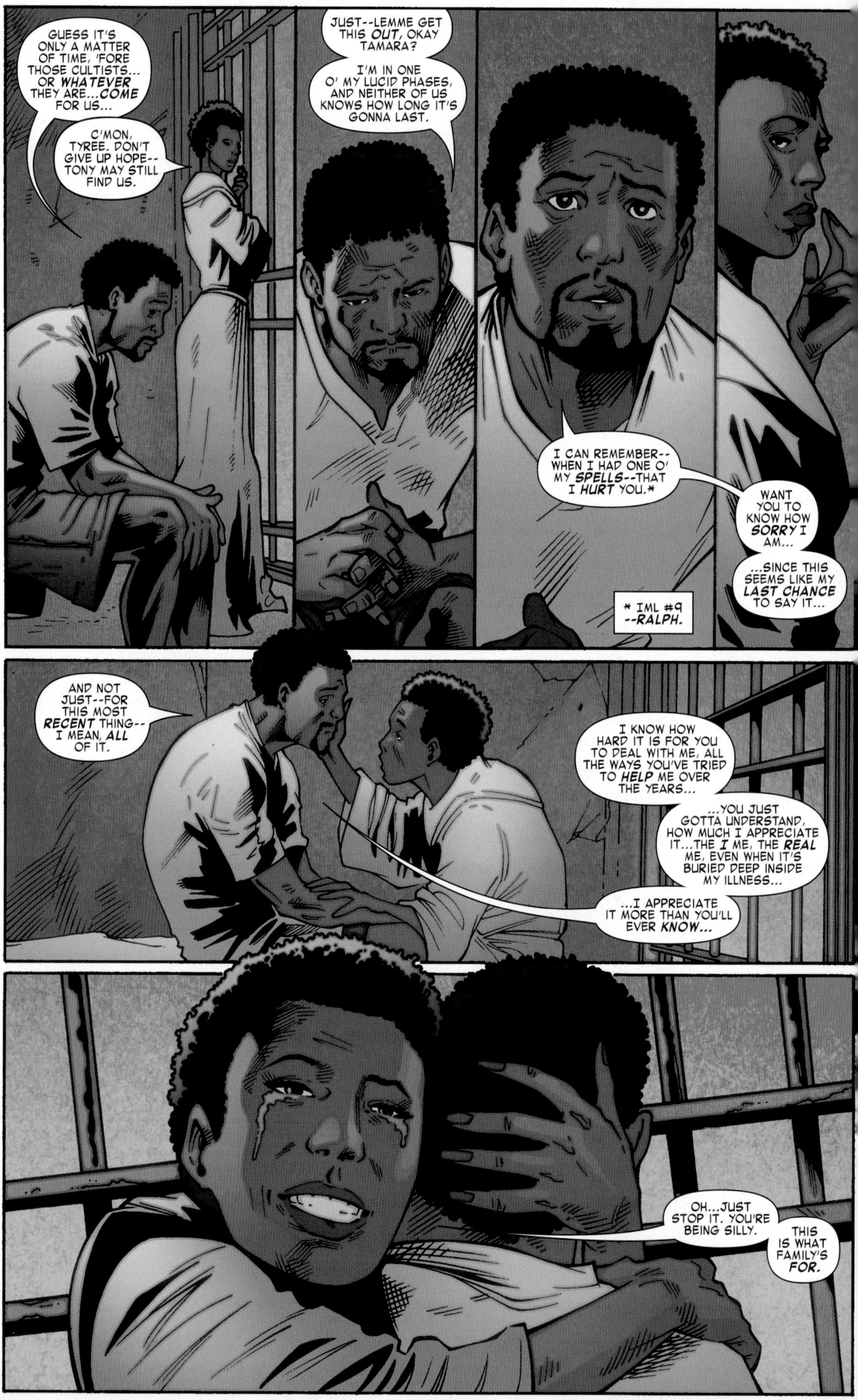
GUESS IT'S ONLY A MATTER OF TIME, 'FORE THOSE CULTISTS... OR WHATEVER THEY ARE...COME FOR US...
C'MON, TYREE. DON'T GIVE UP HOPE--TONY MAY STILL FIND US.
JUST--LEMME GET THIS OUT, OKAY TAMARA?
I'M IN ONE O' MY LUCID PHASES, AND NEITHER OF US KNOWS HOW LONG IT'S GONNA LAST.
I CAN REMEMBER--WHEN I HAD ONE O' MY SPELLS--THAT I HURT YOU.*
* IML #9 --RALPH.
WANT YOU TO KNOW HOW SORRY I AM...
...SINCE THIS SEEMS LIKE MY LAST CHANCE TO SAY IT...
AND NOT JUST--FOR THIS MOST RECENT THING--I MEAN, ALL OF IT.
I KNOW HOW HARD IT IS FOR YOU TO DEAL WITH ME, ALL THE WAYS YOU'VE TRIED TO HELP ME OVER THE YEARS...
...YOU JUST GOTTA UNDERSTAND, HOW MUCH I APPRECIATE IT...THE I ME, THE REAL ME, EVEN WHEN IT'S BURIED DEEP INSIDE MY ILLNESS...
...I APPRECIATE IT MORE THAN YOU'LL EVER KNOW...
OH...JUST STOP IT. YOU'RE BEING SILLY.
THIS IS WHAT FAMILY'S FOR.

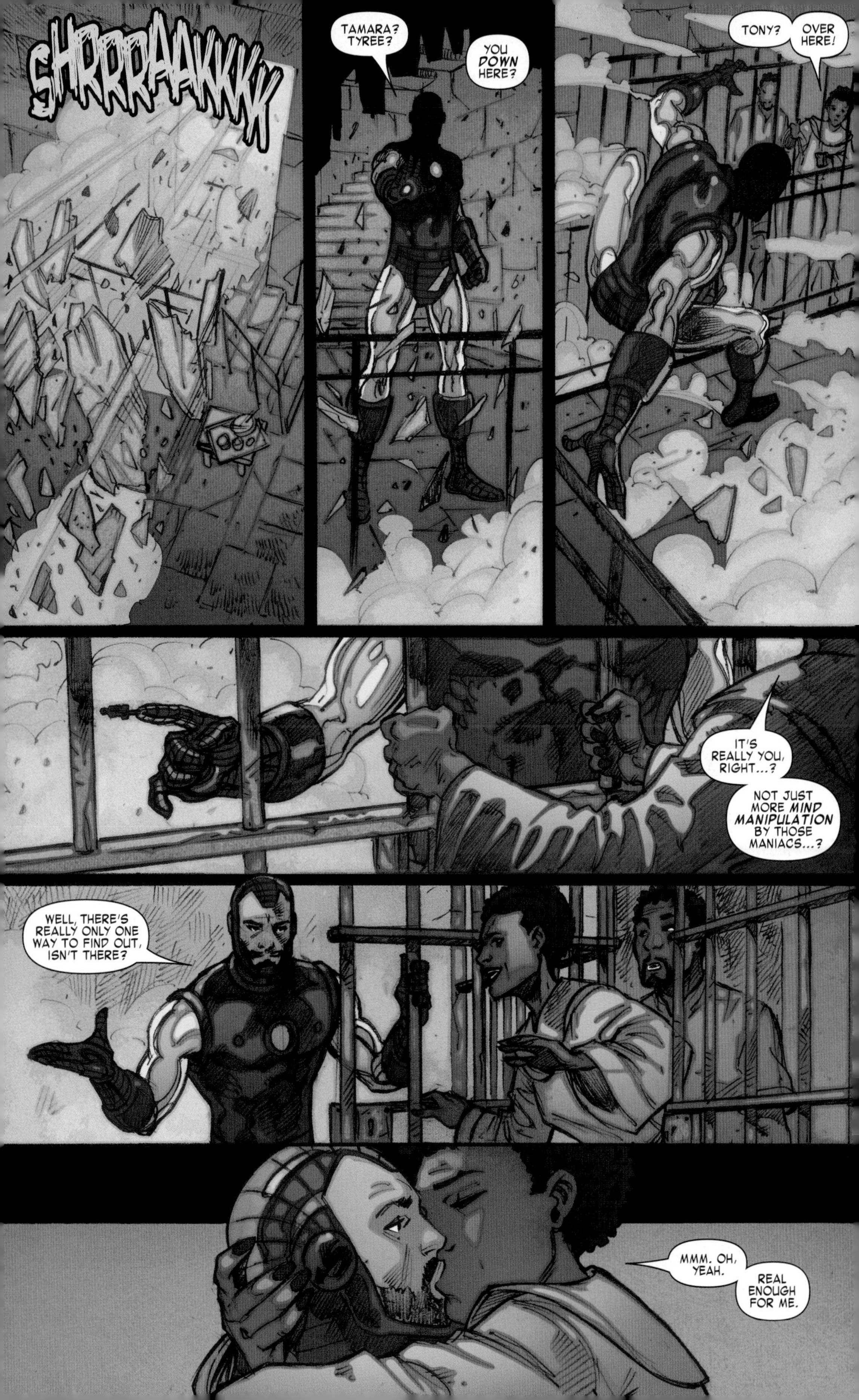
SHRRRAAKKKK
TAMARA? TYREE?
YOU DOWN HERE?
TONY?
OVER HERE!
IT'S REALLY YOU, RIGHT...?
NOT JUST MORE MIND MANIPULATION BY THOSE MANIACS...?
WELL, THERE'S REALLY ONLY ONE WAY TO FIND OUT, ISN'T THERE?
MMM. OH, YEAH.
REAL ENOUGH FOR ME.

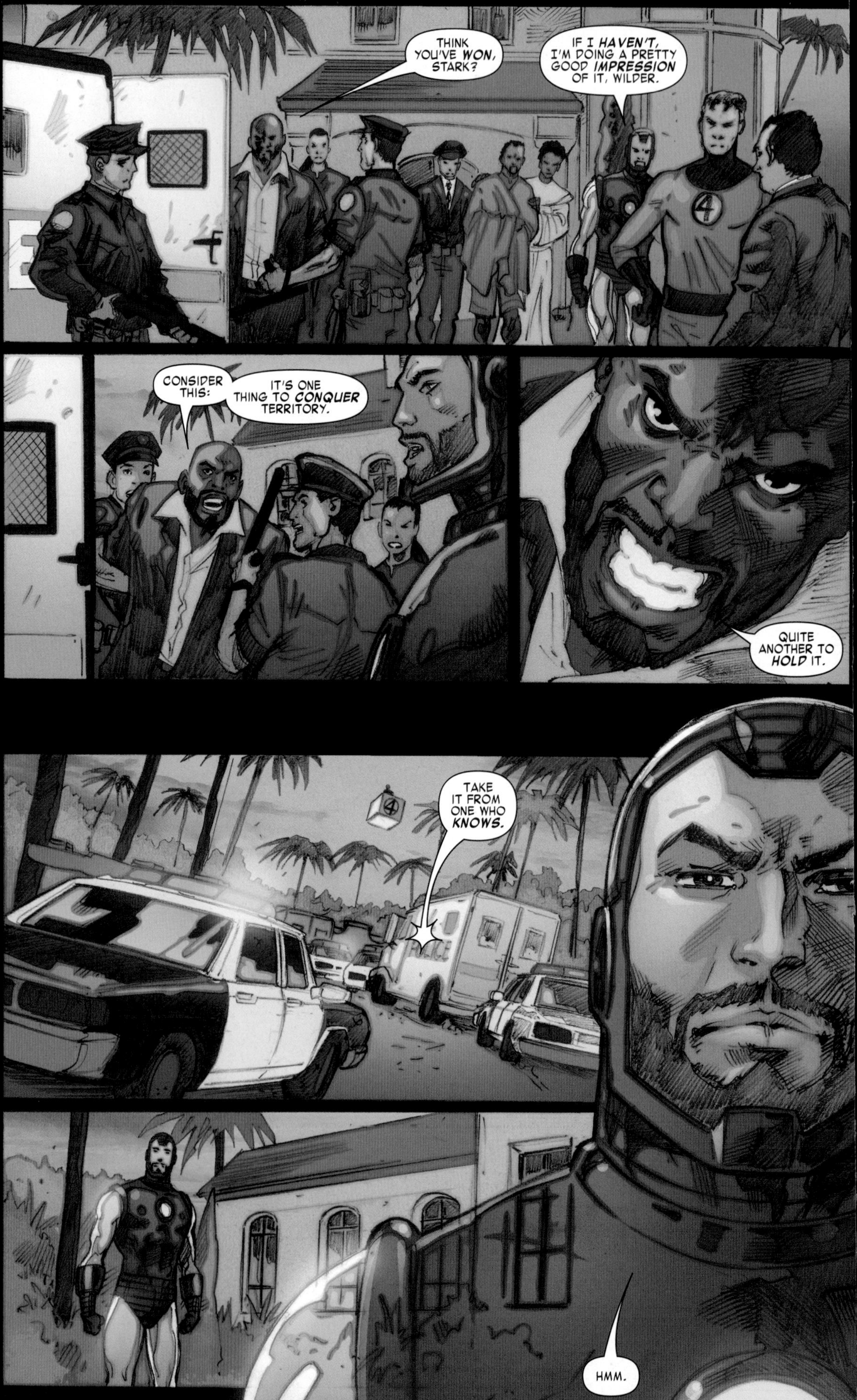
THINK YOU'VE WON, STARK?
IF I HAVEN'T, I'M DOING A PRETTY GOOD IMPRESSION OF IT, WILDER.
CONSIDER THIS:
IT'S ONE THING TO CONQUER TERRITORY.
QUITE ANOTHER TO HOLD IT.
TAKE IT FROM ONE WHO KNOWS.
HMM.

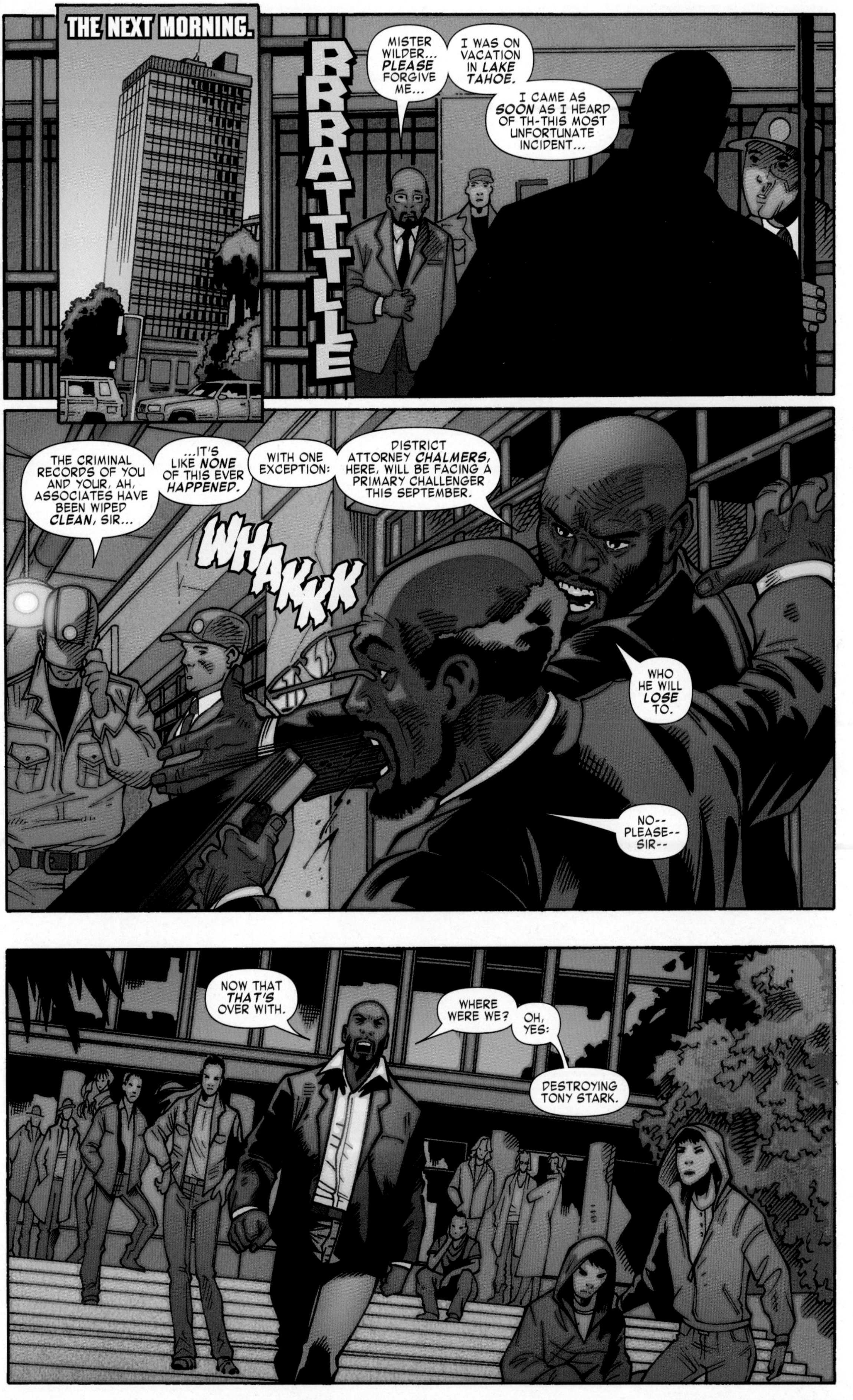
THE NEXT MORNING.
RRRATTTLLE
MISTER WILDER... PLEASE FORGIVE ME...
I WAS ON VACATION IN LAKE TAHOE.
I CAME AS SOON AS I HEARD OF TH-THIS MOST UNFORTUNATE INCIDENT...
THE CRIMINAL RECORDS OF YOU AND YOUR, AH, ASSOCIATES HAVE BEEN WIPED CLEAN, SIR...
...IT'S LIKE NONE OF THIS EVER HAPPENED.
WITH ONE EXCEPTION:
DISTRICT ATTORNEY CHALMERS, HERE, WILL BE FACING A PRIMARY CHALLENGER THIS SEPTEMBER.
WHAKKK
WHO HE WILL LOSE TO.
NO-- PLEASE-- SIR--
NOW THAT THAT'S OVER WITH.
WHERE WERE WE?
OH, YES:
DESTROYING TONY STARK.

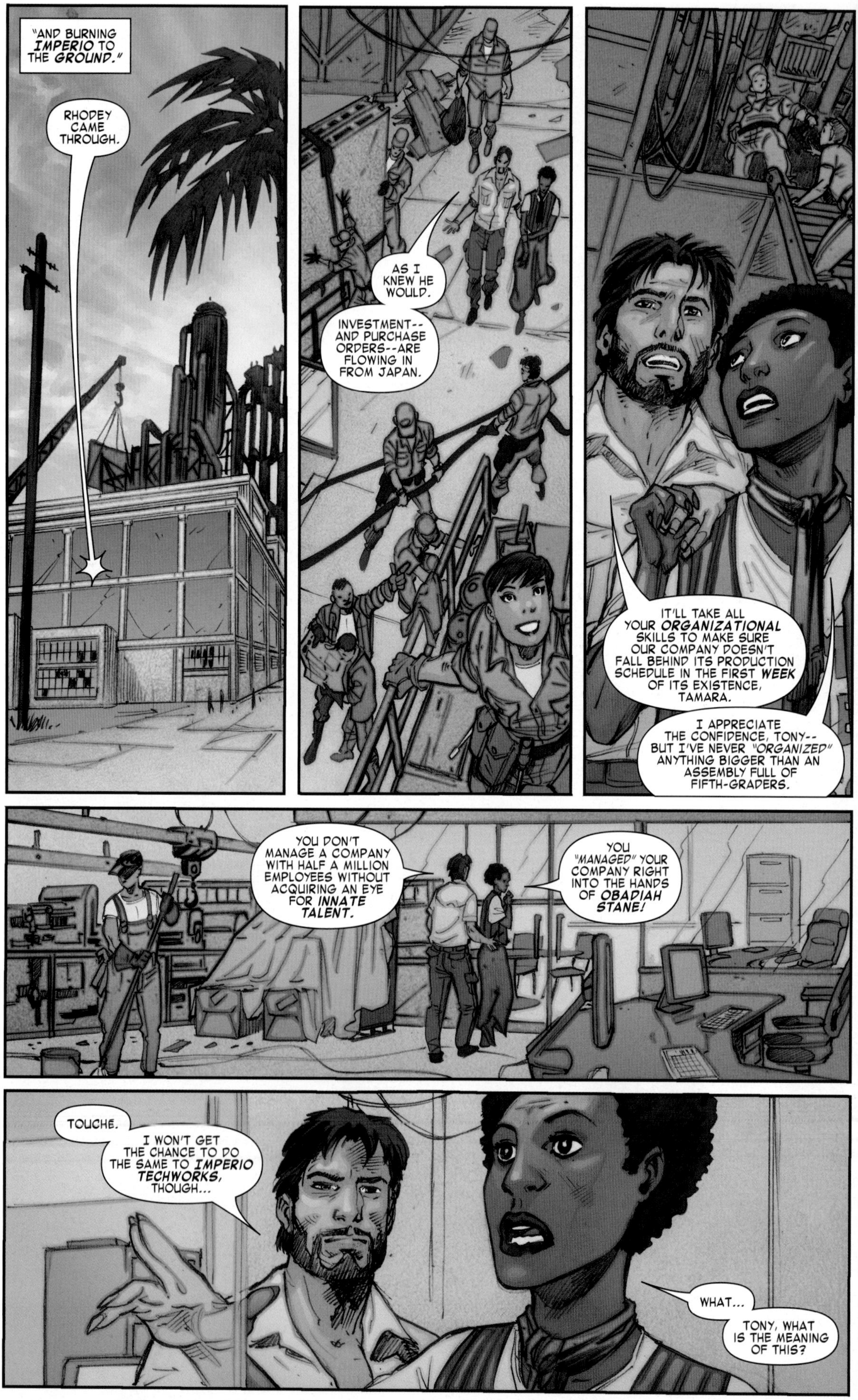
"AND BURNING IMPERIO TO THE GROUND."
RHODEY CAME THROUGH.
AS I KNEW HE WOULD.
INVESTMENT--AND PURCHASE ORDERS--ARE FLOWING IN FROM JAPAN.
IT'LL TAKE ALL YOUR ORGANIZATIONAL SKILLS TO MAKE SURE OUR COMPANY DOESN'T FALL BEHIND ITS PRODUCTION SCHEDULE IN THE FIRST WEEK OF ITS EXISTENCE, TAMARA.
I APPRECIATE THE CONFIDENCE, TONY--BUT I'VE NEVER "ORGANIZED" ANYTHING BIGGER THAN AN ASSEMBLY FULL OF FIFTH-GRADERS.
YOU DON'T MANAGE A COMPANY WITH HALF A MILLION EMPLOYEES WITHOUT ACQUIRING AN EYE FOR INNATE TALENT.
YOU "MANAGED" YOUR COMPANY RIGHT INTO THE HANDS OF OBADIAH STANE!
TOUCHÉ.
I WON'T GET THE CHANCE TO DO THE SAME TO IMPERIO TECHWORKS, THOUGH...
WHAT...
TONY, WHAT IS THE MEANING OF THIS?

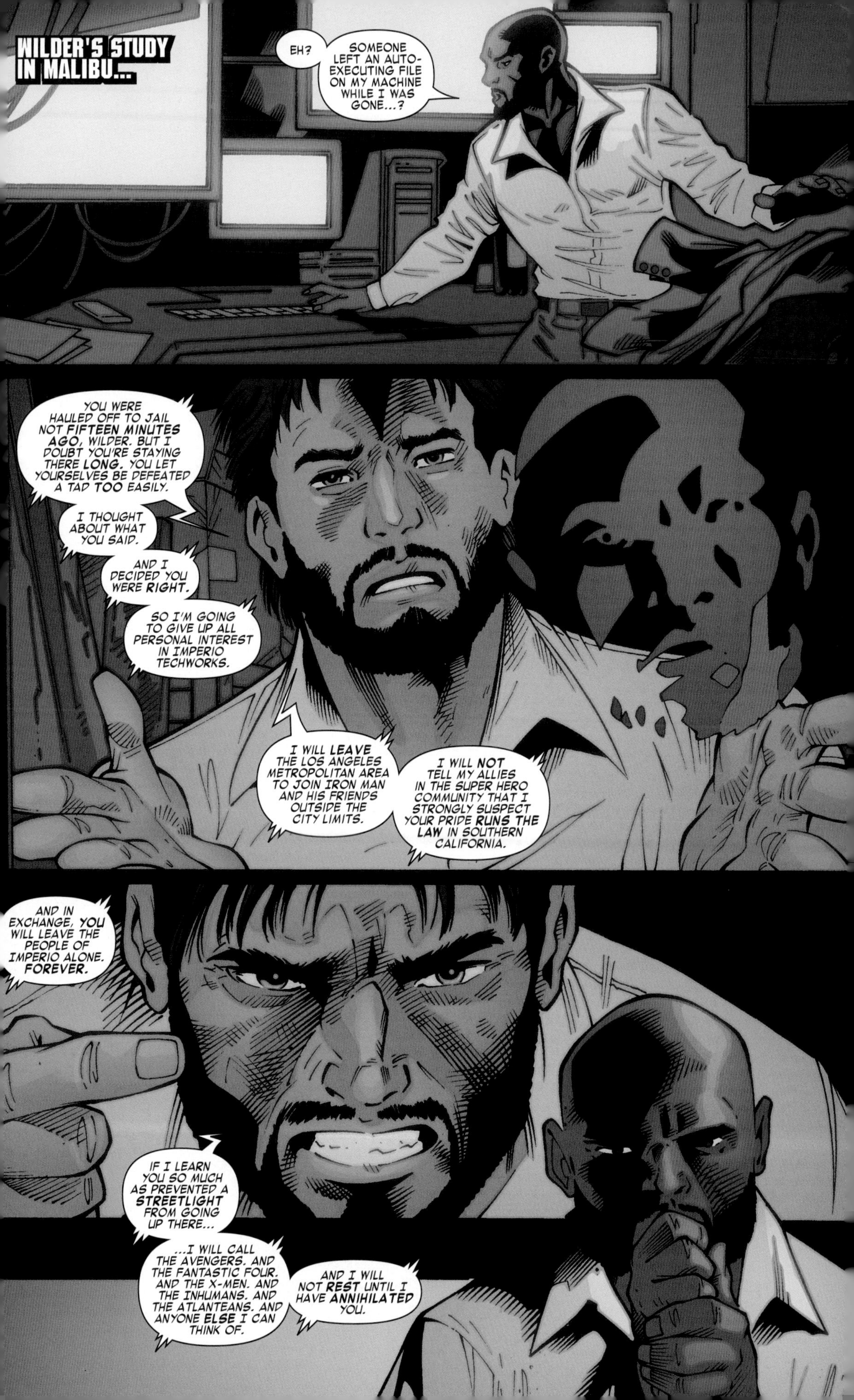
WILDER'S STUDY IN MALIBU...
EH?
SOMEONE LEFT AN AUTO-EXECUTING FILE ON MY MACHINE WHILE I WAS GONE...?
YOU WERE HAULED OFF TO JAIL NOT FIFTEEN MINUTES AGO, WILDER. BUT I DOUBT YOU'RE STAYING THERE LONG. YOU LET YOURSELVES BE DEFEATED A TAD TOO EASILY.
I THOUGHT ABOUT WHAT YOU SAID.
AND I DECIDED YOU WERE RIGHT.
SO I'M GOING TO GIVE UP ALL PERSONAL INTEREST IN IMPERIO TECHWORKS.
I WILL LEAVE THE LOS ANGELES METROPOLITAN AREA TO JOIN IRON MAN AND HIS FRIENDS OUTSIDE THE CITY LIMITS.
I WILL NOT TELL MY ALLIES IN THE SUPER HERO COMMUNITY THAT I STRONGLY SUSPECT YOUR PRIDE RUNS THE LAW IN SOUTHERN CALIFORNIA.
AND IN EXCHANGE, YOU WILL LEAVE THE PEOPLE OF IMPERIO ALONE. FOREVER.
IF I LEARN YOU SO MUCH AS PREVENTED A STREETLIGHT FROM GOING UP THERE...
...I WILL CALL THE AVENGERS. AND THE FANTASTIC FOUR. AND THE X-MEN. AND THE INHUMANS. AND THE ATLANTEANS. AND ANYONE ELSE I CAN THINK OF.
AND I WILL NOT REST UNTIL I HAVE ANNIHILATED YOU.

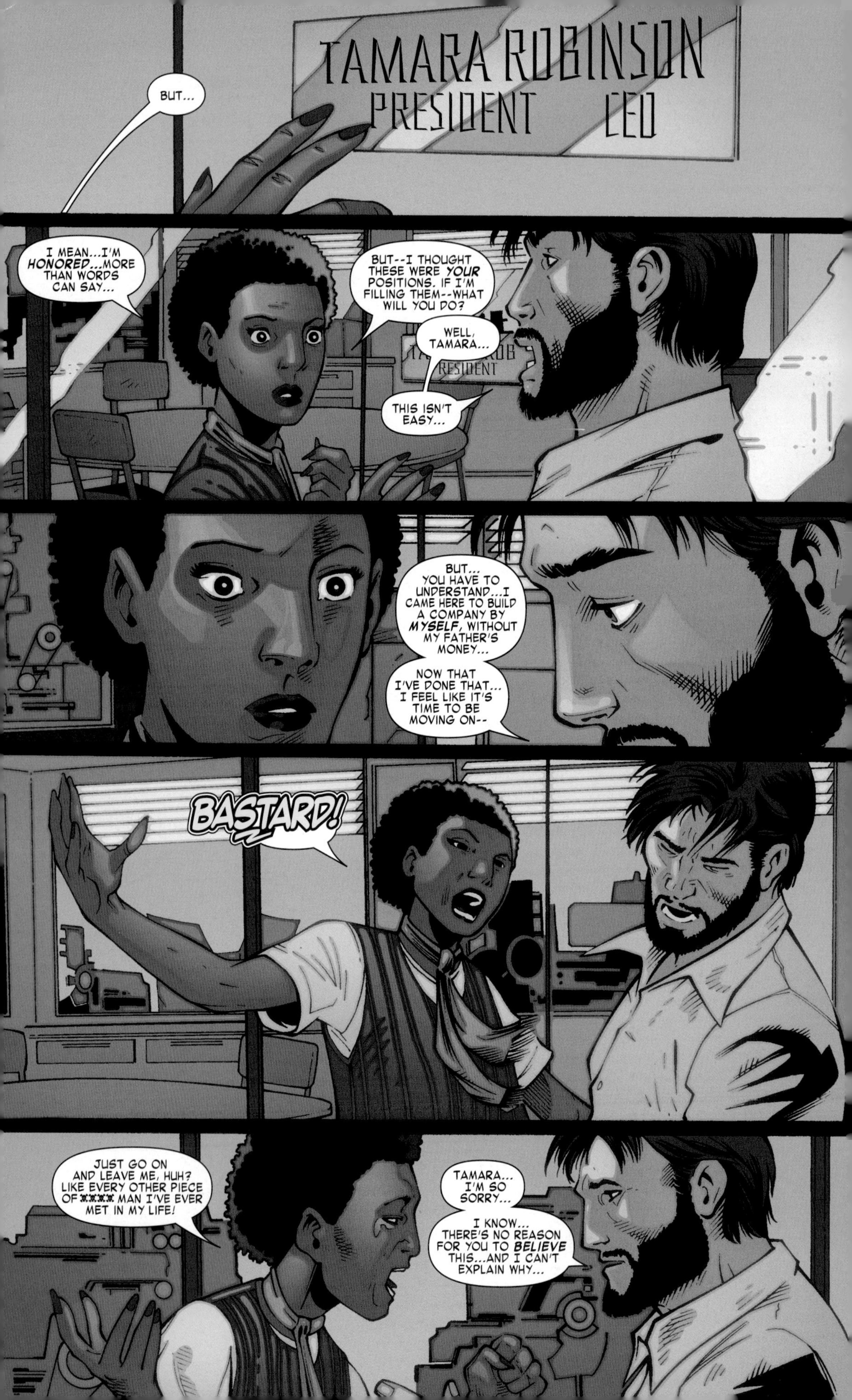
TAMARA ROBINSON
PRESIDENT CEO
BUT...
I MEAN...I'M *HONORED*...MORE THAN WORDS CAN SAY...
BUT--I THOUGHT THESE WERE *YOUR* POSITIONS. IF I'M FILLING THEM--WHAT WILL YOU DO?
WELL, TAMARA...
THIS ISN'T EASY...
BUT... YOU HAVE TO UNDERSTAND...I CAME HERE TO BUILD A COMPANY BY *MYSELF*, WITHOUT MY FATHER'S MONEY...
NOW THAT I'VE DONE THAT... I FEEL LIKE IT'S TIME TO BE MOVING ON--
BASTARD!
JUST GO ON AND LEAVE ME, HUH? LIKE EVERY OTHER PIECE OF ☠☠☠☠ MAN I'VE EVER MET IN MY LIFE!
TAMARA... I'M SO SORRY...
I KNOW... THERE'S NO REASON FOR YOU TO *BELIEVE* THIS...AND I CAN'T EXPLAIN WHY...

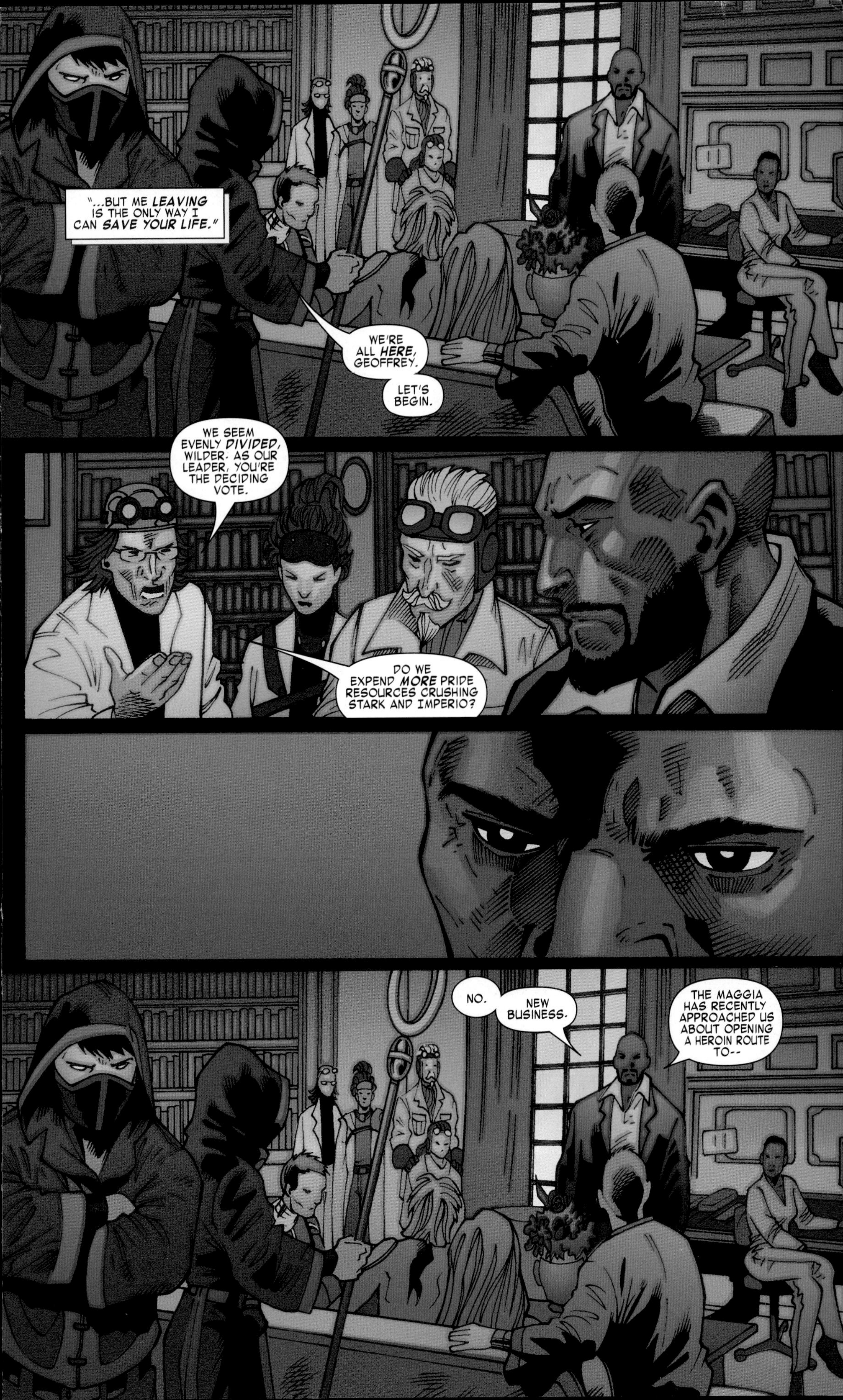
"...BUT ME *LEAVING* IS THE ONLY WAY I CAN *SAVE YOUR LIFE.*"
WE'RE ALL *HERE*, GEOFFREY.
LET'S BEGIN.
WE SEEM EVENLY *DIVIDED*, WILDER. AS OUR LEADER, YOU'RE THE DECIDING VOTE.
DO WE EXPEND *MORE* PRIDE RESOURCES CRUSHING STARK AND IMPERIO?
NO.
NEW BUSINESS.
THE MAGGIA HAS RECENTLY APPROACHED US ABOUT OPENING A HEROIN ROUTE TO--

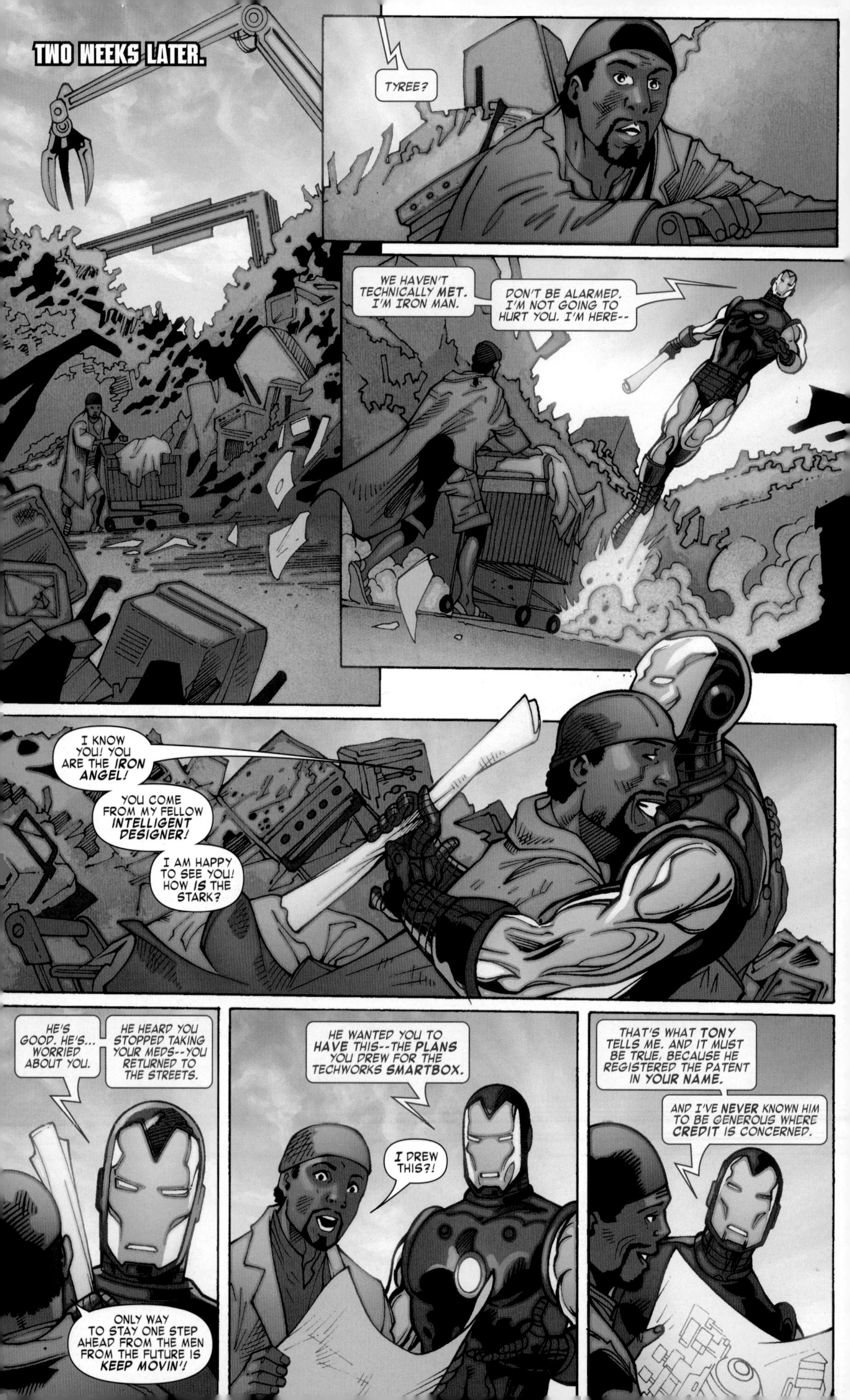
TWO WEEKS LATER.
TYREE?
WE HAVEN'T TECHNICALLY MET. I'M IRON MAN.
DON'T BE ALARMED. I'M NOT GOING TO HURT YOU. I'M HERE--
I KNOW YOU! YOU ARE THE IRON ANGEL!
YOU COME FROM MY FELLOW INTELLIGENT DESIGNER!
I AM HAPPY TO SEE YOU! HOW IS THE STARK?
HE'S GOOD. HE'S... WORRIED ABOUT YOU.
HE HEARD YOU STOPPED TAKING YOUR MEDS--YOU RETURNED TO THE STREETS.
ONLY WAY TO STAY ONE STEP AHEAD FROM THE MEN FROM THE FUTURE IS KEEP MOVIN'!
HE WANTED YOU TO HAVE THIS--THE PLANS YOU DREW FOR THE TECHWORKS SMARTBOX.
I DREW THIS?!
THAT'S WHAT TONY TELLS ME. AND IT MUST BE TRUE, BECAUSE HE REGISTERED THE PATENT IN YOUR NAME.
AND I'VE NEVER KNOWN HIM TO BE GENEROUS WHERE CREDIT IS CONCERNED.

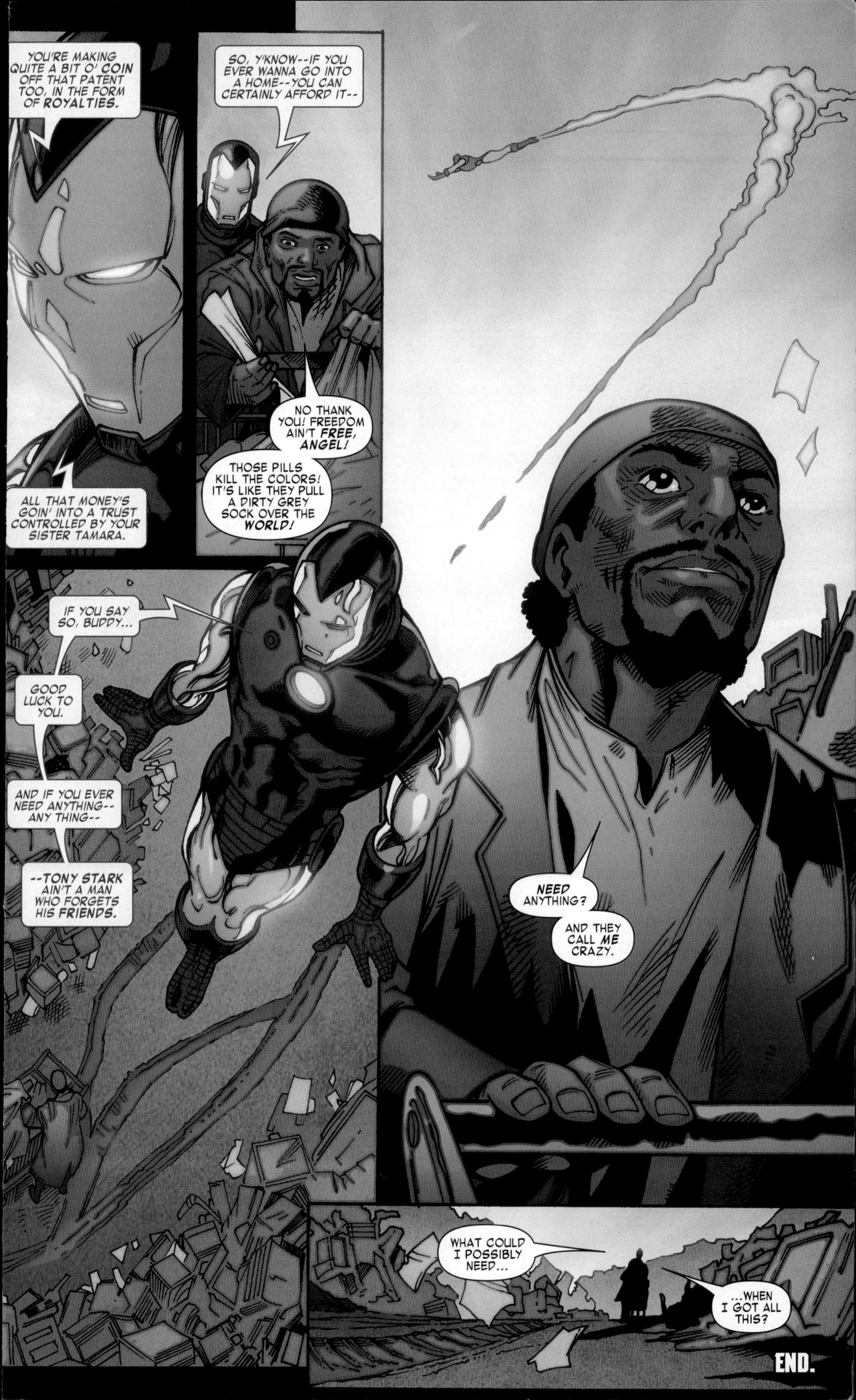
YOU'RE MAKING QUITE A BIT O' COIN OFF THAT PATENT TOO, IN THE FORM OF ROYALTIES.
ALL THAT MONEY'S GOIN' INTO A TRUST CONTROLLED BY YOUR SISTER TAMARA.
SO, Y'KNOW--IF YOU EVER WANNA GO INTO A HOME--YOU CAN CERTAINLY AFFORD IT--
NO THANK YOU! FREEDOM AIN'T FREE, ANGEL!
THOSE PILLS KILL THE COLORS! IT'S LIKE THEY PULL A DIRTY GREY SOCK OVER THE WORLD!
IF YOU SAY SO, BUDDY...
GOOD LUCK TO YOU.
AND IF YOU EVER NEED ANYTHING-- ANY THING--
--TONY STARK AIN'T A MAN WHO FORGETS HIS FRIENDS.
NEED ANYTHING?
AND THEY CALL ME CRAZY.
WHAT COULD I POSSIBLY NEED...
...WHEN I GOT ALL THIS?
END.

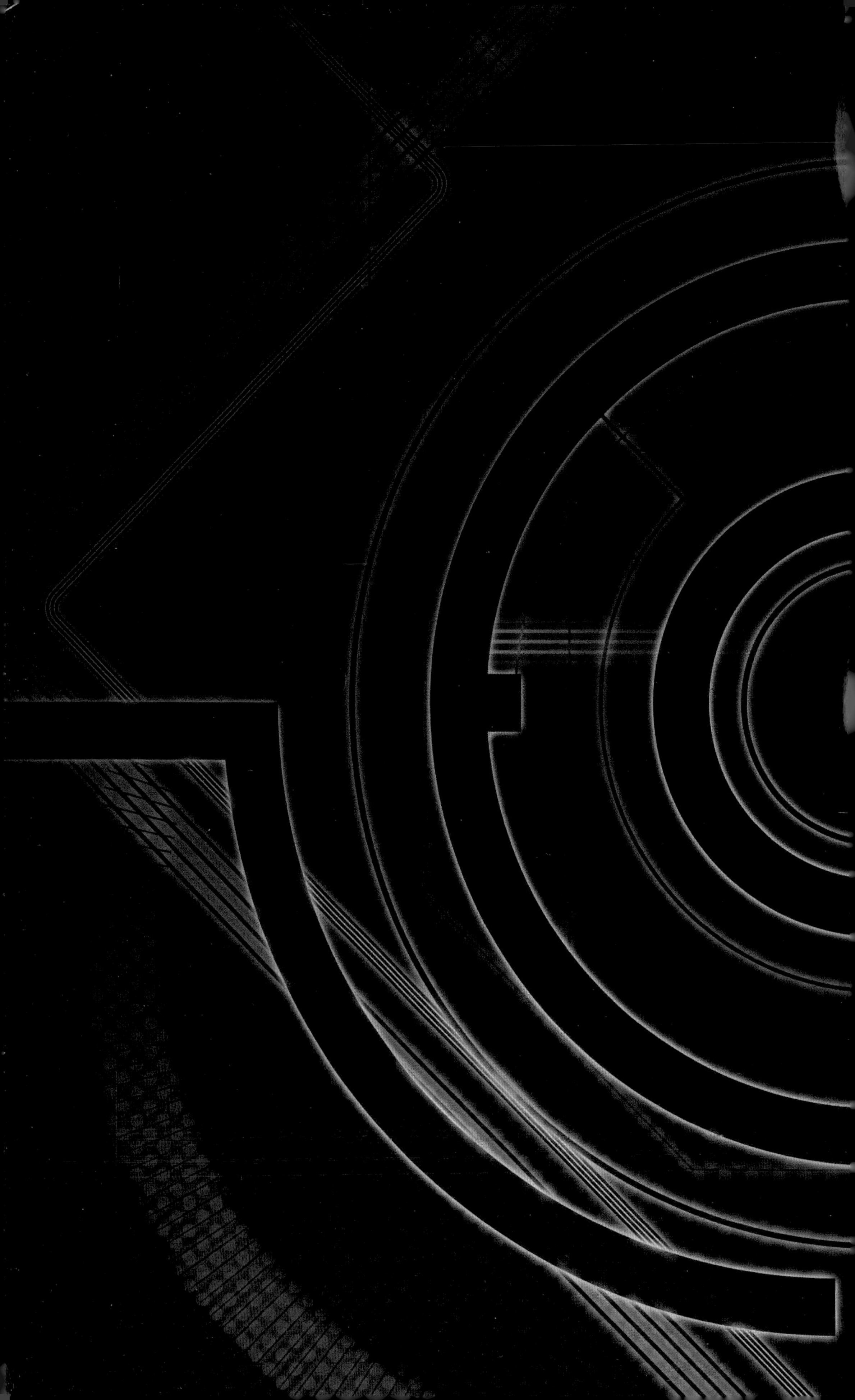